Don’t Act, Just Dance

Don't Act, Just Dance

The Metapolitics of Cold War Culture

CATHERINE GUNTHER KODAT

Rutgers University Press
New Brunswick, New Jersey, and London

A Cataloging-in-Publication record is available from the Library of Congress

A British Cataloging-in-Publication record for this book is available from the British Library.

Visit our website: http://rutgerspress.rutgers.edu

Manufactured in the United States of America

For Alex

. . . more, more, every day more . . .

Contents

Preface

For three days in April 1996, a group of historians and literary scholars gathered in Toledo for a conference on U.S. politics and culture during the cold war. The fall of the Berlin Wall, the collapse of the Soviet Union, the election of Boris Yeltsin: these were relatively recent events, and there was exhilaration in the air, the sense that a still-emerging field within American Studies—cold war cultural studies—was about to expand in exciting new directions. Most of the participants were tenured senior professors, several from large prestigious universities. I was in the second semester of my first year of full-time teaching at a small liberal arts college in upstate New York, and I couldn't shake the feeling that I'd gotten into the conference by mistake. It wasn't only my lack of seniority and institutional clout that had me worried. A paper on *The Nutcracker?* What had I been thinking? Certainly I believed I had something to say that was worth hearing. But could the ballet hold its own among such heavy-hitters as *Silent Spring,* Alfred Hitchcock, *Invisible Man,* the Venona Project, and George F. Kennan's "Long Telegram"? And not just this ballet—*any* ballet. To be sure, dance history is an acknowledged discipline, and the more theoretically inflected field of dance studies had been on the rise since the mid-1980s. Still, despite a reputation for being uniquely open to fresh subjects and interdisciplinary study, American Studies was not exactly humming with dance-related scholarship. I was not sure why, though I had some ideas. Happily, however, my paper got a friendly hearing—and folks weren't just being polite.[1] Maybe, I began to hope, dance was on the way toward drawing the serious scholarly attention it so obviously deserved.

Time has shown that this hope was well-founded: during the past decade scholarly publication in dance has steadily, if slowly, risen, winning the art form (and its academic study) long-overdue respect. Yet a post-conference encounter in the airport tempered the optimism of the moment. My interlocutor was a well-known Marxist literary scholar whose brilliant critical interrogations of canon formation championed overlooked or disdained literary works. I was star-struck and flattered that he wanted to chat. After we exchanged a few pleasantries and agreed on the overall excellence of the conference, he turned to me with mild incredulity: "You're really interested in ballet?"

"Oh, yes," I replied.

He shook his head. "You know, I *hate* ballet. It's so . . . so. . . ." He paused, fixing me with what Henry James might have called a speaking look. "So *fake,*" he concluded. He waved his hand dismissively. "So *elitist,*" he added. "You know what I mean?"

I was pretty sure I did know what he meant—though I'm not sure that *he* knew. For his words and tone put me in mind of a passage I had recently come across in Pierre Bourdieu's *Distinction,* in which the sociologist notes, almost in passing, why men with a certain class consciousness deem particular forms of "aesthetic refinement" unacceptable.

> This is not only because aesthetic refinement, particularly as regards clothing or cosmetics, is reserved for women or because it is more or less clearly associated with dispositions and manners seen as characteristic of the bourgeoisie ("airs and graces," "la-di-da," etc.) or of those who are willing to submit to bourgeois demands so as to win acceptance, of which the "toadies," "lick-spittles," and "pansies" of everyday invective represent the limit. It is also because a surrender to demands perceived as simultaneously feminine and bourgeois appears as the index of a dual repudiation of virility (382).[2]

While not explicitly condemning the ballet as the exclusive preserve of dancing fairies and imperiled princesses (of whatever sex), my interlocutor's quick summary of the form as a pretentious celebration of artifice—so fake, so elitist; in other words, so "simultaneously feminine and bourgeois"—was only a step away from Bourdieu's toad- and pansy-filled landscape. However inadvertently or unconsciously, his closing remark asked exactly the question about ballet that, as a good leftist, he never would have uttered directly. What he *did* say seemed plain enough: as a "fake" and "elitist" cultural discourse, ballet could hardly be said to have an aesthetics, let alone a politics, worthy of intellectual engagement. Rooted in falsity, it could never hope to reveal truth; an elitist entertainment, it would never speak to the people. The implication was clear: why was I bothering with something so frivolous and inconsequential—with a cultural practice whose politics, assuming it even had a politics, could only be retrograde? Shouldn't I be studying something *important?*

I can't remember now what I said—indeed, whether I said anything at all. But I do remember thinking I'd been shown, pretty clearly, that ballet (and probably also dance as a whole) still had some way to go before it could be regarded as a serious art form. This man was no macho poser but a respected scholar who would have been shocked and dismayed to hear that his scorn for the ballet might have seemed a wee bit homophobic.

Mulling over the exchange on my flight home, considering how the conference as a whole had intensified my budding interest in the politics of cold war culture, and feeling even more certain (after all, I'd been provoked!) that ballet needed to play a role in any future research project, I set off on the path to this book. It goes without saying that the path has not been smooth or direct: anyone who has written a book knows that nothing ever turns out as planned. However, *Don't Act, Just Dance* busted more than the usual number of unexpected moves, so much so that I found myself, midway through what I'd imagined would be a fairly straightforward process, having to completely rethink my initial assumptions about the relationship between cold war art and politics. Since I describe those assumptions in some detail in this book, suffice it to say here that I was a firm believer in the complicity thesis of cold war cultural productions. In other words, I believed (as many did and some still do) that the steep rise of cultural development and export during the era of federally funded programs was prima facie evidence that artwork produced and distributed under the aegis of such programs was a species of government agent, something like an artbot for the burgeoning American imperial project. According to this view, even cold war artworks produced without government support were symptomatic of the larger social surround, "stained," as Fredric Jameson said, with the guilt of their historical moment (299).

Coming to terms with the politics of cold war modernist dance is what made me change my tune. Although I began by simply trying to give dance its due within cold war culture, my work eventually shifted to showing how it reveals the terrific complexity of the era's politics of modern art. Those politics are suggested in the Balanchine catchphrase that titles this book, a paradoxical exhortation that invites two contradictory interpretations. First, dancing is not acting; the *activities* of the dance should never be confused with *action* of any kind, let alone political action. Second, dancing is the *quintessence* of human action; political to its very bones, dance is most effective when it is most itself. At a key point in my struggle to come to grips with the polysemy of Balanchine's phrase, I discovered the work of Jacques Rancière and his concept of art's metapolitics. That discovery—and the connections and rereadings that followed—came quite late in my research, but it was worth the wait.

It would not be entirely accurate to say that *Don't Act, Just Dance* was born in a waiting room at Toledo Express Airport. But that was where the flight began.

Don't Act, Just Dance took a long time to complete. Were it not for the help I received along the way, it would not have been finished at all. I am particularly thankful for two fellowships I received early in the project, when, as the mother of triplets, I needed time simply to read, look, listen, and think. The Woodrow Wilson National Fellowship Foundation's Millicent McIntosh Flexible Fellowship gave me both financial support and a leave from teaching. And by providing me with an office, a computer, and unlimited access to the University of Oxford's extraordinary library, a residential fellowship at the Rothermere American Institute at the University of Oxford allowed me to devote myself to research in an atmosphere of superb intellectual stimulation.

During much of the project, I was a member of the English and Creative Writing Department at Hamilton College, and I am grateful for two faculty development grants (one funded through the Mellon Foundation, the other drawn from the dean of faculty's discretionary fund) to support my research. I was also the fortunate recipient of a research support stipend from a fund established by the late Richard M. Couper, a good friend of Hamilton and a wonderful champion of the faculty. In my seventeen years at Hamilton I was lucky to have the support of four outstanding deans—Bobby Fong, David Paris, Joseph Urgo, and Patrick Reynolds—and the gift of warm and generous faculty colleagues always willing to read a chapter or talk out a theoretical problem. Steve Yao and Dana Luciano both read early, awful drafts of the Spartacus chapter; I'm grateful for their criticism and their forbearance. Maurice Isserman, Shoshana Keller, Sam Pellman, Rob Hopkins, Monk Rowe, and "Doctuh" Mike Woods patiently answered my questions or gave research advice about the Red Scare; ethnic politics in the Soviet Union; and atonality, bop, and the State Department's sponsored jazz tours. John Bartle, Frank Sciacca, Barbara Gold, Joe Molloy, Jens Vossmeier, and Marta Folio helped with translations from Russian, Latin, and German. Librarians Glynis Asu, Julia B. Dickinson, Lynn M. Mayo, Kristin L. Strohmeyer, and Karen Ingeman provided brilliant research assistance. I signed on for the cold war conference in Toledo largely because of the encouragement of Peter Rabinowitz. He and Nancy Rabinowitz were patient sounding boards and offered steadfast encouragement in the early phases of my research. And I am thankful for the warm friendship and support of Roberta Krueger and Thomas Bass.

To Eugene M. Tobin, Margaret O. Thickstun, and G. Roberts Kolb I owe the incredible gift of Hamilton College itself. This is a odd thing to say, I know—but they understand what I mean.

My debts beyond Hamilton College are many. Thanks to Martin Manning, former public information officer for the now-defunct U.S. Information Agency (USIA), for his early research advice; to Betty Austin and Vera Ekechukwu for their assistance in locating materials in the U.S. State Department/

USIA archives held in the Fulbright Collection at the University of Arkansas; to Amy Fitch at the Rockefeller Archive; to Timothy A. Edwards, Head of Operations at the UCLA Music Library Special Collections; to Karen Schoenewaldt and Patrick J. Rodgers at the Rosenbach Museum; to Linda C. Leavell for help in tracking down Marianne Moore materials; to Jonathan M. Bloom for answering questions about Arthur Upham Pope; and to Paul DiMaggio for early advice that helped me sharpen the focus of my analysis. Carl Serpa and David Cannata generously helped me find answers to the questions I posted about Aram Khachaturian on the American Musicological Society listserv.

Thanks are also due to Jamie Barlow, Michael Coyle, Bernard Gendron, Mark Hertsgaard, Adam Lutzker, Russ Reising, and Thomas Hill Schaub for their encouragement and enthusiasm. Alan Nadel generously stepped in with advice and guidance at a critical point in the project's development.

While it was born and raised at Hamilton College, *Don't Act, Just Dance* came of age at the University of the Arts. My thanks to Associate Provost Carol Graney, also director of the university's library, and Provost Kirk Pillow for their support as the manuscript reached completion. In Philadelphia, Nelson Cárdenas provided translations of Spanish and Portuguese reviews of the Merce Cunningham Dance Company's 1968 South American tour.

To Lisa Boyajian at Rutgers University Press: many, many thanks.

I am also grateful to the following individuals and organizations for their permission to quote or reproduce copyrighted material:

The George Balanchine Trust and Ellen Sorrin, director of the trust, for permission to reproduce photographs of Balanchine's choreography for *The Figure in the Carpet*

The Merce Cunningham Trust and Lynn Wichern, executive director of the trust, for permission to reproduce a photograph from the Merce Cunningham Dance Company's rehearsal for the 1972 Persepolis Event

Nicholas Jenkins, Lincoln Kirstein's literary executor, for granting access to the Lincoln Kirstein papers held in the Dance Collection at the New York Public Library and for permission to quote from them

Gabriel Pinski, for permission to reproduce Fred Fehl's photograph of Jacques d'Amboise and Melissa Hayden in *The Figure in the Carpet*

David M. Moore, administrator of the literary estate of Marianne C. Moore, and Penguin Group, U.S.A., for permission to quote from Moore's published and unpublished work

In addition, an early version of chapter 6 was published as "I'm Spartacus!" in James Phelan and Peter Rabinowitz, eds., *A Companion to Narrative Theory* (Oxford: Blackwell, 2005), 484–498. I am grateful to Wiley-Blackwell for permission to reprint portions of that earlier work.

Don't Act, Just Dance was conceived when my children, Axel, Dexter, and Madeleine, were small. They and the book grew up together; and, like my academic colleagues and professional research assistants, they made contributions to the project. It was Axel who suggested that I include *Nixon in China* in my analysis. Dexter's willingness to join me in multiple viewings of multiple versions of *Spartacus* not only resulted in good conversation about the story but also laid the foundation for our later shared viewing of *The Wire.* When I wondered about the wisdom of the book's interdisciplinary reach, Madeleine, with her twin passions for dance and poetry, assured me that I was on the right track. While I was often riven with doubts about the project, my children always expected that I would finish the book. Their confidence helped keep me going.

My greatest debt of all is reflected in the dedication. From our first meeting in a Baltimore ballet class, through various jobs, homes, and dance studios in West Newton, Somerville, Clinton, and Philadelphia, Alex has been my rock. Without his love and support, *Don't Act, Just Dance* would never have been started, much less finished. How lucky I am to owe him so much. And how inexpressibly thankful.

Part I

Rethinking Cold War Culture

1

Combat Cultural

The Moiseyev Dance Company of the Soviet Union made its U.S. premiere at the old Metropolitan Opera House in New York City on Saturday, April 19, 1958. The troupe's visit had been organized by the charismatic impresario Sol Hurok, whose energetic courtship of Soviet cultural officials had begun two years earlier, but the company arrived in Manhattan just three months after the signing of the nations' first bilateral cultural exchange agreement (a circumstance that delighted Hurok because it not only endowed the privately arranged booking with a certain official gravitas but also set the stage for similarly lucrative opportunities in the future).[1] When New Yorkers opened their Sunday papers to rave reviews by the *New York Times*'s John Martin and the *Herald Tribune*'s Walter Terry, the public's already strong interest in the company developed into near-mania. The Moiseyev played to a sold-out house through the rest of its New York City engagement, and Ed Sullivan dedicated an entire evening's broadcast to the troupe (Martin, "The Dance: A la Moiseyev"; Terry, "Dance: Russians Blaze").[2]

Among those who made their way to the opera house was poet Marianne Moore, who was also a guest at Hurok's Saint Regis Hotel luncheon for company founder and artistic director Igor Moiseyev on the day of the troupe's last performance.[3] On June 6, 1959, a little more than a year after her night at the Met and her afternoon at the Saint Regis, Moore published "Combat Cultural," a seven-stanza rumination on this momentous Russian season, in *The New Yorker*. Moore had an extraordinary zest for revision: over the course of almost fifty years she whittled "Poetry" from five stanzas to just three lines; when compiling her final collection, she set aside more than half of her work.

Yet she kept "Combat Cultural" largely intact when she republished it in her 1959 collection *O to Be a Dragon*. After making a few more changes (small but, as we will see, not insignificant), she included "Combat Cultural" in her ruthlessly edited *Complete Poems*. (Recall that collection's famous epigraph: "Omissions are not accidents.")[4] It seems safe to assume, then, that the poem had some significance for a writer who was not especially reverent about her own past work. Still, the poem drew scant critical interest during Moore's lifetime or in the earliest efforts to assess her *oeuvre* following her death in 1972. More recent scholarship has accorded it almost no attention whatsoever.[5]

"Combat Cultural" is something of a *pièce d'occasion;* like Moore's more famous "Hometown Piece for Messrs. Alston and Reese" it draws mostly apologetic side-glances from the handful of critics who have chosen to acknowledge it.[6] Fewer than forty pages of scholarship have been devoted to "Combat Cultural," and they present two possible approaches to the poem. According to the first view, it is one of several entertaining but minor poems that "indicate [Moore's] pleasure in devising ever-changing rhymes and meters for the service of the arts," a somewhat patronizing approach that ignores or misconstrues crucial aspects of the event that inspired the piece. The second view connects it to philosophical concerns addressed in other Moore poems, a well-intentioned effort that also blunts the work's historical relevance (Stapleton 198).[7]

Granted, no amount of fancy critical footwork will turn "Combat Cultural" into "What Are Years." Even so, it makes some difference to understand what the poem describes—not only the actual event that provided its central image but also the peculiar Moiseyev approach to folk dance and the political conditions that shaped it. "Combat Cultural" deserves analysis that makes clear the connections linking its subject, the circumstances that occasioned its creation, and its formal properties. Despite its teasing conclusion that the dance it describes (and so, by extension, the poem itself) "may . . . point a moral," "Combat Cultural" is best understood not as a claim about some universal property of wisdom but rather as a meditation on the relationship between artistic and political regimes of representation, a meditation so steeped in the event it describes that the reader who knows nothing about U.S. and Soviet government efforts to enlist the arts in the cold war may find the poem incomprehensible.

What is worth knowing, then, about the arts of the cold war if one is to understand "Combat Cultural"? We could start with the poem's manifest (though never directly named) subject, the Moiseyev Dance Company. Igor Moiseyev (who died in 2007 at age 101) trained at the Bolshoi Ballet school and spent his early dance career entirely within the confines of the Russian ballet. He founded his company in 1937, a year after being appointed director of the Moscow Theatre for Folk Art. As the founding date hints, and as a glance at the company's repertory makes clear, Moiseyev was quite mindful of the Soviet government's rapidly-growing suspicion of modernist, "Western," aesthetic values, a suspicion that burgeoned into the Stalinist *zhdanovshchina* aesthetic. Moore, herself a modernist with a keen understanding of dance, would have recognized that even though popular and folk material did inform certain advanced artistic practices of the period (say, the work of Charles Ives and Béla Bartók), Moiseyev's choreography could not be termed modernist. Emphasizing technical virtuosity and bravura physical display, the repertory of the Moiseyev Dance Company favored the broad, flat road of the circus act, its folk details working largely to solicit state sanction of production values more in the spirit of Radio City Music Hall than of a collectivized farm or factory.[8] As Moore's poem slyly (but non-judgmentally) observes, Moiseyev's was not the kind of "high quality" art "unlikely to command high sales." On the contrary, his dances were built to deliver mass-appeal spectacle—what "one likes to see."[9]

"Combat Cultural" offers brief, single-stanza sketches of two Moiseyev dances that neatly represent popular 1950s American notions of Russia: "a documentary / of Cossacks" points to the stoical Red solidarity of the company's celebrated "Partisans," while the "aimlessly drooping handkerchief" signals the czarist affectations of "City Quadrille." From this introduction the poem moves to its main image, taken (as Moore explains in the footnotes to her final version) from "Two Boys in a Fight," a choreographic one-liner that for years was one of the most popular works in the company's repertory.[10] Moiseyev Dance Company programs routinely claim that the piece reproduces the wrestling style of "the Nanayan people" of "the frozen regions of the Northern Soviet Union," and "Combat Cultural" provides an accurate description of the piece (*Moiseyev Dance Company* 16).[11] What appear to be two small figures clenched together and swathed in fur-trimmed Arctic native garb wrestle back and forth across the stage. The dance proceeds through a comic series of leg holds and falls, including a bit of apparent wall walking and a moment of literal brinksmanship at the edge of the orchestra pit, before its conclusion, when the costume pops open to show that the two identically dressed "battlers" are in fact "just-one-person." The slapstick contest between adversaries so perfectly matched as to be "seeming twins" is, then, only half of the joke: With the trick of the dance revealed, viewers realize that the joke has been on them, and the register of their enjoyment shifts from laughter at the farcical antics of two boys in a fight to wonder at the skill of the single dancer who so ably carried off the deception.[12]

In rendering "the favorite sport and constant pastime" of a Siberian native people as music hall shtick, "Two Boys in a Fight," despite its seeming oddity, is representative of the Moiseyev approach to folk dance (*Moiseyev Dance Company* 16). Shortly after founding his troupe, Moiseyev articulated its four aims: to "create classic national dances . . . reject everything extraneous . . . raise the skill of the performance of folk dances to the highest artistic level, and . . . improve ancient dances in such a way as to influence the creation of new national dances" (*Moiseyev Dance Company* 4). The company's mission was not, then, to preserve vanishing cultural treasures (riven as they often were with politically problematic, "extraneous" material) but to streamline and modernize (without making modernist) "ancient," ethnic dances so that they would embody, in ways that were both inspiring and reassuring, a Soviet vision of cultural unity-in-diversity. As anyone who has seen the Moiseyev knows, this involves adding gymnastic and ballet values to what otherwise are quite simple steps.

The technical and stylistic gulf between actual folk dance and Moiseyev folk dance did not go unnoticed during the company's Met season. John Martin commented on it in his review, though he found both the dancers' extraordinary technical facility and Moiseyev's creative approach to his raw material entirely praiseworthy, and most dance critics covering the 1958 season joined him in applauding Moiseyev's artistic vision. "Of the present repertoire some of the numbers are highly selective arrangements and formalizations of an 'authentic' folk dance," Martin wrote. "The hand of the choreographer . . . is clearly seen in them" ("The Dance: A la Moiseyev").[13] In accepting this substitution of deliberately arranged, highly schooled movement for more heterogeneous homegrown gesture, Martin and his fellow critics likewise accepted Moiseyev's implicit claim (which amounted to a rewriting in dance terms of Russocentric Soviet policies) that the diversity of U.S.S.R. folk-dance forms could legitimately be subsumed under the category of Russian folk dance—a reclassification that in turn nicely licensed the revising, government-approved "hand of the choreographer."[14] That intervening hand is obvious in "Two Boys in a Fight," a work that is much less a folk dance than an ethnic novelty act, one that in April 1958 translated particularly well from Russian to American. What had been written as "Samoyedic" in the Soviet Union could be read as "Eskimo" in an Arctic-fascinated United States, where, just three months after the Moiseyev season, President Dwight D. Eisenhower would sign the Alaska Statehood Act. The two nations' parallel projects of extending national sovereignty into territory above the Arctic circle were indeed "seeming twins"—and not only geographically.[15]

Moore was almost certainly not familiar with the tragic facts of Nganasan life under Russian (later Soviet) rule, but she did know something about dance.[16] It is revealing, then, that of all the works she saw during the Moiseyev's Metropolitan Opera season she chose to apotheosize the piece with the least purely choreographic interest. For as its title indicates, and as drafts of the poem make clear, "Combat Cultural" is not centrally concerned with detailing the visual pleasures of the dance. The first stanza of the poem does cast the

Moiseyev season as a specific example of the enjoyment offered by demonstrations of physical grace and athletic prowess, but two late typescript versions show that Moore saw this stanza as expendable.[17] Rather, the poem subtly addresses the Moiseyev season as an aspect of the growing practice of using art as a tool to promote strategic national goals. Moore was not alone in seeing the Moiseyev as an invitation to consider the relationship between the arts and politics: most of Walter Terry's *Herald Tribune* review of the company's opening night performance was a polemic in favor of expanding U.S. cultural diplomacy. "One need not delve deeply into the political implications of the visit to come up with the simple fact that the Russians have made a mighty effective move in sending us a mass of smiling, richly talented ambassadors," he wrote. "Only the United States government, if it recognizes the ambassadorial powers of the dance (and it should by this time), can see to it that the Russian people enjoy as stirring a glimpse of us as we have of them in the persons of the Moiseyev artists" ("Dance: Russians Blaze"). But while both critic and poet recognized the large issues afoot in the Moiseyev season, "Combat Cultural" shows Moore hesitant to tread where Terry rushes in. The poem has no interest in presenting the dancers' "explosive exuberance and stunning virtuosity" as proof of the need for increased government "exploitation" of the arts ("Dance: Russians Blaze"). Instead, "Combat Cultural" takes up the representational challenge presented by "Two Boys in a Fight" to examine (rather than applaud, deplore, or quietly accept) the notion that the arts and politics should be seen as "battlers dressed identically."

As a mode of artistic practice and scholarly exegesis, allegory is one of the oldest and most direct methods of linking artistic form to political event. Certainly, Moore's description of the Moiseyev's stagy Arctic wrestling match can be read as an allegory of the contemporaneous, extra-theatrical, and similarly "cold" U.S.-Soviet conflict. But following her allegory's deepest implications leads a reader to the unexpected proposition that what looks like a struggle between two diametrically opposed political systems may be better understood as a *trompe l'oeil* rendering of a single phenomenon of aggression. I say unexpected because Moore's poetry is not generally mined for its geopolitical insight. Yet as both David Caute and Odd Arne Westad have made clear, the cold war came about in no small degree thanks to the acres of political, cultural, and ideological common ground shared by the Soviet Union and the United States. Westad describes a "Russian exceptionalism" that, like its U.S. counterpart, entailed a belief in the "[Soviet] mission as part of a world-historical process." Likewise, Caute observes that the cultural front of the cold war "was possible only because both sides were agreed on cultural values to an extent that may seem astonishing, given the huge divide between a 'totalitarian' system and a pluralistic democracy" (Westad 72; Caute, *The Dancer Defects* 4). On the whole, Westad's and Caute's studies have markedly different aims and take irreconcilable positions on the most substantive consequences of the cold war. Whereas Westad emphasizes its effects on the postcolonial fortunes of so-called "third world" nations whose internal political conflicts became bloody proxy wars between the superpowers, Caute claims that, "in forty-five years of cold war, Americans and Russians brought down the occasional plane, little more" (5). Given these differences, their shared point about U.S.-Soviet resemblance is all the more striking.

Moore's multiple drafts of "Combat Cultural" show that U.S.-Soviet cold war politics and the Moiseyev's cold "battlers" comprised the poem's theme and subject from its conception. "People to People / Person to Person" appears in the center of the single sheet of handwritten notes that were almost certainly her first approach to the poem. Distributed around these words are the phrases "in breathless contortion," "bunnyhug," "boy grapplers," and "this remote cold Russia" (Moore Collection). Completely unrecognizable as verse, the notes show Moore following a line of associations stemming from Eisenhower's early foray into cold war cultural combat: the People to People program of "citizen diplomacy" that had been launched with fanfare just two years before the Moiseyev season.[18] An extremely rough typescript draft (possibly her first effort to transmute her impressions into verse) shows her widening the subject of the poem to include other dances ("A dance of the sabres—just for two"; "The dancer of old Russia for me: / with aimlessly drooping handkerchief"), toying with a title ("Old Russia Cold Russia," "The (Cultural) ~~Guests Fight~~ Combat"), and adding an early version of the stanza that denies an inverse relationship between high-quality art and high sales by appealing to the manifest skill of "Two Boys in a Fight." In this draft the poem's final stanza begins to take shape: "Old Russia, did I say? Cold Russia / this time. matching tusslers / have to be two parts of one objective / wrestlers of old Russia / are *symbolic* not satiric." Squeezed in between this stanza and several hastily scrawled stabs at a description of "Two Boys in a Fight" ("the bunnyhug," "twisters in a rug," "wrestlers in a rug") are, again, the words "people to people / person to person" (Moore Collection).

"Combat Cultural" is topical, but its effects resonate beyond its immediate moment thanks to that final stanza, which adopts a skeptical view of the assumed genetic correspondence between cultural text and political pretext that is foundational not only to allegorical reading but also to any diplomatic or strategic use of the arts. Taken together, the poem's central image and closing moral emphasize art's power to *mis*represent or alter reality, as the recognition that we have mistaken one for two opens onto its opposed (or twinned) realization: unities, too, may be seen as temporary, even imaginary, once we understand how the symmetry and wholeness of a work of art (Moore's "objective symbolic of *sagesse*") is an effect of a studied technical virtuosity, of cunningly worked "cement."[19] By casting "Two Boys in a Fight" as both an emblem of cold war superpower relations and a lesson on the craftiness of aesthetic wisdom, the poem pushes us to consider the complex and paradoxical relationship between politics and art, modes of organizing human life that simultaneously endorse and critique each other. Political entities may literally set the stage for the making, disseminating, and experiencing of art, thereby seeming to establish not only the conditions of an artist's production but also the terms in which her work is presented. Yet they rarely succeed in dictating or controlling its reception or interpretation. Fourteen years after the Moiseyev's New York season, in what could be understood as a mid–cold war philosophical treatise, Jacques Derrida insisted on writing's combativeness, its ability to speak beyond, even to contravene, the intentions of its governing-authoring "father." Though he focused on the word, his arguments hold true for the nonliterary texts of music, dance, film, and painting, as well.[20] In truth, Moore's poem configures the field of cultural production as a battleground in which deception in one register becomes illumination in another. For the "combat" of "Combat Cultural" is not only a battle for global political hegemony conducted in displaced fashion via cultural ploughshares beaten into ideological swords. It is also a battle over the politics of aesthetic signification, staged as much within the artworks themselves as within the opera house.

As Moore built up "Combat Cultural" from its early drafts, her bald references to Eisenhower's cold war cultural program rapidly fell away. But close attention to the typescript drafts and to her minute revisions between *The New Yorker* version and the one that appears in the *Complete Poems* indicates that the concept and its uncanny relationship to the subject of "Two Boys in a Fight" continued to haunt the poem. Moore's painstaking attention to the final stanza produced a satisfactory version relatively early in the writing process, so her chief compositional challenge involved shaping the poem so as to lead it properly to this conclusion.[21] Comparing *The New Yorker* version to those published later in *O to Be a Dragon* and the *Complete Poems* shows that she recast the rhetorical questions of the opening stanza into a more general claim while restoring the explanatory footnotes cut by *The New Yorker*. The main focus of her revisions, however, was punctuation. The various published versions show Moore worrying over subtle distinctions among commas, colons, semicolons, and dashes as they linked, or divided, claims and observations, with the hyphen becoming a particular focus of concern.

Begun in the copyediting stage of *The New Yorker* version (as a typesetter's copy of "Combat Cultural" indicates) her work of revision—of interrogation, really—continued straight through to the publication of the final version.[22] Some hyphens are dropped ("frock-coat-skirt" becomes "frock-coat skirt"), while others are added ("platform piece" becomes "platform-piece"). Some hyphenated words are fused into a single entity ("flip-flop" becomes "flipflop"). Some compound constructions separate ("just-one-person" becomes "just one person"). Moore's fiddling with the hyphen suggests an immersion in the question of how, or whether, unrelated and even oppositional bits of raw material might be "cemented" to form a new, seemingly harmonious unity. We might say that the hyphen in "Combat Cultural" does the work of the costume in "Two Boys in a Fight" or of Eisenhower's People to People campaign. It is a trick that, once discovered, compels us to consider how our ability to distinguish between articulated parts and seamless wholes depends on where we believe a line has been drawn (or withdrawn). It emphasizes the protean powers of aesthetic form and heightens the hermeneutic challenge at the core of any effort to grasp the relationship between art and politics. The struggle described in Moore's poem encompasses not only the obvious issue of the political use of art (the efforts of cold war governments and politicians to make art do ideological work) but also the uncanny capacity of artworks to articulate, even embody, sharp political tensions without resolving them. A work of art about the political use of art that itself both proposes and frustrates an exclusively political reading, "Combat Cultural" muses over the ways in which even the most smoothly cemented vessels of containment may rupture in unexpected revelation.

"Combat Cultural" nimbly touches on many of the key historical, formal, and theoretical concerns that I will take up and examine, in more prosaic detail, in the ensuing pages. The poem has been long considered a minor piece by an artist generally not seen as having much interest in political events.[23] Yet I read it as a thoughtful and candid response to immediate geopolitical issues and how they affect larger, longstanding concerns about the correlation (easily felt, less easily defined or described) between art and politics. A meditation on the fraught entanglements of aesthetic principles and political realities, "Combat Cultural" simultaneously reflects and interrogates its sociopolitical frame. These mimetic cross-currents become apparent through a reading that not only filters formal understanding through historical event to reveal the former's debt to the latter—by now the expected and necessary gesture of American cultural analysis—but also takes seriously the possibility that a work of art might challenge, complicate, or even contradict what we think we know about that history.

With its mind-boggling richness of event, its superfluity of arresting (in some cases almost unbelievable) personalities, its multiple national archives packed with records in unprecedentedly varying formats (photographic, video, and audio in addition to print), the cold war turned out to be a supremely narratable event in the years following its mooted conclusion in a U.S. "victory" that, it was somewhat disquietingly postulated, entailed nothing less than an end to history.[24] Tony Judt has pointed out one popular version of the cold war narrative, which sees the forty-five-year-long deadlock between the superpowers as an "inevitable and necessary" (if also "nerve-wracking") stalemate finally broken when, "thanks to greater resources, a vastly more attractive political and economic model, and the initiative of a few good men (and one good woman)—the right side won" (Judt, *Reappraisals* 368–369).[25] The ideological investments of this triumphalist narrative are plain enough. For Judt, this is "a history of *America*'s cold war: as seen from America, as experienced in America, and told in a way most agreeable to many American readers" (371).

The ringing anaphora of Judt's pronouncement is certainly appealing, even as his insinuation of a homogeneous American experience and understanding of the cold war flirts with the same narrow view it means to denounce. It is true that the parochialism of much American cold war political history is shared by many American cold war cultural histories. (The period's technological advances in transportation and telecommunications made the creation and dissemination of literature, film, visual art, music, and dance an unprecedentedly international affair, yet what counts as cold war culture in these studies is by and large an exclusively domestic product.)[26] Still, it is remarkable how few of these cultural histories sound the note of righteous triumphalism. On the contrary, many set out to explore "the power of large cultural narratives to unify, codify, and contain—perhaps *intimidate* is the best word—the personal narratives of [the U.S.] population" (Nadel 4). Thus, while American political histories tend to see the end of the cold war as a vindication of U.S. political and economic values, cultural histories are more interested in exploring how those values were articulated, packaged, and sold. Not surprisingly, such research focuses on the detection and analysis of techniques of persuasion, expressions of patriotism, and the effects of political spin, both as manifested in the works themselves and as practiced by the cultural brokers (from Paramount Pictures and the Museum of Modern Art to the State Department, the Central Intelligence Agency, and the National Endowment for the Arts) who commissioned or presented the work to the public, both in the United States and abroad.

To be sure, there are many differences between political history and cultural studies: in methodology, theoretical orientation, and disciplinary understanding of what constitutes pertinent evidence within the field. All help account for dramatically contrasting interpretive approaches. A more consequential factor, however, lies in the much earlier formulation of cold war cultural studies as a subfield within the humanities. Cold war culture emerged as a special object of analysis years before the fall of the Berlin Wall; its study thus had nothing to do with explaining or justifying a U.S. triumph. A phenomenon of what is sometimes called the "second cold war," the scholarly discovery of American cold war culture announced itself in the back-to-back appearances of Serge Guilbaut's *How New York Stole the Idea of Modern Art: Abstract Expressionism, Freedom, and the Cold War* (1983) and Michael Rogin's "Kiss

Me Deadly: Communism, Motherhood, and Cold War Movies" (1984).[27] Published in the shadow of Fredric Jameson's *The Political Unconscious* and putting many of Jameson's central theoretical claims into brilliant interpretive practice, Guilbaut's and Rogin's analyses set the parameters for the study of cold war cultural productions (what they are, what they do, and how they matter) in terms highly critical of American cold war politics.[28] Rogin's essay, especially, put into play three powerful interpretive criteria. First, the paradigmatic American cold war cultural productions are narrative works (primarily films and novels) that address, either directly or analogously, geopolitical concerns specific to the superpower tensions of the era. Second, these narratives stage this address through formal and rhetorical strategies that reflect a historically specific political demonology, tapping into a paranoid, exclusionary undercurrent in the U.S. polity that, while predating the cold war, finds fresh life within it. Third, the contemporary cultural value of these works accordingly lies in their status as cautionary tales of the power of cultural productions to mobilize public assent to a repressive, anti-democratic politics. Adding to these interpretive guidelines Guilbaut's description of abstract expressionism's capture by an expansionist, neo-imperialist U.S. agenda in early cold war cultural diplomacy "gives us access," as Rogin put it, "to the cold war discourse within which we continue to speak" (238). Undeniably, attaining a more sharply critical cultural self-awareness constituted something of an urgent political necessity at the time: Ronald Reagan delivered his "evil empire" speech to the National Association of Evangelicals on March 8, 1983, and proposed the Strategic Defense Initiative (also known as the Star Wars program) just two weeks later. With the 1970s atmosphere of détente dissolving in a reheated 1950s American militarism promulgated by a president prone to draw on movie plots as foreign policy rationales, the notion that cold war culture could foster a paranoid, rabidly anti-communist ideology rapidly took root.

The collapse of the Soviet Union did produce some studies that sought to complicate this picture by exploring ways in which cold war U.S. cultural productions engaged aspects of the political landscape in manners often more paradoxical than propagandistic.[29] However, the publication of Frances Stonor Saunders's *The Cultural Cold War: The CIA in the World of Arts and Letters* breathed fresh life into notions of cold war cultural complicity by reviving, for a new generation of scholars, the history of how the CIA covertly funded many putatively independent cultural organizations. The most famous and embarrassing instance, given the number of distinguished writers who were caught unawares in its net, was Michael Josselson's and Melvin Lasky's Congress for Cultural Freedom, an infiltration first reported in the *New York Times* in 1966 and soon subjected to withering critical analysis in Christopher Lasch's *The Agony of the American Left*.[30] Lasch's somewhat theoretical interest lay in exploring what this system of funding revealed about both the government that created it and the intellectuals who participated in it. Saunders, by contrast, cast the literature, films, paintings, and music promoted by involved organizations as themselves fundamentally tainted: "Someone once said that if a dog pisses on Notre-Dame, it doesn't mean there's anything wrong with the cathedral. But there's another proverb: . . . 'You can't jump into the lake and come out dry'" (415). A strong antipathy to modernism runs through Saunders's study and is clearly an important aspect of her argument (at times she seems to feel that postwar modernism was itself a CIA plot), but it has drawn little critical attention. Rather, her study largely reenergizes claims made by Reagan-era critics of the left that "abstract" or "atonal" cold war cultural productions were politically opportunistic. Thus, while the cold war may have ended, what the phrase cold war culture signifies has hardly changed. To a considerable degree, discussions of cold war culture remain discussions of a cowering (best case) or co-opted (worst) culture.

Faced, on the one hand, with triumphalist narratives of U.S. cold war victory in which the cultural productions of the era appear chiefly to set a scene or illustrate a political point (the defection of Soviet ballet dancers, the jamming of Voice of America transmissions of jazz music), and, on the other, with exposés of U.S. cold war cultural complicity in which artworks are reduced to instruments of propaganda or ideological stalking horses, I seek to tell a different story. In doing so I have no interest in denying the continuing appropriateness of Rogin's interpretive model for certain works or (turning to post–cold war political histories that include a cultural accounting of the dissolution of the Soviet Union) of dismissing the importance of a study such as Walter L. Hixson's *Parting the Curtain*. Rather, my aim is to broaden what up to now has been a fairly monophonic rendering of cold war culture: roughly faithful to the live event but limited in its range and vulnerable to distortion. Cold war culture deserves a fuller accounting. Indeed, this book's guiding assumption is that cold war culture merits the same sort of sustained, sensitive critical attention that characterizes study of the cultures of Elizabethan England or Weimar Germany. Like cold war America, such labels designate historical periods of cultural production using a kind of political shorthand. While a grasp of Germany's doomed experiment in republican government is a crucial precondition for understanding Bauhaus design, few would be content with an analysis of the school that described it solely as a symptom of political circumstance. Likewise, no one would accept a definition of Elizabethan culture that placed much of the era's music, dance, and poetry outside an established interpretive model. Yet despite a handful of recent, notable exceptions, most analyses of cold war culture have been limited in just this fashion, privileging a barometric connection between the era's literary and cinematic narratives and its political, social, or economic weather in a manner that leaves cultural productions in other media *hors de combat* while assuming that the complex question of the relationship between aesthetic form and political formation, a particularly vexed instance of the question of aesthetic autonomy, has been long settled.[31] In contrast, I aim to show that the question of the relationship between the arts and politics of the cold war remains very much alive. Indeed, it was one of the era's central concerns, as Moore's "Combat Cultural" indicates. By adding ballet and modern dance to the established cold war canon of literature and film, and by reading these works in terms of their critical engagements with two of the most striking developments in cold war American culture—the institutionalization of modernism and the related, explosive growth of government funding of the arts—*Don't Act, Just Dance* proposes the rediscovery of that culture in an expanded field.

The essay by Tony Judt pinpointing the limitations of a certain U.S. cold war historical narrative demonstrates what's at stake in constructing such an expanded field—in particular, the consequences for our understanding of the "end" of the cold war. For Judt, a better accounting involves acknowledging how "the cold war and the post–cold war eras" are "intimately intertwined" (372). Though he does not name specific examples of scholarship that offers such an accounting, he almost certainly had in mind Westad's impressive *The Global Cold War*, which explores how superpower military and political interventions in the developing nations of Africa, Latin America, and Southeast Asia "creat[ed] today's world," an inquiry that, Westad grants, produces "an unabashedly presentist . . . historical account" (1). My study does not take Westad's work as a template to be filled in with selected cultural articulations of specific political struggles; to do so would be to practice, on a grand scale, a certain style of cold war cultural symptomatology I want to avoid. Rather, *Don't Act, Just Dance* shares with *The Global Cold War* a conviction that habits forged in response to the conflict continue to operate today despite their steadily decreasing effectiveness under dramatically changed conditions. Westad's concern is with continued superpower intervention in the politics of other nations, mine with a certain mode of politically engaged cultural hermeneutics.[32] Understanding the rise of cold war cultural studies as itself a phenomenon of the cold war should suggest how the scholarly habit of ferreting out evidence of ideological complicity in U.S. cold war cultural productions is, too, a cold war cultural practice, one rooted in a critical posture (the so-called "hermeneutics of suspicion") that harmonized perfectly with the era's rampant paranoia.[33] This isomorphism has been easy to miss in cold war cultural studies, given the widely shared understanding of contextualist scholarship as a necessary corrective to the faux-naïve cultural politics of those formalist scholars generally viewed as (and condemned for) practicing the epitome of cold war cultural criticism (the New Critics in literature, Clement Greenberg in visual art). Yet it's worth acknowledging the degree to which the forced choice between contextualism and formalism proceeds from a flawed understanding of the nature of the relationship between art and politics.

Castigated by some contextualist scholarship as the essence of political escapism, the notion of aesthetic autonomy has recently emerged as a new category for rethinking the relationship between artistic form and political meaning. For Jacques Rancière, "art is not, in the first instance, political because of the messages and sentiments it conveys concerning the state of the world. Neither is it political because of the manner in which it might choose to represent society's structures, or social groups, their conflicts or identities. It is political because of the very distance it takes with respect to these functions, because of the type of space and time that it institutes, and the manner in which it frames this time and peoples this space" (*Aesthetics and its Discontents* 23). Thus, a more dialectical view of the relationship between cold war formalism and the various politically aware contextualisms that have replaced it suggests a habit of managing deep-seated anxieties about the politics of art by setting to one side the possibility that a work's aesthetic "distance" from "the state of the world" might itself be political. Indeed, for Rancière, such distance represents art's particular *meta*politics, a discourse of the political whose truth is to be found in its ability to reveal the "radical falseness" of what so often passes for politics.[34] *Don't Act, Just Dance* certainly offers readings that explore individual artworks' investments in, or hostility to, a particular political regime or set of social conditions. But my aim here is also to explore how the forms and effects of a certain cool, quintessentially modernist aesthetic distance might themselves constitute an important, if heretofore largely overlooked, political characteristic of cold war cultural productions.

Contextualism and formalism are not only two terms of a false dichotomy; they also are other names for history and theory. The correspondence is not exact, of course, but the tensions structuring the relationship between each pair of terms are similar, and they structure the dialectical reading practice at the heart of this book. Obviously, to identify cold war culture as a subject of study is to accept in advance certain principles of historically grounded cultural analysis; thus, I parse my readings with the aid of a theoretical grammar distilled from philosophical writings that were themselves produced either during the cold war or in its shadow. From this overture, then, part 1 proceeds in three movements: History, Theory, Dancing. First, I describe the political instrumentalization of the arts during the cold war by placing it in the context of the dramatic rise in U.S. government involvement in the arts and concomitant institutionalization (a term I mean to indicate both the effort to make official and the determination to lock up and silence) of modernist aesthetic values. This particular aspect of cold war history was itself historically produced, as efforts to enlist the arts in building the postwar American imperium were rooted in attitudes shaped during the New Deal. Next, I discuss certain key theoretical concepts of Rancière and Theodor W. Adorno, philosophers whose interests in the relationship between art and politics were deeply inflected by the cold war in ways at once complementary and interrogatory. Finally, I explain how this weaving together of history and theory into a new matrix for the study of cold war cultural production shaped my thinking in selecting artwork for analysis—and why, as Marianne Moore so shrewdly recognized, dance lies at the center of that matrix as one of the most potent articulations of the metapolitics of cold war culture.

2

History

From the WPA to the NEA (through the CIA)

Government support of the arts in the United States has several traits that make it unusual in the history of public arts patronage. Wealthy Americans have always collected and commissioned artworks and acted as sustaining patrons for individual writers, painters, and composers, yet such discrete and often idiosyncratic practices do not correspond to the quasi-public, institutionalized traditions of royal and religious patronage that were fundamental to the development of modern European and Asian programs of government arts funding.[1] Rather, Federal One, the first systematic public arts program in the United States, was begun as an employment project during the Great Depression, a condition of emergence that had been enabled by (and, through that enabling, has preserved and perpetuated) a deliberate entanglement of artworks with social work.[2] This entanglement was probably a necessary precondition for the creation of any publicly-funded arts program in the United States, where, as Harriet F. Senie and Sally Webster note, the arts in general have tended to be seen as "a luxury incompatible with republican values" and public art in particular is "regarded with distrust" (xi). Even the most cursory review of the history of government arts funding provides ample evidence supporting their observation while also exposing the peculiarly American character of this distrust. In fact, by identifying an assumed connection to luxury as the most un-American aspect of the arts, Senie and Webster invite a sympathetic, almost patriotic, reading of this wariness.

Many politicians know that populist hostility to luxury can easily be made to register as a robust defense of classically American virtues such as thrift, industry, and democratic egalitarianism. Unsurprisingly, then, the architects of Federal One relied heavily on the rhetoric of democracy in describing the aims and expected benefits of the program, a reliance that A. Joan Saab has shrewdly described and analyzed. Although appeals to democratic virtue are hardly watertight (as recent events in the history of government arts funding vividly illustrate), they played a significant role in the 1935 establishment of Federal One. Saab outlines how the desperate straits of the Depression created conditions under which a set of rather abstract claims about the inevitable expansion of art's "power . . . to do good" could finally make the leap from theory to practice (8, 2). This ambition to recruit art to the task of increasing social good hastened a process Saab calls "desacralization": a demystification of art that was well under way before the 1930s and visible in the favored subjects of The Eight (particularly among the Ashcan School painters: William Glackens, George Luks, Robert Henri, John French Sloan, and Everett Shinn) and in the formal experimentation of artists such as Charles Demuth, Georgia O'Keeffe, Alfred Stieglitz, and Paul Strand (5–6). Saab acknowledges that the formal and thematic aspects of this work were strongly influenced by European modernism.[3] However, she is less interested in tracking the consequences of U.S. adoption of modernist European artistic practices and theories of the artwork (consequences that, arguably, would not be fully visible until the cold war) than in tracing how a certain limited engagement with some of those practices and theories—especially those calling for the abandonment of reverential views of the artwork—became part of an American reconsideration of art's status within a republican democracy. "With the Depression as a backdrop, many deliberately tried to use art in the service of democracy," Saab writes. "People as diverse as government administrators, social workers, established artists, farmers, museum personnel, university professors, industrial designers, urban planners, schoolteachers, doctors, patients, journalists, novelists, clergymen, rabbis, and housewives actively debated the definitions, uses, and significance of art in daily life, and in the process challenged aesthetic categories and transformed traditional ideas of American cultural production" (9). Saab's rhetorical turn to the Whitman catalog, one of the favorite devices of progressive Depression-era political rhetoric, effectively signals her sympathy for the democratic claims of this desacralization project. Unsurprisingly, perhaps, she only obliquely acknowledges the elite roots of this drive to challenge "aesthetic categories," which (as she notes) first found expression in the work of highly trained visual artists and the erudite writings of scholars and critics such as Lewis Mumford, Van Wyck Brooks, and John Dewey.[4] Rather, she explores the desacralization process via the "pedagogies of production" informing the Community Art Center Program, a relatively understudied aspect of Federal One—a move that furthers the perception that the WPA arts programs emerged in response to a grassroots effort to "think differently about the place of art in everyday life" (66), as does her description of the rise of a countervailing (and, with the 1939 termination of Federal One, eventually triumphant) resacralization of the artwork expressed in the canny purchasing, exhibition, and educational practices of the Museum of Modern Art.

Opening less than two weeks after the 1929 stock market crash, MoMA faced from the start the problem of making its mission compelling to an American public inclined, now more than ever, to view art as a luxury. Alfred H. Barr, Jr., the museum's first director, saw the problem as an opportunity "to create a new art institution, one that included not only the traditional fine arts of painting and sculpture but also posters, photographs, and cups and saucers" (Saab 88). MoMA's strategic blurring of the conventional boundaries between high and low aesthetic categories has much in common with the desacralization project of the WPA art programs, as Saab acknowledges. However, she also sees Barr establishing an institutional "commitment to formalism" that, over time, instilled "resacralizing" principles of alienated spectatorship (rather than "desacralizing" modes of individual creative activity) that led MoMA to embrace a "pedagogy of consumption" as the answer to the question of the place of art in American democracy. Rather than create conditions under which many more Americans might now *make* art (the aim of the Community Art Center Program), MoMA's mission was to make it possible for many more Americans than ever before to *see* art.

At issue were the difficult and deeply intertwined problems of deciding what counts as art and what counts as a democratic experience of it. Saab perceptively describes the contradictory effects of the 1930s' most spectacular effort to produce the definitive democratic artwork and art experience: the weird blend of public service and private entrepreneurship that was the 1939 World's Fair Exhibition. Enthusiastically described in a May 1939 *Art Digest* editorial as "a new twentieth-century art form . . . [and] an independent expression of a people," the fair was also, Saab observes, "a model of [art in] democracy firmly grounded in consumer capitalism" (133, 135). Saab's neat binary approach breaks art into sharply opposed and politically charged regimes of production and consumption, each with an allied participatory or spectator-based mode of appreciation (182–183). This model does not describe better or worse strategies for the creation of a democratic art experience but rather outlines dialectically related aspects of modern artworks' entanglements with capital and industry.[5] Importantly, however, her analysis demonstrates that an affirmative instrumentalization of art—an intense, shared governmental and commercial interest in harnessing the power of art to do good—lies at the heart of both of these allegedly opposed strategies for democratizing art.

William F. McDonald also stresses the importance of this instrumentalization in the creation of Federal One. For him, however, the community enrichment programs of the late nineteenth-century settlement house movement were the wellspring.

> In the social-settlement movement the settlement worker served, so to speak, as a staff officer, to coordinate the activities of the caseworker and to relate them to each other and to the whole within a limited social continuum. His consequent concern with groups and varieties of group expression led him naturally to emphasize those outward forms in which, in complex as well as in simple societies, friendly people express the bonds that bind them together. Music, the dance, the pageant, art, handicraft, and the theatre were stressed, not as media in which the maestro and the diva expressed their superiority, but as spontaneous and natural manifestations of the élan of the group.
>
> This emphasis upon the democratic rather than the aristocratic qualities of culture . . . had its origin in the social settlement movement (9).[6]

Like Saab, then, McDonald sees Federal One as legitimizing government support for the arts through appeals to democratic values, more sharply defined as the values underlying the reformist egalitarianism of the settlement house movement. Emphasizing the program's roots in the settlement worker's therapeutic or adaptive uses of art, however, allows McDonald to get a bead on the class anxieties and resentments released by the effort to expand this settlement house vision of culturally-enabled uplift to include so-called "white collar" WPA relief programs, like Federal One, that Saab's analysis misses. Long before the House Committee on Un-American Activities brought down Federal One amid charges of communist agitation and fellow traveling within its programs, white-collar relief, "which employed women as well as men and which busied itself with educational and recreational activities," was "distinctly less popular" with the public than the manual labor programs. The need for such relief "was not so apparent, and the product of [these] activities was in many cases . . . in the lay mind, a luxury." McDonald notes, "what was true of the white collar projects in general was true of the arts programs in particular. Music, drama, literary activity, painting, and sculpture were in the layman's mind avocations that existed either for the delectation of those who could pay for them or for the self-satisfaction of those who engaged in them" (113).

Predictably, then, public attacks against white-collar relief appeared "at the very beginning of the WPA." McDonald cites a report of a 1934 meeting of the New York City Board of Aldermen in which government-funded "cartographic studies, semantics, [and] classes in eurhythmic dancing" were denounced as "boondoggles" (114). Rather than divide the interwar American experiment in public arts support into competing philosophies of participatory versus spectator-based, then, McDonald explores how the attempt to mount a large-scale public arts program on the comparatively modest and distinctly utilitarian cultural foundations of the settlement house movement failed to alter an entrenched American perception of art as a luxury. Like Saab, he sees the Community Art Center Program as a success for the WPA, but he describes its history quite differently. The centers were "a late development in the Federal Art Project and represented a by-product of its main emphasis" (227), which was, as WPA director Harry Hopkins explained in a 1937 letter to President Roosevelt, "the democratization of cultural *opportunities*" (227, 226; emphasis added). This broad construal of Federal One's mandate embraces *both* the making of art and its delectation. Whereas Saab sees a bottom-up movement of participatory democratic arts creation that reached its apotheosis in the Community Art Center Program, McDonald sees a last-ditch effort to save a beleaguered Federal One that involved deliberately minimizing the more avocational aspects of its mission so as to engineer a return to the ministering, instrumentalist approaches to art creation and experience that characterized the settlement house movement.

My point here is not to decide which of these two explanations of the rise and fall of Federal One is the more correct but rather to emphasize how the view of art as a tool for promoting social welfare—a welfare described almost entirely in the affirmative terms of job creation and the celebration of community—was a fundamental enabling condition for the establishment of the first program of government arts funding in the U.S. Both Saab and McDonald show that participants, organizers, and supporters of government arts funding routinely linked this instrumentalization to uniquely American democratic values. Of course, there is nothing inherently democratic in a utilitarian view of art and, in fact, opponents of Federal One also appealed to "democracy" and "America" in their counterarguments. While it is possible to explore these objections in terms of their fit (or lack thereof) with various First Amendment guarantees (a preferred approach during the late 1980s–early 1990s resurgence of ideological objections to government funding of the arts), my interest here is simply to acknowledge how easy it was for an American distrust of art to be revived and redeployed through the very terms used to eliminate that distrust.

The Depression-era experiment in harnessing art's power to promote a particular kind of social good, then, was effective in getting Americans to give a thought to government arts patronage—no small accomplishment—but it was not effective in getting them to keep that thought. Federal One's emphasis on narrowly domestic, increasingly short-term goals offered no firm rationale for arts funding as a worthwhile government endeavor (even though Federal One's most ardent supporters, Eleanor Roosevelt among them, held this view), a weakness that was compounded by the defensive appeals to job creation and community enrichment that characterized Federal One's responses to its conservative critics. In retrospect, however, it is possible to detect, in the critics' repeated expressions of concern about the more cosmopolitan and international ("un-American") aspects of art's power to do good—a power incoherently denounced as at once communistic and elitist—precisely the expanded terms in which the arts again would be instrumentalized, and public support for them justified, in the next program of U.S. government arts funding.

In July 1938, just a month before the opening of the House Un-American Committee hearings that led to the dismantling of Federal One, President Roosevelt approved the establishment of the State Department's Division of Cultural Relations. The first chief of CU (as it was known) was Ben M. Cherrington, who viewed cultural diplomacy as "a mechanism for real exchange and understanding rather than a bullhorn for the American way" (Cull 11). Well intended but untimely, his dialogical approach to cultural diplomacy went into eclipse two years after his appointment when, in an effort to combat growing Nazi propaganda in Latin America, Roosevelt created the Office of the Coordinator of Inter-American Affairs under the aegis of wealthy, energetic, and ferociously ambitious Nelson Rockefeller. The agency acronym was CIAA, "but most people referred to it simply as the 'Rockefeller Office'" (12). Adopting a "heavily ideological and emphatically one-way approach to information work," Rockefeller fundamentally altered the tone and rapidly expanded both the scope and types of South American programs established by Cherrington's more academic and trade-oriented approach to cultural relations (12). Rockefeller's contributions included the publication of a photomagazine, *En Guardia,* modeled on *Life,* which enjoyed such success that Germany launched a counter-journal, *De Guardia.* CIAA also produced Spanish-language shortwave radio broadcasts ("bombastic, sugar coated" and distinctly less popular than the "honest, frank and uncolored" programs of the BBC) and created a funding front, Prencinradio, to promote radio and film projects sympathetic to U.S. interests (12–13).[7]

As its mass-media emphasis makes clear, the CIAA mission was structured along the lines of a modern sales campaign. Rockefeller drew on the forms and methods of American propaganda that had been established during World War I by George Creel's Committee on Public Information ("in all things from first to last . . . a vast enterprise in salesmanship, the world's greatest adventure in advertising"), techniques later refined and elaborated by public relations maestro Edward L. Bernays (Henderson 24).[8] In the two years of its existence, Creel's committee had invented almost the entire range of techniques in what he euphemistically called white or gray "information services," and during the cold war they dominated "public diplomacy" (the favored term in the Eisenhower years). To sell a foreign war to the American public and manage pro-U.S. propaganda overseas, Creel had "recruited university scholars, made films, set up exhibits, . . . invented the 'handout' for public information, developed pictorial publicity, propaganda cartoons and memorable posters, lined up historians and intellectuals, co-opted labor leaders, and adapted a raft of other practices unknown before 1917" (Arndt 29). An unapologetic hard-sell, the approach was unpopular with Congress, and the CPI was closed down almost immediately after the war. Roosevelt's undersecretary of state and chief foreign policy advisor Sumner Welles explicitly rejected its methods (xi–xii, 31). But those methods were exactly right for the flamboyant, emphatic Rockefeller, whose family's public relations advisor, Ivy Lee, came from the CPI, and he kept faith with the program despite its predictably mixed results (31). As Brazil's exhausted minister of external relations, Oswaldo Aranha, is said to have quipped in 1941 after a series of meetings with "symphony conductors, film stars, and even the 'short-pants ambassador' of the Boys Club of America," "One more goodwill mission and Brazil will declare war on the U.S.A." (Cull 13).

Though government patronage of the arts was by no means the central aim of the CIAA office, its key innovation and lasting contribution was to include the fine and performing arts among the range of products deemed to be suitable vehicles for pro-American propaganda. Drawing on his extensive contacts within the world of American fine and performing arts (his mother, Abby Aldrich Rockefeller, was one of the founders of MoMA; Rockefeller himself had been elected president of the museum's board in 1939, one year before the creation of the CIAA), Rockefeller established a system of government assistance of traveling exhibitions of contemporary U.S. art and performing artists that was, in fact if not in name, a state-sponsored program of arts patronage. In 1941, in one of its most consequential endeavors, the office sponsored a twenty-eight-week tour of the nonce troupe American Ballet Caravan, comprised of professional dancers culled from Lincoln Kirstein's failed Ballet Caravan and George Balanchine's defunct American Ballet, supplemented by advanced students from the School of American Ballet (at that point Kirstein's and Balanchine's sole surviving endeavor). "The first officially sponsored overseas performing arts event in U.S. history," the tour had a decisive impact on the development of Balanchine's career (Arndt 403). Two of his most celebrated works, *Ballet Imperial* and *Concerto Barocco,* were made for it, and the experience taught Kirstein a never-to-be-forgotten lesson in the value of government sponsorship.[9]

It is tempting to credit this information-services colonization of the arts to Rockefeller's outsized vanity or see it as a chapter in the larger narrative of his family's pursuit of global economic power. But doing so overlooks the important precedent of Federal One. Historian Frank Ninkovich draws a clear connection between the use of the fine and performing arts in the CIAA programs and the previously established "federal role in culture . . . created by the WPA" (12). Indeed, precisely as federal commitment to a program of domestic arts funding waned, interest grew in government use of the arts within an international, pro-American information service. The focus on exploiting the power of art to do good was not lost; it was simply relocated.

This practice of yoking artwork to a more pointedly political, internationally imagined "social work," briefly eclipsed by the exigencies of military propaganda and intelligence during World War II (though the 1942 creation of Voice of America under the supervision of former Federal Theatre director John Houseman bears noting), grew at a tremendous rate in the early years of the cold war. Consider the pace of congressional legislation and executive action: the passage of the 1946 Fulbright Act (the year in which the "Rockefeller Office" was subsumed into the State Department); 1948 Smith-Mundt Act; the 1953 founding of the U.S. Information Agency; and the 1954 creation of Eisenhower's 5 million dollar emergency fund for the rapid, massive expansion of cultural exchange programs that would, the president hoped, "demonstrate the superiority of the products and cultural values of our system of free enterprise" (Osgood 214).[10] The State Department's recruiting (some might say exploitation) of William Faulkner as one of its earliest and most highly-publicized international goodwill ambassadors is among the most well-known early chapters in this history. Faulkner traveled every year in the five years following his 1950 appearance in Stockholm to receive the Nobel Prize in literature, making journeys at State's behest to destinations as various as Lima, São Paulo, Tokyo, Manila, Rome, London, and Reykjavik.[11]

This newly internationalist instrumentalizing of the arts did not escape the charges of un-Americanism that had helped to scuttle Federal One. Cultural exchange programs and overseas information services were early and favorite targets of the resurgent, vociferous, and vicious anti-communist hysteria that marked the opening years of the cold war; the combined effects of Senator Joseph McCarthy's claims of communist subversion within the State Department and Congressman George A. Dondero's attacks on the "subversive," "un-American" nature of modernist art destroyed or severely crippled many early efforts in cultural diplomacy. An early casualty was Advancing American Art, a 1946 experiment in federal arts patronage in which the State Department directly purchased 118 paintings by forty-seven artists to create a traveling exhibition of contemporary U.S. art. The show featured works by Georgia O'Keeffe, Arthur Dove, John Marin, Romare Bearden, and Ben Shahn, and the predominance of work in a modernist idiom was attacked by the artistically conservative (and likely envious) members of the American Artists Professional League, who "violently protested" the use of American tax dollars to purchase "a lot of radical and un-American art" (Genauer, "Still Life" 89).[12] When congressional investigations into the artists' political backgrounds revealed that several were or had been persons of interest in recent House Un-American Committee hearings, Secretary of State George C. Marshall recalled the show from Czechoslovakia. The paintings were declared government surplus and sold. Marshall pledged never again to spend public funds on art, and the State Department took the further step of deciding that no artist thought to be a communist would be allowed to participate in government-sponsored exhibitions. Advancing American Art precipitated a national furor that, for many Europeans, confirmed exactly the suspicions of American philistinism it had been designed to discredit. Those suspicions were hardly allayed by McCarthy's 1953 campaign to root out communist infiltration at the Voice of America and purge literary works by suspected communists from the State Department's International Information Administration network of European libraries (also known as America Houses). The latter, in particular, was a public-relations nightmare for the United States.[13]

It has been argued that the Central Intelligence Agency got into the business of arts patronage precisely to sidestep this internationally embarrassing, politically opportunistic eagerness to ferret out communist subversion within the nation's earliest cold war expressions of "soft power."[14] This was the claim of the brash and unapologetic Thomas W. Braden, a CIA operative and architect of the "vast and secret" network of agency-allied cultural programs managed by the Orwellian-named International Organization Division (IO). His aggressive *Saturday Evening Post* response to 1966 revelations of CIA involvement in a wide range of national and international labor, student, cultural, and intellectual organizations claimed that covert operations to fund symphony tours, bribe labor leaders, and create CIA-controlled citizen action groups were not only necessary but fundamentally all of a piece. Strategically speaking, a successful concert by an American symphony did exactly the same political work as a dummy student union.

> As for the theory advanced by the editorial writers that there ought to have been a Government foundation devoted to helping good causes agreed upon by Congress—this may seem sound, but it wouldn't work for a minute. Does anyone really think that congressmen would foster a foreign tour by an artist who has or has had left-wing connections? . . . Back in the early 1950s, when the cold war was really hot, the idea that Congress would have approved many of our projects was about as likely as the John Birch Society's approving Medicare. . . .
>
> I remember the enormous joy I felt when the Boston Symphony Orchestra won more acclaim for the U.S. in Paris than John Foster Dulles or Dwight D. Eisenhower could have brought with a hundred speeches. . . .
>
> I remember with great pleasure the day an agent came in with the news that four national student organizations had broken away from the Communist International Union of Students and joined our student outfit instead. I

> remember how Eleanor Roosevelt, glad to help our new International Committee of Women, answered point for point the charges about germ warfare that the Communist women's organization had put forward. I remember the organization of seamen's unions in India and in the Baltic ports. (10, 14)

A publicity hound given to extreme and eminently quotable pronouncements, Braden was, personally and ideologically, a chip off the "Rockefeller Office" block.[15] His subsequent media career dimmed public memory of his early CIA work. (After his death in 2009, most obituaries identified him only as the author of *Eight Is Enough* and Pat Buchanan's sparring partner on *Crossfire.)* But his gregariousness and his lively defense of the agency's line on nonmilitary covert operations have made him a seminal figure in cold war cultural studies.[16] Braden's claims (not to mention his seeming personification of the ideological links connecting the CIA, MoMA, and the Rockefellers) are foundational to Serge Guilbaut's influential *How New York Stole the Idea of Modern Art*. By focusing on the actions of American politicians, patrons, editors, gallery owners, museum directors, and foundation heads eager to promote an anti-communist (and neo-imperialist) agenda by exploiting the work of U.S. artists, Guilbaut offers insight into the assumptions these various arts handlers shared concerning the social and political functions of "modernist," "difficult," "challenging," or "abstract" art, assumptions that made efforts to turn art into propaganda seem both plausible and possible.

Widely heralded in 1983 as groundbreaking scholarship, the book's central arguments were not new, a fact that Guilbaut ingeniously, if circuitously, acknowledges when he discusses the 1970s studies of Max Kozloff, Eva Cockcroft, and David Shapiro and Cecile Shapiro, all deeply influenced by the reports of covert CIA involvement in seemingly benign projects of cultural exchange (11).[17] Together with these so-called revisionist historians of post–World War II American visual art, he has made claims about the rise of abstract expressionism that have since come under considerable critical scrutiny.[18] Although Michael Kimmelman, Michael Leja, Ann Eden Gibson, and David Craven have contributed to this critique, the impact of their work on cold war cultural studies has not, for the most part, matched the force and range of its impact among art historians, where the revisionist reading of abstract expressionism as political puppet has largely fallen out of favor (Kimmelman 4).[19]

In truth, Braden's account of the rationale and successes of CIA-funded cultural operations needs to be taken with several grains of salt. As Hugh Wilford observes, his insistence that congressional Red baiting justified CIA involvement in international cultural programs ignores the fact that several front organizations had been established well before the Red Scare. It also minimizes the significant strategic advantage these organizations enjoyed when they maintained a seeming independence in countries that would have viewed a clear American connection with suspicion or hostility (250).[20] Even more dubious (though, until now, never seriously questioned) is Braden's insistence that events such as the Boston Symphony Orchestra's 1952 Paris performance of Igor Stravinsky's *Le Sacre du Printemps* at the Congress for Cultural Freedom–sponsored *Oeuvres du XXe Siècle* spoke for strategic American interests in the same tone, and to the same effect, as did the labor and student leaders who had been drafted monetarily or ideologically to the anti-communist cause.[21] The insinuation that hearing an American orchestra play *Le Sacre* might somehow lead Parisian leftists to reconsider their allegiance to the *Parti communiste français* bears more than a passing resemblance to the "feebleminded . . . common sense" that Theodor Adorno identifies as the hallmark of a thoroughly rationalized, quantified, and consumerist approach to art and aesthetic experience (13).[22] I explore the theoretical critique of this common sense in some detail in chapter 3. Here, I want to emphasize how this confident belief in the arts' utility to a program of political propaganda continues the Depression-era American interest in tapping the power of art to do good by matching the country's cold war-intensified conflation of democracy and capitalism to a similar effort to fuse art and propaganda.

The implosion of McCarthyism and the subsequent softening of hardline anti-communism into a more centrist "liberal consensus" cleared the way for increased public spending on State Department and U.S. Information Agency efforts at cultural diplomacy while slowing (without ever quite ending) the creation of covert CIA-sponsored initiatives. But while public funding for international programs in arts and culture increased, the philosophy behind them remained unchanged. U.S. government arts patronage as practiced under the mantle of cold war cultural diplomacy was more strongly influenced by the values of culture industry than Federal One had been, an effect of the CPI's focus on information service as a mode of advertising. During the cold war, government arts patronage operated on the assumption that *all* American cultural endeavors were, in Eisenhower's words, propaganda for "the superiority of the products and cultural values of [the American] system of free enterprise." His linking of products and cultural values reflects a fundamental faith that "America" can find powerful, affirming, and equivalent expression in both a glass of Pepsi-Cola and an Arthur Dove canvas.[23] In this view, art is indeed little more than the "product" of a larger, pre-existing set of social, economic, or political conditions, the "values" of which it is the speaking symptom. Thus, soft drinks and painting have the identical power to do good for the United States; their differences lie primarily in issues of demographics and market share—useful differences for public diplomacy, since it is in America's strategic interest to draw on the broadest array of products in service to the cause.

The public face of cold war cultural diplomacy was unremittingly upbeat, and until quite recently the scholarship has largely reproduced without question the somewhat implausible claims promulgated by the internal memoranda that served as the chief means of programmatic assessment within the State Department and the USIA (for instance, the assertion that a U.S. movie star's comments about Cyprus's political sovereignty directly "forwarded American objectives" in Turkey).[24] Inclination to accept such claims undoubtedly stems from the appealing conceptual tidiness of imagining these programs as small-scale rearticulations, in a soft (feminized, seductive) cultural key, of hard (masculinized, coercive) strategic initiatives—those cold war military, political, and economic interventions undertaken in Guatemala, Iran, Vietnam, Chile, and elsewhere. Yet early on there was considerable evidence that cultural diplomacy, particularly efforts that emphasized American accomplishments in the visual and performing arts, was largely ineffective as an instrument of political propaganda. Sometimes it was even counterproductive. Odd Arne Westad and Nicholas Cull have shown that international educational exchange, the arm of cold war public diplomacy many believed most likely to produce advocates for the American way, had its share of failures, students whose experiences in the U.S. either awakened a committed opposition to capitalism or deepened preexisting anti-American convictions. Probably the most well-known instance of this type of diplomatic "failure" is Sayyid Qutb, founder of Egypt's Islamist Muslim Brotherhood and, in the view of some, the "intellectual grandfather of al-Qaeda" (Cull 503); always devout, Qutb was radicalized by his studies and travels in the U.S. between 1948 and 1950.[25]

The U.S. Information Service (USIS) "was routinely known as 'useless' in State Department slang" (Cull 502; also see note 10 in this chapter for the distinction between USIA and USIS). Even Richard T. Arndt, a former Fulbright Association president whose passionate dedication to the ideals of genuine cultural exchange remain undimmed despite what he himself calls the "meretricious rhetoric" of "USIA puffery," has confessed to being "unprepared for the shock of mediocrity" that greeted him when he entered the agency in 1961 (xxi, xiv). He discovered that few of his fellow agents had much genuine interest in or understanding of the educational and fine arts aspects of their mission:

> USIA's six-week training session grouped two overlapping teams of thirty "lateral-entrants," highly selected we were told [and] . . . allegedly experienced in some area of "interest" to USIA and its work. In fact, most came from journalism or public relations backgrounds . . . or from domestic political work—one from a trade union, one from public policy advocacy, one from non-university military history. I was alone in representing a research university. [Arndt had been a professor of French at Columbia.] Among us, eight at most spoke a foreign language with any proficiency. . . . More than half had left their futures behind. Some had trouble with alcohol, some were shedding families, some were in full career crisis. (xiv)

An "accidental, ill-defined and contradictory mix of cultural relations and propaganda" (Arndt 85) formulated as "a way to address the world rather than a mechanism for understanding it" (Cull 489) and sustained by "flamboyant claims of success" that were, and remain, fundamentally "impossible to prove or disprove" (Arndt 84), U.S. cold war cultural diplomacy "forwarded American objectives" much less frequently than has been supposed. As Arndt puts it, "expecting a cultural program to . . . influence a parliamentarian's vote is like assuming all Stanford graduates will vote for the same presidential candidate" (xix). Obviously untenable in the field of education, the confident expectation of consistently favorable strategic outcomes for American public diplomacy begins to seem a kind of ideologically induced fantasy when the "diplomats" come from the world of the fine and performing arts.

Funding for the arts has never amounted to more than 2 percent of the budget for public diplomacy (Arndt xviii). But these State Department and USIA programs, which constituted the nation's only system of government arts patronage between Eisenhower's 1954 creation of the emergency fund and the 1965 establishment of the National Foundation on the Arts and Humanities, drew disproportionate attention from Congress and the public, and efforts to make art and artists serve established policy needs were correspondingly strong. Several untoward events, however, indicate that this was easier said than done.[26] Victoria Phillips Geduld's recent analysis of the Martha Graham Dance Company's 1955 State Department–sponsored tour of Asia describes multiple instances of audience confusion and hostile local reviews; for Geduld, these appearances "backfired" diplomatically (66).[27] And as Penny Von Eschen's groundbreaking study of the fortunes of the cold war jazz ambassadors has made clear, for artists such as Louis Armstrong, Dizzy Gillespie, Randy Weston, and Duke Ellington, accepting government arts patronage hardly entailed unquestioning acceptance of U.S. foreign policy objectives, much less an assumption of responsibility for forwarding "American interests" as construed by the State Department. Von Eschen's study introduces an important complicating chapter into the long-established narrative of American jazz as an especially robust form of pro-U.S. propaganda during the cold war, in part because she focuses on the experiences of the touring artists and the effects of their on- and offstage appearances in Africa, South America, Eastern Europe, and the Far East rather than on the fortunes of Willis Conover's Voice of America program "Music U.S.A."[28] By revealing the artists' indifference and sometimes active hostility to U.S. foreign policy objectives, her portrait of cultural diplomacy's political effects raises serious questions about the common belief that the arts are an especially persuasive form of propaganda.

> While the performing arts tours [of the State Department and USIA] accompanied America's post–World War II pursuit of political and economic control through policies of modernization and development, control over the export of culture remained elusive. The State Department failed to anticipate that people would interact in unforeseen ways. . . .
>
> Intended as a color-blind promotion of American democracy, the tours . . . led just as often to the fostering of collaboration and solidarity throughout the African diaspora. . . . As the government recognized the power of African American culture and tried to harness it to project an image of U.S. racial progress abroad, the State Department's cultural programs and tours in fact helped to nurture the development of oppositional transnational and Afro-diasporic sensibilities. (255, 256)

Von Eschen is frank about her limitations when it comes to analyzing the formal aspects of jazz, yet the strong implication of *Satchmo Blows Up the World* is that some inherent property of both the music and its artists is uniquely conducive to an independent and politically critical aesthetic experience. Here she follows an established interpretive line within contemporary jazz cultural studies that focuses on the sociopolitical aspects of the music's emergence within U.S. racial history. The approach has considerable merit, but it may minimize or ignore those politically less straightforward aspects of the art form that a more thorough-going analysis of jazz's complex and simultaneous formal engagements with modernist aesthetics and the imperatives of culture industry would make apparent.[29] What Von Eschen presents as a politics unique to the jazz aesthetic might be more fully understood as jazz's signal articulation of the metapolitics of modernism. As chapter 3 will show, this is a more active and political aesthetic formation than many have commonly supposed.

Americans had barely recovered from the impact of the spectacular 1958 Moiseyev Dance Company season when, in April 1959, the Bolshoi Ballet made its astonishing Metropolitan Opera House debut.[30] By then, public discussions of government funding for the arts had moved well beyond the incendiary mid-1950s denunciations of cultural diplomacy's "blunders and baloney."[31] Rather, such discussions had become so infused with the spirit, expressed in Walter Terry's Moiseyev review, that the time had come for increased government "exploitation" of the arts that New York Republican senator Jacob K. Javits was moved to publish in the *New York Times* an impassioned call for "the establishment of a United States Arts Foundation that would bring the prestige of the Federal Government to bear to develop more fully and to disseminate more widely our cultural heritage . . . [so that], in self-defense, if for no less selfish reason, we [will be] prepared to meet the cultural challenge of our competitors. . . . If we are to measure up to the stature of leader of the free world, we must act as such, as a nation's civilization is equated in many places with its degree of culture" (21).[32]

Historians have well described the strong connection between the rapid growth of a cultural front in the cold war and the 1965 creation of the National Foundation on the Arts and Humanities, the parent agency of the National Endowments for the Arts and the Humanities.[33] In 1959, that connection made itself audible in Javits's oddly military-industrialist appeal for government arts patronage in the cause of "self-defense" against "the cultural challenge of our competitors." Transposed into a more diplomatic key, the cold war note could be detected as late as 1988 in Livingston Biddle's description of the arts as "our unfailing ambassadors, . . . perpetual allies" able to "enter portals otherwise closed" (516).[34] Borrowing a metaphor from Yeats and Americanizing it in pointedly patriotic fashion, Michael Straight, deputy chief of the NEA during the agency's golden age under Richard M. Nixon, declared that the arts had become politically invaluable "twigs for an eagle's nest."[35]

Accepting the role the cultural cold war played in the establishment of America's most comprehensive program of government arts patronage entails considering the possibility that the crumbling of the communist Eastern Bloc and rapid disintegration of the Soviet Union, far more than the "offensive" artwork of Robert Mapplethorpe, Andres Serrano, or Karen Finley, were the most salient factors in the late 1980s–early 1990s collapse of congressional support for the NEA—a collapse from which the agency has yet to fully recover.[36] This is the view of art critic Michael Brenson, who frames his analysis in a canny reading of John F. Kennedy's October 26, 1963, address at the dedication of Amherst College's Robert Frost Library. There, the president shrewdly aligned that most ideological of American self-understandings—the notion that the United States "is, at its core, a nonideological nation"—with the romantic/modernist image of the artist as the "last champion of the individual mind and sensibility against an intrusive society and an officious state" (Brenson 18, 16).[37] "Art is not a form of propaganda, it is a form of truth," Kennedy proclaimed, his syntax reflecting the binary logic at the core of American cold war anti-communism. "In a free society art is not a weapon and it does not belong to the sphere of polemics and ideology." Taking direct aim at the cultural politics of the Soviet Union, he declared, "Artists are not engineers of the soul" (18).[38]

Less than a month after delivering this speech (the most heart-felt statement yet from a president whose personal and political attention to the arts had been much noted in the press), Kennedy was dead. Though Lyndon Johnson signed the bill establishing the National Foundation on the Arts and Humanities, the program's creation was widely viewed as the fulfillment of Kennedy's vision. Brenson is right, then, to see his Amherst speech as crucial to establishing artistic "free expression . . . [as] a cornerstone of the NEA" and to attribute this move to cold war imperatives (Brenson 19). For if artists "were not independent, and if the government did not demonstrate that it was confident enough to allow them to criticize, even attack, American institutions, [they] could not help ground the country during this win-at-all-cost moment that required the government to adopt an ends-justify-the-means mentality in order to survive, and they would not be effective ideological weapons" (17). Even so, in the more pragmatic political discussions surrounding the NEA's creation, the critical capacities of art, though dutifully acknowledged, were emphatically relegated to the background. Rather, the preferred rhetorical mode tapped into the same quasi-Arnoldian, democratic grandiloquence that had accompanied the creation of Federal One and the development of cultural diplomacy: proponents of the legislation praised the arts for their uplifting, affirmative qualities, making America "a more beautiful . . . [and] *happier* nation" (20).

> Although the Cold War climate in America demanded tolerance for radical challenges to convention, whatever form they took, the Kennedy oratory, and congressional arguments for the Endowment, were most comfortable with the belief that art was ennobling and transcendent. As the Cold War wound down, and President Ronald Reagan's America, chest-thumpingly proud of its God-fearing economic and military empire, assumed, correctly, that it no longer needed to prove its tolerance for free expression to win the hearts and minds of the rest of the world, the Kennedy and NEA balance between an ennobling view of art . . . and a commitment to artistic free expression . . . became increasingly unstable. After the Cold War ended in 1989, the willingness of Congress to tolerate NEA support for free expression . . . disappeared. (20–21)

Unsurprisingly, perhaps, the end of the cold war brought about the end of most programs of cultural diplomacy. The USIA was closed without much fanfare in 1999, and most of its few remaining services were folded into the State Department.[39]

Still, in accepting Brenson's point, I do not mean to claim that cold war cultural combat was the *primary* factor in the historic establishment, rapid expansion, and remarkable contraction of a comprehensive program of U.S. federal arts patronage—though the fact that it took a nuclear doomsday scenario to persuade Americans that the time had come to make a formal commitment to public funding of the arts certainly deserves acknowledgment. Rather, by situating cold war–inspired government arts programs in the context of a historical narrative that begins in the 1930s, I want to emphasize a peculiarly American instrumentalization of the arts, one that informed both Depression-era and cold war understandings of art's role in public life. The postwar formalism of the New Critics and Clement Greenberg is often cast as the antithesis of both the 1930s realist aesthetic and an associated style of political activism in the arts. But uncovering the common ideological taproot of government-supported arts programs between the 1930s and the 1960s has allowed me to identify and isolate a shared core assumption that the only viable program of American government arts patronage is one in which the arts earn their public keep. They must either produce specific, measurable social improvements, or they must celebrate and affirm preconstituted national or community values. Thus, enthusiasm for government arts patronage rises in proportion to the growth of social or political problems that the arts might conceivably address (say, relieving unemployment or fighting communism), and ebbs when those problems subside (the economy recovers) or disappear (the United States "wins" the cold war).[40]

In 1968, the NEA asked art historian Francis V. O'Connor to assess the legacy of the WPA visual arts programs in New York. His conclusions contain an uneasy admission that the creation of the NEA had been driven by expediencies not all that different from those that had characterized Federal One as well as later diplomatic uses of the visual and performing arts. Asked by the NEA to review New Deal arts projects with the goal of formulating recommendations for contemporary government patronage policy, O'Connor produced a rich and suggestive 226-page report that includes a guide to New Deal art inventories and indices, excepts from interviews with WPA artists (whose memories of their experiences ranged from nostalgic recollections of artistic community to bitterness at the destruction of work deemed government surplus), and an assessment of Federal One's effectiveness in providing employment and economic relief. O'Connor's concluding list of eighteen policy recommendations has the following preface:

> Since the government will probably never face in the future a situation so similar to the thirties that it will have the abject destitution of the nation's artists to justify and make expedient its patronage, it will have to grow even more willing than it was then to risk and to waste its resources. Indeed, if the Federal government cannot bring itself to risk the imponderables of artistic expression and development, and to waste, perhaps, a small fraction of its immense resources, . . . then it should not seek to support art at all.
>
> Implicit in this is the reality that all future Federal support of the visual arts must be based on an increasingly comprehensive and deepening willingness to value these arts for their own sakes rather than to subsidize them solely for the sake of something else. (110–111)[41]

Clearly, O'Connor was criticizing the utilitarianism that had informed Federal One and cautioning against continued reliance on instrumentalist rationales for government arts patronage. Some might see his call for government support of art for its own sake as articulating an "openly elitist . . . autonomous aesthetic of modernist formalism" (Blake 203)—an expressive mode that, it's often claimed, enjoyed special favor in cold war government arts programs "because [the art] was abstract [and thus] . . . unlikely to be interpreted in ways potentially disrupting to the political and cultural consensus" (Binkiewicz 223). Rooted in Guilbaut's *How New York Stole the Idea of Modern Art*, this notion of abstract modernist art as an "elitist" quintessence of art for art's sake that is also inherently non- or apolitical has become, over the past twenty years, the favored explanation for the perceived dominance of work in a modernist idiom (in dance, music, and literature as well as visual art) within cold war U.S. programs of government arts patronage. Donna M. Binkiewicz, for example, has claimed that "tried-and-true . . . politically consensus-oriented . . . high modernist" work enjoyed a degree of government support that "more inclusive," "more figurative" and "politically more critical" "postmodern" work did not.[42] To illustrate her point, she contrasts the politically explicit "new aesthetic" of Willie F. Herrón III and Glugio Nicandro (known as Gronk)'s 1973 *Black and White Moratorium Mural* in East Los Angeles with "older forms of abstract expressionism, such as [Robert] Motherwell's *Elegies,* [which] had become the accepted cannon [*sic*] but were no longer on the cutting edge" (223). Modernism is a received idea through Binkiewicz's study (as is her tidy opposition of "modernist" elitism and "postmodernist" "pluralism"), and her critique is tellingly confused here: canonical works are, *eo ipso,* not "cutting edge," and while the more than 150 large canvases Motherwell produced in his *Elegy to the Spanish Republic* series are, indeed, modernist abstractions, they can hardly be termed apolitical—as the project's full title indicates. Rather than attribute O'Connor's views to cultural elitism, then, we would do better to take seriously his fear that the government's mid–cold war embrace of the role of patron might turn out to be just as contingent and expedient as had earlier experiments in arts funding. Indeed, the NEA's post–cold war fortunes have shown that fear to have been well founded.

Then, too, the limits of the notion that the American distrust of art is rooted in an democratically egalitarian suspicion of its connections to non- or anti-republican luxury or elitism are finally becoming clear. While interesting, an emphasis on the moralizing and religious rhetoric within congress members' extraordinary expressions of hostility and disgust about specific works seems, in itself, insufficiently illuminating, simply enlarging the appeal to populist egalitarianism by adding an equally predictable gesture toward a puritanical American suspicion of sensual pleasure.[43] We might do better to consider the fact that the wrangling over the NEA unfolded in the early years of what is now recognized as the onset of an unprecedented postwar explosion in income inequality that saw increasingly large fortunes being amassed by an increasingly small percentage of the American population.[44] While it did not go completely unremarked in the early 1990s, it was far less of a target for populist outrage than was the work of Mapplethorpe, Serrano, and Finley. Whatever concerns may have informed the skeptical view of art held by the nation's earliest citizens, then, Americans during the immediate post–cold war years did not have trouble reconciling luxury and elitism with the reigning "[R]epublican values."

Yet Americans not only continued to distrust art: they denounced it, often with extraordinary vehemence. There may well be something unique within the American character that accounts for this attitude. But can it account for it completely? Might something about the art object itself—or, to put it more exactly, something about the demands made on the subject who experiences modern art within the cold war political frame—also be at play?

3

Theory

Adorno and Rancière (Abstraction, Modernism, Gender, Sexuality)

To the contemporary American academic humanist reared under the command "always historicize," Jacques Rancière's 2003 assertion that "there is no criterion, . . . no formula" for determining the correlation of politics and aesthetics may seem willfully naïve or deliberately provocative.[1] Along with his observation that "there is no such thing" as historical necessity, his claim seems to dismiss current beliefs about the best scholarly practices for uncovering and interpreting connections between art and politics (Rancière, *Dissensus* 201). Certainly, it is neither accurate nor fair to characterize current wisdom as *entirely* governed by the perception that artwork is a symptom or reflection of the political, economic, and social conditions of its moment of production and circulation. Nevertheless, art's effects are portrayed as subordinate to larger forces, whether revolutionary or repressive, to a degree that would be striking if it were less ubiquitous.

The three most common views of the relationship between art and politics do convey a sense that the arts are a thoroughly second-order phenomenon. First, there is the view of art's connection to politics as ornamental at best, but more often "useless" (recall the State Department's nickname for the USIS, discussed in chapter 2) when it isn't a dangerously deceitful seduction or a consciousness-blunting drug. According to the second view, art inhabits, maybe even constitutes, a transcendent, elevated plane that is emphatically separate from the world of politics but obliquely related insofar as the ennobling capacities of "good" art help build better citizens. These competing formulations appear across the ideological spectrum in versions tweaked to fit political agendas on both the right and the left, and they continue to dominate public discussions in the United States. The third view holds sway in the more rarified precincts of the academy. Here, autonomous artworks are seen as species within the larger genus of expressive cultural practices. In this view, artworks, along with sport, religious ritual, cuisine, and fashion, function chiefly as manifestations of deep social forces. This sociological or anthropological view of art, sometimes descriptive, sometimes prescriptive, tends to emphasize art's grounding in and forwarding of the operating assumptions of the status quo. It often comes close to expressing the correlation between art and politics as a formula, complete with equal sign: that is, an artwork's immediate social context *is* its meaning.

Of course, although it may seem simple in the abstract, this task of historicist/contextualist interpretation is rarely simple in practice. The challenge lies in deciding which of a work's many possible contextual frames is *most* determining. Any given artwork bears the marks of multiple contextual pressures, which frequently invite competing, even contradictory, interpretations. Thus, the hermeneutic task is complex. Yet even when the interpretive aim is to account for art's ability to embody or engender resistance to the dominant sociopolitical conditions of its production (as in Stuart Hall's program for cultural studies, for instance), emphasis tends to lean in one of two directions.[2] One emphasizes the resisting listeners'/readers'/viewers' capacities for critically creative revision, usually understood as being expressed collectively and thereby deepening the anthropological or sociological aspect of contextualist reading. The other investigates an artist's own political investments, typically portrayed as a function of her socioeconomic station, race, gender, or sexuality.

The artwork itself, as a gateway into an often unpredictable but politically consequential *aesthetic* experience, is rarely credited with fostering such interrogatory power. Especially in cold war cultural studies, scholars tend to see aesthetic experience as a figment of false consciousness: at best a compensatory politics, at worst an ideological narcotic. Rancière aside, much study in the field has proceeded under the assumption that there *is* a formula for the appropriate correlation of art and politics: Walter Benjamin's proposition that "there is no document of culture that is not at the same time a document of barbarism" ("Theses" 256). An inconvenient truth in any age, his observation is particularly incisive when applied to the post–World War II, post-Fordist, late modern cultural order, which was born in the shadows of Auschwitz and Hiroshima and drew its first breaths in the poisonous atmospheres of McCarthyism and the gulag. As Fredric Jameson declares in *The Political Unconscious,* "the meaning of the greatest cultural monuments cannot be separated from a passionate and partisan assessment of everything that is oppressive in them and that knows complicity with privilege and class domination, stained with the guilt not merely of culture in particular but of History itself as one long nightmare" (299). As his readers know, modernist cultural monuments are among the most complicit (though it is James Joyce's *Ulysses* that supplies the view of history as a nightmare). The politically engaged cultural critic must therefore expose the specific terms of that complicity, and in cold war cultural studies those terms often turn out to be the acronyms of government agencies (CIA, CCF, DOS, USIS) that sought to enlist the arts in federally funded programs of anti-communist propaganda.

Still, the redeployment of Benjamin's diction in Theodor Adorno's (widely misread, often misquoted) apothegm—"to write poetry after Auschwitz is barbaric" ("Cultural Criticism and Society" 34)—points to an understanding of the relationship between cold war art and politics quite different from Jameson's symptomatological reworking of key Frankfurt School texts (which is more than a little tinged with the antithetical cultural Marxism of György Lukács, which I will turn to shortly.)[3] The limits of the symptomatological approach were described years ago when Hall observed that "partial, part-for-the-whole, types of explanations, . . . which allow us only to abstract one element out . . . and explain that, . . . are inadequate precisely on those grounds. For that reason alone, they may be considered 'false'" (Morley and Chen 39). Hall made this point by way of explaining his own understanding of the political as a realm of ceaseless contestation and change. Derived from the works of Valentin Vološinov, Antonio Gramsci, and Ernesto Laclau, this understanding is manifested in the central cultural studies concept of articulation, which for Hall is "a way of thinking the structures of what we know as a play of correspondences, non-correspondences, and contradictions," of comprehending culture and politics as discourses that have unintended effects (112). Hall believes that a proper understanding of the discursive nature of both cultural productions and political formations renders claims of unalterable correspondence between "'ruling ideas' and 'ruling classes'" untenable, including "the proposition that particular ideas and concepts 'belong' exclusively to one particular class" and express the values and beliefs of that class exclusively (40). Applying his view of the mutable, contestatory nature of political and cultural discourses to the problem of determining the relationship between cold war art and politics helps illuminate why readings that assume a straightforward ideological connection between the strategic interests of a government and the art that government funds or exports—in particular, readings that see modernist artworks as elitist abstractions constitutively incapable of speaking against their patron—rapidly reach an interpretive *cul-de-sac.*[4] Elaborate investigations of indirect, coded, or confused (that is, unconscious) correspondences between art and politics may take longer to reach this dead end, but they are similarly haunted by an instrumentalist reductionism that sees artworks as essentially passive constructs destined to register the effects of presumably more powerful forces—a view often expressed through gendered concepts and sexualized language, a point I develop later in this chapter.

A full appreciation of Hall's understanding of the discursive aspects of the relationship between politics and art paves the way for a more critical reading of interpretive strategies founded on assumptions and methodologies derived from Pierre Bourdieu's early work.[5] This quantitative-empirical mode of analysis primarily sees the arts as cultural goods producing cultural capital within a symbolic economy of power and privilege. It drew considerable interest in the decade or so after the 1989 congressional attacks on the NEA, when researchers were trying to predict the future of any central cultural authority in the United States, publicly funded or not.[6] The approach may seem to be suited to a discussion of cold war culture concerned with the rise of government involvement in the arts, and I do grant its main premise: that the arts have been and will continue to be recruited as enforcers of class privilege, signifiers of social stratification, and instruments of political propaganda. Yet I cannot agree with the second and third premises implied by much of this scholarship: that the political and social effects of an artwork are limited, *a priori,* to the intentions of its patron and/or handlers (publishers, museums, booking agents, gallery owners) and that to comprehend the history and variety of art's service to power is to grasp all that is worth knowing about art and its effects. In its reliance on market survey data and tendency to describe aesthetic experience as consumption rather than, say, thought, affective engagement, critique, or politics, such an approach perpetuates precisely the instrumentalist attitude toward art that needs questioning.[7] Bourdieu's subtly gendered and sexualized characterization of artists and the arts as a dominated sector of the dominant class, elaborated in some detail in *The Rules of Art* and discussed at a later point in this chapter, presents a related objection since however much such analogies may be intended as simply illustrative, they nonetheless participate in the longstanding habit of discounting art's claim on a politically active mode of experience by feminizing it.

In contrast, Rancière and Adorno take exception to the sociological claim that art's primary function is as helpmate or apologia for the reigning social, economic, or political order, doing so in ways that connect the limitations of this view to a parallel set of problems within Jameson's approach. For Rancière, these two reigning assumptions within the academy (art as the unconscious of politics, art as the marker and enforcer of class stratification) fail to rise to the interpretive demands of the task they set for themselves. Moreover, in rendering this correlation formulaically, they straiten our separate understandings of politics and art in ways that reveal the intellectual will to power that grounds much cultural analysis. In *The Philosopher and His Poor,* Rancière explains how Bourdieu's program of sociological demystification grounds itself in the same discourse of mastery that informs the more abstract philosophical uses of the Marxist reflection theory that it holds in such contempt.[8] Rancière first expressed his reservations about this demystifying mode of critique in his 1969 essay "On the Theory of Ideology," in which he publicly broke with his teacher Louis Althusser.[9] For Rancière, the theory of ideology propounded by Althusser, Bourdieu, Sartre, and others is itself ideological and in need of interrogation. Most problematic is its assumption of a proletariat "necessarily deceived as a function—even as a condition of possibility—of [revolutionary] action," which posits a "'class struggle' functioning only at the price of not leaving to the classes a point where they could even meet" (Swenson 260; Rancière, *The Philosopher and His Poor* 195).

Rancière's 1981 *The Nights of Labor* is a crucial text for understanding his critique of this particular style of leftist cultural analysis. As he explains:

> It is not knowledge of exploitation that the worker needs in order "to stand tall in the face of that which is ready to devour him." What he lacks and needs is a knowledge of self that reveals to him a being dedicated to something else besides exploitation, a revelation of self that comes circuitously by way of the secret of others.
>
> . . . What justifies our claim to see the realm of representation neatly divided between manipulators and manipulated, to see the laboring class as necessarily duped by what it believes? (20, 22)

For him, "the realm of representation" is quintessentially the realm of art, the home of "the secret of others" and the place where the worker stands to gain the necessary knowledge of a self beyond exploited laborer. It is not surprising, then, that Rancière has little patience for programs of cultural critique invested in demonstrating art's function as symbolic capital or bringing to light a "stain" of originary "guilt" invisible to all but the master critic (Jameson 299). Such demonstrations of an artwork's "complicity with privilege and class domination" risk becoming further exercises in privilege and domination, invested as they can be in the very discourses they pretend to disrupt and indifferent as they sometimes are not only to the actual aesthetic experiences of the working classes (which are often described both nostalgically and nationalistically) but also to the interrogatory, emancipatory effects of art itself (299).[10] Entertaining the possibility that these effects, as functions of the formal properties of the individual artwork, may make themselves felt even in those cultural productions believed to be most politically compromised (such as abstract late-modernist art, supposedly the star of postwar America's program for global domination by cultural means) is to start to shift the contours of the cold war cultural landscape in ways that open up new paths for understanding correlations between the era's art and politics.

Adorno and Rancière brought that new landscape into focus largely by working through their dissatisfactions with received Marxist understandings of the relationship between art and politics, and by far the clearest example of that received understanding is Serge Guilbaut's *How New York Stole the Idea of Modern Art*. The impact of his analysis has been profound. It set the terms for a similarly influential study, Lawrence H. Schwartz's *Creating Faulkner's Reputation,* and no proper accounting of cold war cultural studies can ignore it. A work of social history that favors analysis of U.S. artists' economic and political situations over discussion of their work, *How New York Stole the Idea of Modern Art* examines the early cold war emergence and eventual critical celebration of abstract expressionism. According to Guilbaut, the abstract, late modernist, New York School paintings of Willem de Kooning, Barnett Newman, Mark Rothko, and paradigmatically Jackson Pollock "succeeded because the work and the ideology that supported it . . . coincided fairly closely with the ideology that came to dominate American political life after the 1948 presidential elections" (3). In support, he offers critical readings of the postwar liberal consensus described in Arthur M. Schlesinger, Jr.'s, 1949 *The Vital Center;* the purchasing and exhibition practices at MoMA (which, as I mentioned in chapter 2, was founded and largely controlled by the Rockefellers); and the forcefully expressed, strongly formalist aesthetic values of Clement Greenberg, an early champion of abstract expressionism and an important member of *Partisan Review*'s stable of anti-Stalinist cultural critics. He links a late-1930s "de-Marxization" of New York's leftist intellectuals to the rising postwar fortunes of an abstruse, technically complex, modernist art that, thanks to its "political apoliticism," became a darling of U.S. liberal cultural imperialists during the cold war (2). Guilbaut concludes that "without really wanting to, the avant-garde lined up behind the ideology that had only recently become dominant. . . . By 1948 their once disturbing vision could be integrated into the new anti-Communist rhetoric. Avant-garde radicalism did not really 'sell out,' it was borrowed for the anti-Communist cause" (202).

Likewise, Schwartz claims that "Faulkner's work was championed and canonized because his often supremely individualistic themes and technically difficult prose served an ideological cause" (210). Rather than analyzing the novelist's formal accomplishments (which, he implies, are besides the point: "in every era, there are many excellent writers who never achieve widespread recognition"), he investigates political and economic conditions in the years before Faulkner's 1950 receipt of the Nobel Prize (3). According to Schwartz, the postwar anti-communist liberal political consensus made itself felt in literary circles through a conflation of the formalist values of the rightist New Critics (chiefly Southern writers such as Allen Tate, Robert Penn Warren, and

John Crowe Ransom) and the leftist anti-communism of the New York intellectuals (such as Philip Rahv, William Phillips, and Lionel Trilling). This conflation was hastened by a timely and politically motivated series of Rockefeller Foundation grants to the *Sewanee Review* (for the Southerners) and the *Partisan Review* (for the New Yorkers) designed to further scholarship promoting literary modernism, whose aesthetics, Schwartz claims, "not only reflected [an anti-communist] political ideology but helped to legitimize it as well" (201).[11] This well-funded politicization of modernist aesthetics, he argues, led to the remarkable turnaround in Faulkner's literary reputation. Scorned during the 1930s as crudely gothic, politically retrograde, willfully recondite fictions, his novels were widely praised as humanist masterpieces by the late 1940s.

Schwartz's study differs somewhat from Guilbaut's in its stance toward modernist difficulty. As Guilbaut's title implies, his complaint is less with the formal values of modern art than with what he sees as the postwar American perversion of them. Still, both authors express similarly jaundiced views of the politics of modern art in cold war America, stressing how such work's abstraction or difficulty rendered it politically mute and an easy target for co-optation. They unite in stressing the artists' inability to resist (even, sometimes, to recognize) political manipulation as well as the semiological pliancy of the artwork once it falls into the hands of government. This is a seduction scenario: the co-optation happens unintentionally; art makes the ideological case "without really wanting to." Though Schwartz and Guilbaut do not characterize either the artists or the work in obviously feminized terms, it is easy to link their insistence on the artworks' hapless passivity with what Isobel Armstrong has described as the "insistently denigrating . . . connection of the aesthetic and the feminine" (29). I will return to this point later in the chapter. For now, I am concerned with how Guilbaut's and Schwartz's studies, which present themselves as works of historicist criticism with little interest in cultural theory, owe a large, if mostly unacknowledged, debt to the cultural Marxism of György Lukács.

In something of a return of the art historical repressed, Guilbaut's account of the emergence of abstract expressionism in the post–World War II United States recapitulates the central point of Lukács's indictment of expressionism in post–World War I Germany. In Lukács's view, the chief and fatal flaw of expressionism—a flaw which, in his diagnosis, subtends all modernist aesthetic practices—is its "abstraction away from reality" into a "purely subjective," "one dimensional" view of the social totality, a movement that can only be seen as a politically quietist turning away from the artist's responsibility "to represent reality as it truly is" (for Lukács, an entirely possible task and the artist's chief ethical obligation) toward the "subjectivist distortions," the "decadent manifestations," of capitalist imperialism (38, 40, 43, 33, 57, 58). In Guilbaut's view, abstract expressionism concretized a similarly rightward subjectivist withdrawal from political reality in the postwar United States: "Marxism gave way to psychiatry. The individual moved into the place of history and social relations" (165). Schwartz likewise sees the postwar celebration of Faulkner as part of a coordinated, politically motivated effort "to eclipse the rebellious tradition of realism/naturalism" by overvaluing modernist "stylistic innovation and personal perception" (199, 202). These observations are accurate descriptions of one aspect of the postwar U.S. imaginary, which saw a general rise in discourses of individualism, not only in politically strategic, anti-communist polemics but also in the rhetoric of the civil rights movement—although the latter is seldom acknowledged as a complication of any effort to define postwar U.S. individualism solely as right-leaning, capitalistic, false consciousness.

Lukács's analysis was produced almost fifty years earlier than Guilbaut's and Schwartz's and under quite different historical, political, and economic conditions. Yet the vexed tone that they share, along with their similar diagnoses of modernism's individualist, psychologizing problem, raises the possibility that at least some of the persuasive power of Guilbaut's and Schwartz's readings derives from their clever repurposing of an established complaint. In other words, the diagnosis sounds right because it sounds familiar. In truth, both *How New York Stole the Idea of Modern Art* and *Creating Faulkner's Reputation* draw much of their eristic power by reactivating the anxieties that have long attended efforts to interpret abstract art—anxieties that led Lukács to dismiss such work out of hand as politically impotent (best case) or actively reactionary (worst). Guilbaut and Schwartz harness that argument to an updated leftist populism that dismisses cold war modernist art as little more than formalist mystification.

Consider Lukács's 1938 essay "Realism in the Balance" and its dismissal of montage, which he correctly takes as a synecdoche ("the pinnacle of this movement") for the formal and structural transformations involved in the shift from a realist aesthetic to a more abstract representational practice. Perhaps an awareness of Sergei Eisenstein's theory of cinematic montage as politically progressive in the extreme was behind Lukács's admission that "photomontage . . . is capable of striking effects, and on occasion it can even become a powerful political weapon."[12] But he cannot quite shake a suspicion that the "technique of juxtaposing heterogeneous, unrelated pieces of reality torn from their context" amounts to little more than a "joke." Anxious to make clear that the joke isn't on him, eager to prove he is no dupe, he sums up the "final effect" of montage as "profound monotony." He declares, "The details may be dazzlingly colourful in their diversity, but the whole will never be more than an unrelieved grey on grey. After all, a puddle can never be more than dirty water, even though it may contain rainbow tints" (43). Lukács labors to ground his critique in a scrupulous Marxist analysis of cultural production, but his dismissal of modernism's formal "monotony," expressed as a squeamishness about its filthy unformed (or deformed) puddlings, seems less a function of his political commitment than a reconfiguration of the hostile responses of traditionalists to experimental artwork so as to accommodate a particular party demand. Modernism, he implies, requires no real skill. It offers nothing of value, and those who claim to see something in it are either gullible fools, masters of cynical calculation, or filth-loving decadents.

The more adventitious aspects of Lukács's Marxist theoretical armature become clear as he moves from his condescending view of modernism's regrettable monotony to a more heated denunciation of "chaos" as "the intellectual cornerstone of modernist art" (44). The ideological high ground crumbles away completely later in the essay, when he abruptly complains about "the very narrow doorway which leads to Joyce or other representatives of avant-garde literature: one needs a certain 'knack' to see just what their game is." Lukács intends to make an unflattering comparison between the limited appeal of modernism and the presumably more politically progressive accessibility of realism: "In realism, the wealth of created life provides answers to the questions put by the readers themselves," whereas the "taxing struggle to understand the art of the avant-garde" makes such art "quite beyond" the comprehension of "ordinary people" (57). But his admission that such seemingly chaotic literature may, after all, possess an organizing principle apparent to those with the knack to see it—that its "juxtaposed . . . pieces of reality" might not, after all, be "heterogeneous" and "unrelated" but deliberately selected and carefully arranged—undercuts his critique in two ways. It sounds a note of personal vexation at not having that knack himself and, more disturbingly, assumes that limited powers of comprehension are constitutive of "ordinary people" rather than a consequence of the political and economic exploitation that made (and keeps) them ordinary. Lukács here reifies notions about the aesthetic and intellectual capacities of the working class that Marxism, in its most radical aspects, supposedly means to falsify. As we will see, this is an aspect of traditional Marxist cultural criticism that deeply disturbed Rancière. Thus, Lukács's argument, for all its erudition in service to the reigning Soviet line on cultural production, is less a principled call for an art that serves the people than a manifestation of the epistemological anxiety that sprang up in the wake of the twentieth-century collapse of the Enlightenment's "coming to know" narrative that was the central prop of nineteenth-century bourgeois realism. It was an anxiety that modernism acknowledged and articulated but could not allay.[13] Lukács's sense that some properties of modernism are cultural reifications of aspects of capitalist economic relations is not without truth, but his nostalgic partiality for a prior aesthetic practice and for a related, dependable ordinariness in the working subject it both addresses and depicts amounts to a defensive reaction to this epistemological collapse, a determination to persist in believing that it is possible for a single totalizing perspective to capture "reality as it truly is."

It is clear that Guilbaut and Schwartz share Lukács's commitment to artistic interventions into political life that, in revealing how things "truly" are, might mobilize political change. It seems equally plain that both also see the meaning and significance of cultural productions as not only determined by but also delimited to the conditions of their emergence. As Raymond Williams once said, in a similarly traditional Marxist formulation, "you cannot understand an intellectual or artistic project without also understanding its formation; . . . the relation between a project and its formation is always decisive" (151). Acknowledging that this belief is rooted in the conviction that it is possible, through a single privileged vantage point, to grasp the totality of "reality as it truly is" helps us see the reason for the disdain that Guilbaut and Lukács, in particular, share for the analytics of individualist psychiatry. (For Lukács, writing in 1938, this unquestionably meant psychoanalysis; in 1983, this was still almost certainly also the case for Guilbaut.) The psychoanalytic discovery of the unconscious and its accompanying central assertion that subjectivity itself is "not one" has radical consequences for any theory of politics that sees nature and history as thoroughly knowable subjects of human making. However, Lukács (and Guilbaut after him) is mistaken in assuming that the psychoanalytic interrogation of the dreams of human mastery amounts to a retreat into solipsism and a renunciation of historically grounded political struggle. For psychoanalysis, "the basic epistemological idea [is] that while concepts have a history through which they come into being, their conceptual value exceeds the conditions and processes of their historical emergence" (Dean, *Beyond Sexuality* 23). As provocative as this formulation is for politics, I want to draw attention here to its implications for any effort to interpret artworks that aims to recognize both their historicity and their mutability in a manner that would not valorize one over the other but seek to grasp the dialectical nature of their relationship.

Adorno's understanding of how this dialectic finds formal expression precisely through the most forbidding aspects of modernist atonality is what distinguishes his cultural analysis from Lukács's. (I here use *atonality* metonymically to indicate exactly that unmoored quality of avant-garde art that Lukács finds most distressing.) Adorno's well-known disagreement with Lukács on the ideology of modernism does not derive, as is commonly supposed, from a mandarin admiration for the interpretive challenges presented by innovations such as montage (about which Adorno, too, had reservations). Rather, he was willing to entertain psychological, individualistic explanations for social and cultural phenomena alongside—indeed, in dialectical engagement with—the more traditional Marxist view.[14] Such an approach made it possible for Adorno to detect, embedded in the jagged aural contours and fragmented textual forms of "apolitical" modernist work, what might be described as a Marxist individualism, a negative assertion whose power derives from the political obliquity that Lukács denounces as "subjectivist tendencies." As Robert Hullot-Kentor has said, for Adorno such work bodies forth "the fundamental capacity of art: . . . the possibility of turning the powers of the world against itself" (*Things beyond Resemblance* 207). Such a capacity is nothing if not political, perhaps especially when its "answers to the questions put by life itself" are not prescriptive but interrogative (Lukács 57).

Thus, Lukács's imperative that art must represent social relations so as to forward economic and political transformation along predetermined lines and his corollary insistence that any art that fails to do so clearly and unambiguously is little more than bourgeois mystification are countered by Adorno's denial of the imperative mode as such, a denial that rests precisely on the impossibility of properly understanding (let along representing) totality. This is not to deny the possibility of any kind of cultural analysis: "the mind is indeed not capable of producing or grasping the totality of the real, but it may be possible to penetrate the detail, to explode in miniature the mass of merely existing reality" ("The Actuality of Philosophy" 38). An interest in the critical possibilities of the detail was not, for Adorno, an effort to cast the artwork as itself the telling detail of "merely existing reality" so that the wished-for comprehension of totality materializes under cover of trope (the artwork as metaphor, metonym, symbol, or symptom of the social whole). Rather, he rejects the quasi-instrumentalist insistence that art represent the social totality in a certain masterful way.

One might conclude, then, that the disagreement between Lukács and Adorno on the merits of modernist aesthetic practices—not only montage but also dissonance, irony, and abstraction—amounts to the difference between assertion and acknowledgment and the posture towards dominance entailed in that difference. Lukács's assertive belief in the fundamental truth of realism left him unable to fully address the suturing of the proletariat to Italian and German fascism via the strategic cultural recycling of the most comfortingly familiar realist tropes and techniques. Nor could he grasp how a capitalist culture industry also depended on the consolatory repetition of narratives and images drawn from nineteenth-century classics. In contrast, Adorno's acknowledgment of the constitutive limitations of realism allowed him to recognize precisely how its claim to say all may amount to a delimitation in advance of what is sayable. Precisely by acknowledging the dialectical tensions fundamental both to Freud's model of subjectivity and to Marx's objective understanding of capitalism, Adorno is able to fathom, in abstraction's often bruised, twisted, and roughened mimesis, the deep politics—the insistent "it shall be different"—sheltered within even the most ostensibly apolitical works of modern art.

Adorno's chief artistic interests were music and literature. Yet J. M. Bernstein maintains that if he "had turned his attention to art, to painting and sculpture, he would have, could have, only deployed the resources of abstract expressionism for his purposes," not least because such art "embraces its incapacity" (146, 248). Bernstein's implication is that an Adornian reading of abstract expressionism would lead not to Guilbaut's charge of political apathy but toward a political understanding of the works' formal strategies as resolute negations of the hubristic certainty underlying any claim to represent total truth. Such a reading would, in turn, open onto an understanding of abstract expressionism's relationship to the postwar U.S. imperium that would be properly histori*cal* and thus "incommensurable with histori*cism*," that faulty interpretive mode that "instead of following [the artworks'] own historical content, reduces them to their external history" (*Aesthetic Theory,* 1997, 182–183). Unfortunately, the approach to cold war cultural productions that Schwartz and Guilbaut have adopted risks precisely this sort of reduction.

Adorno's declaration that "art, even as something tolerated in the administered world, embodies what does not allow itself to be managed and what total management suppresses" describes not only a great deal of cold war modernist art but also the interpretive efforts to manage it characteristic of the many overlapping, administered worlds—museum, government agency, university classroom—in which it has been permitted to spend its delimited life (*Aesthetic Theory,* 1997, 234). Guilbaut's and Schwartz's studies do have a great deal to tell us about the politics of those worlds. But to understand the politics of the art itself, we need to draw on theoretical models that move beyond the antimodernist aesthetics of Lukács.

Begun "as a quest for the authentic voice of working-class experience oriented by notions of popular culture, sociability, and [a] working class ethos" (Swenson 263), Rancière's *The Nights of Labor* became a critical interrogation of its opening assumptions of working-class intellectual and cultural unity. An immersion in the writings of French militants of the 1830 revolution and afterward led him to the entirely unforeseen conclusion that these workers "were not representative of anything and did not found their militancy upon . . . any workers' culture" (Swenson 262). Faced with the error of his attempt to construct "a sort of collective worker's body" that would allow him to present these writings as manifestations of an "authentic" workers' consciousness, Rancière decided that "what was at stake here was to account for the constitution of a web of illegitimate discourses, discourses that broke a certain identity, a certain relation between bodies and words. . . . What was at stake was the construction of a story in which we could see not the production of voices by a body but the gradual sketching out of a sort of collective space by voices" (quoted in Swenson 262–263).

Employing a narrative approach derived from Virginia Woolf's *The Waves,* Rancière produced a study that, with its "interlacing cast of characters, prismatically shifting focus, and complete lack of thetic statements, . . . resembles a modernist novel far more closely" than it does a historical or sociological study conventionally conceived and executed (Swenson 263). The move to a modernist mode of discourse was not accidental: Rancière's research led him to conclude that the leftist cold war intellectual's faith in a straight-talking, realist, workers' aesthetic, disdainful of philosophical complexity and hostile to self-consciously cultivated individualist (elitist, effete, abstract) styles and forms, was little more than a primitivist fantasy. "My little story of odd proletarian nights would like to question precisely this jealous concern to preserve popular, plebian, or proletarian purity," he writes, adopting an interrogative posture that underscores the restless questioning that he sees as the most important aspect of aesthetic experience (*The Nights of Labor* x). In his introduction to *The Nights of Labor,* Donald Reid characterizes the studies of aesthetics, literature (especially poetry), film, and visual art published in the thirty years since the work's appearance as elaborations of Rancière's fundamentally political understanding of cultural texts "not as passive objects to be deciphered and categorized, but as active, *constantly posing questions* to the would-be interpreter" (xxxii, emphasis added). This sense of textuality itself as a living, protean force, resisting symptomatological reduction and imbued with the potential to redraw power relations, is rooted in a reading of Plato's *Phaedrus* that is similar to Derrida's, an aspect of Rancière's thought to which I will return.

While Adorno's suspicion of the strictly empirical sociological method and its assumptions is grounded in a larger theoretical framework, it was also strongly influenced by his experiences with Paul Lazarfeld's Princeton Radio Research Project, his first job after arriving in the United States in 1938. Appointed director of the project's music division, Adorno imagined his contribution as a critical engagement with Benjamin's "The Work of Art in the Age of Mechanical Reproduction." His goal was to explore how claims developed in the context of print and visual culture might be applied to a consideration of music in the age of radio transmission, but the program quickly came to grief. As Adorno soon discovered, Lazarfeld's thoroughly instrumentalist project was "a privately-held research venture" designed to "put the new science of sociology at the service of commercial interests" (Hullot-Kentor, *Current of Music* 10). Adorno objected not only to the program's operating assumptions but also to the way in which those assumptions were embodied within its methodology, including the use of a "programme analyser": an "empirical measuring device" that allowed research subjects to press a button to indicate what they "liked or disliked about a particular piece of music" (Müller-Doohm 247). Adorno wrote, "When I was confronted with the requirement, as it was literally stated, 'to measure culture,' I on the contrary reflected that culture is precisely the very condition that excludes a mentality that would wish to measure it" ("Scientific Experiences" 223). While it is tempting to attribute these barbed formulations to the hauteur of a rigidly maintained, peculiarly

European, cultural rarefaction, Adorno never believed that art is an elevated, sacred space untouched by the mundane realities of human existence and so empirically indescribable. Rather, he maintains the more complex, nuanced view that art's "contribution to society is *not* communication with it but rather something extremely mediated: It is resistance in which, by virtue of inner-aesthetic development, social development is reproduced without being imitated" (*Aesthetic Theory,* 1997, 226). In such a view, the work of cultural analysis can hardly be said to begin, much less end, with a push-button tally of what a listener likes or dislikes about a musical work.

While many recognize that Adorno's wartime and cold war American exile influenced his critique of culture industry, fewer understand the degree to which his experiences during those years informed his theories about the political and social aspects of aesthetic autonomy. This is not surprising. As Michael Sullivan and John T. Lysaker have noted, for many years the American reception of Adorno's thought revolved around "charges of pessimism, quietism, and resignation" leveled in support of the "orthodox conclusion" that "progressive thought must abandon Adorno" (87, 88). The reasons for this dismissal were many. They include fallout from the German student movement of 1967–1969, when Adorno was denounced for refusing to align critical theory with the revolutionary praxis of the Sozialistischer Deutscher Studentenbund; the problematic English translations of many of his major works, with a related tendency to take idiosyncratic projects (such as *The Authoritarian Personality*) as representative; and the simplification and attendant annexation of his analysis of culture industry by critics such as Clement Greenberg, a serious distortion of Adorno's thought that continues to inform dismissive characterizations of it as high modernist formalism. Nonetheless, as Peter Uwe Hohendahl observed nearly two decades ago, Adorno's cultural investments do "not easily respond to the conventional dichotomy of high and low," as a careful reading of his extraordinarily wide-ranging writings on culture makes clear (119, 120).[15] During the past decade, a new body of scholarship has gradually emerged, one that aims to dispel misunderstandings, misreadings, and misgivings.[16]

Though one cannot credit any single scholar or allied group with spearheading this revisionary interest in Adorno, Sullivan and Lysacker's 1992 essay did mark out its ground:

> We began with the question: does Adorno provide us with any avenue for positive political action? In thinking through this question we have arrived at the question of art's relation to thoughts on social emancipation. That Adorno believed there is a connection was never in doubt. After all, he wrote: "The notion of artistic objectivity goes hand in hand with social emancipation, the latter being a situation where something frees itself on its own steam from social

> convention and control."[17] What was in doubt, however, was whether this connection could amount to anything. We take our analysis to have shown that it can. We have argued that Adorno's turn to aesthetic theory is a turn to a certain kind of thought experiment, one in which we might envision how the tension between subject and object could be maintained. Art is valuable to the project of emancipation not because it can retrieve, in its imagination, utopia from no-place, but because it can instantiate a subject-object relation that is not wholly forgetful of its own self-formation, one that, in rare and great moments, produces free and autonomous particulars. (120)

If this is to anticipate, through Adorno, Rancière's view of art as a means for expanding the field of what *counts* as politics, it is also to indicate the degree to which modern artworks, for Adorno, signify politically insofar as "unsolved antagonisms of reality return . . . as immanent problems of form" (*Aesthetic Theory,* 1997, 6). Though this can be (and, via Jameson, has been) viewed as a formula whereby political issues are read off the artwork through allegorical readings of its content or of the relationship between its content and its form, Adorno himself rarely adopted such an approach. He preferred instead to emphasize the artwork's ontological status—its rendering of reality *otherwise*—as its critical fundament. For him, "art is the social antithesis of society, not directly reducible from it" (*Aesthetic Theory,* 1997, 8). This irreducibility also encompasses the notion of aesthetic autonomy: art is not utterly heteronymous, but neither is it truly free.

Adorno is well known for his effort to work out a theory of art that would acknowledge the radically altered conditions for poetry after Auschwitz, one that would value art's powers of refusal at least as much as its powers of affirmation—of doing good. This effort was in part a function of his deep engagement with the work of modernist artists who shared an aesthetic of negation (for example, Schoenberg, Kafka, Berg, Beckett, and Celan). However, though modernist art was important to him, his aesthetic theory is not exclusively modernist, let alone elitist in the grand prescriptive manner.[18] His 1951 essay "Cultural Criticism and Society," source of the famous line about poetry after Auschwitz, sets the terms for a rigorously dialectical approach to the question of the politics of the artwork, putting it in relation to an equally sober view of the politics of cultural criticism and critical theory. If writing poetry after Auschwitz is barbaric precisely to the extent that it aims to do good—thereby soliciting "self-satisfied contemplation" in the reader—then the demands of coming to a dialectical understanding of the work of art in the cold war fall on artist and critic equally: "culture is only true when implicitly critical, and the mind which forgets this revenges itself in the critic it breeds" (34, 22). Adorno takes aim here at targets on both sides of the Iron Curtain. Artifacts of capitalist "consumer culture" and "commissar"-regulated socialist realism, the approved cultural productions of "totalitarian regimes of both kinds," similarly seek to harness the power of art to do good and therefore need to be brought to account equally. Yet because "*all* culture shares the guilt of society," criticism devoted solely to unmasking the ideological investments of cultural productions rapidly "becomes superficial" (26). "What distinguishes dialectical from cultural criticism is that it heightens cultural criticism until the notion of culture is itself negated, fulfilled and surmounted in one" (28–29). Thus "a successful work, according to immanent criticism, is not one which resolves objective contradictions in a spurious harmony, but one which expresses the idea of harmony negatively, by embodying the contradictions, pure and uncompromised, in its innermost structure. Confronted with this kind of work, the verdict 'mere ideology' loses its meaning" (32).

In a critical study published in the wake of the fall of the Berlin Wall, Terry Eagleton characterized Adorno's aesthetic philosophy this way: "Dialectical thinking seeks to grasp whatever is heterogeneous to thought as a moment of thought itself, 'reproduced in thought itself as its immanent contradiction.' . . . [Dialectical thinking is an] enterprise . . . always teetering on the brink of blowing itself up" (341). Though Eagleton's tone is condescending, his language, perhaps inadvertently, registers the profoundly historical aspects of Adorno's postwar dialectical thinking, making clear its status as cold war philosophy *par excellence.* A postwar critical reflection that is "always teetering on the brink of blowing itself up" is one that has surrendered itself to its age "without reservation and without the presumption of being superior to it" (Adorno, *Aesthetic Theory,* 1997, 182). Such reflection adopts a posture toward its subject quite different from what often passes for materialist cultural study, wherein the self-protective safety of the critic's superior vantage is the historicist given. Rather, this critical engagement risks self-immolation, not in order to liquidate its other (in some historically determined, mutually assured destruction) but to preserve the other and its testimony to the insufficiency of the critical reflection that seeks to capture it. For Adorno, this tension finds formal expression in those modern, dissonant, abstract works that risk incomprehension, bemusement, or disgust for the sake of realizing their capacity to turn the powers of the world against itself.

Adorno's dialectical approach to a modernist artwork's immanent formal critique of *all* of the conditions of its being invites careful consideration of just what the term *cold war culture* means. Rancière's identification of three different regimes of artistic production and apprehension—the ethical, the representative, and the aesthetic—raises an additional set of complications for historicist methods of cultural analysis. We may, following Gabriel Rockhill, emphasize the evolutionary dimension of this concept, calling it a "genealogy" whose categories can be plotted along a timeline of past theories of the relationship between art and society, Platonic, Aristotelian, and Romantic (4).

At the same time we should recall Rancière's insistence on the contemporary *simultaneity* of these regimes as ways of not only making but also understanding art. For while "art and literature, as we know them today [that is, in the aesthetic regime], have only existed for about two centuries, . . . they did not come into existence as radically new ways of doing but as new regimes of identification," new modes of configuring and, importantly, of perceiving art's relation to the world:

> When Madame de Staël cast forth the word *littérature,* in its new sense, she was very careful to stipulate that she was not proposing a change to the poetics codified by the theoreticians of *belles lettres.* All that she said that she had changed was the conception of the relationship between *lettres* and society. There is, in fact, no historical point of rupture on the basis of which it became impossible to write or to paint in the old fashion and necessary to do it in a new way, no point of [no] return that brought about the shift from an art of representation to an art of presence or of the unrepresentable. But there is a slow re-configuration that provides the same ways of doing/making—a metaphor, a *frottis,* a use of light and of shadows—with a new visibility and a new form of intelligibility on the basis of which new ways of doing/making arise. (*Dissensus* 208)

Rancière deliberately avoids specifying the forces that initiate this "slow re-configuration." Essentially a consequence of transformative *reading,* such reconfigurations may be triggered by any manner of economic, political, biological, philosophical, or technological causes, working individually or in various combinations. Any effort to grasp art's dialogical engagement with the immediate conditions of its emergence entails appreciating how our understanding of those conditions is itself ceaselessly changing and historically evolving, a notion that is closely tied to Rancière's view that the emancipatory force of art lies in its ability to redraw the boundaries of politics itself. If "politics is first of all a way of framing, among sensory data, a specific sphere of experience" ("The Politics of Literature" 10), it is also a way of deciding who speaks and who is spoken about, who acts and who is acted upon, which modes of speech and action are legitimate, which illegitimate. Art alters what counts as politics through its "distribution of the sensible" (*partage du sensible*): its construction, through its formal strategies, of "new landscape[s] of the visible, the sayable, and the doable" (*Dissensus* 149).

To be sure, artistic *poiesis* always entails traversals across the gap between the world itself and the world of the work. For Rancière, however, it is only within the aesthetic regime (that is, only in the past two centuries) that this gap has come to signify *politically.* A fundamental feature of the aesthetic regime (which, as I have mentioned, encompasses ways of making and ways of experiencing art) is its vastly expanded understanding of the unsettling power of writing that Plato first described in *Phaedrus:* its ability "to travel the world without a father to guarantee the discourse, [to] . . . turn right and left without knowing to whom it should and should not speak" (Rancière, *The Flesh of Words* 92). This is the power of art as *techné:* the power of form and style. "The Flaubertian absolutization of literature" that sets fully into motion the aesthetic regime is not "the sovereignty of writing that makes art out of all non-meaning. It is rather the inversion of this sovereignty, the revelation of its secret. And this secret is not the glorious 'pattern in the carpet' which symbolizes the master of fictions playing with the reader's desire. It is the constitutive contradiction of literature . . . [realized in] the equal worth of every subject, . . . the 'absolute way of seeing things' that is called style" (93).

Because the effects of the aesthetic regime operate not only in the immediate historical moment and spatial location of a work's emergence but also beyond those initiating parameters, Rancière has little patience for the scholarly habit of identifying discrete technical or epistemological stages of artistic production, which he believes serves chiefly to limit an artwork's range of effects. Most vexing for him is the supposed split between modernism and postmodernism, but he takes a generally skeptical view of the concept of modernity itself as a distinct category within the aesthetic regime. Modernity is "a questionable notion" insofar as it encourages the belief that there is "only one meaning and direction in history, whereas the temporality specific to the aesthetic regime of the arts is a co-presence of heterogeneous temporalities" (*The Politics of Aesthetics* 26).[19] Rancière's theory of artistic regimes thus demands from the critic a special kind of interpretive double vision, sensitive to historically particular modes of production and dissemination as well as the changing hermeneutic demands arising from the temporal and spatial shifts that accompany art's movements into the multiple geographies and chronographies in which works circulate and find their being.

Those worldly circulations and mutable temporalities are, for Rancière, key aspects of art's autonomy, which he takes to be the engine of the metapolitics of art. He finds support for this view in the famous "paradox and . . . promise" of Friedrich Schiller's *Letters on the Aesthetic Education of Man.* Rancière's reading of this text, which he calls "the 'original scene' of aesthetics," helps us see that neither early cold war New Critical formalist naïveté nor late cold war contextualist suspicion have come to grips with the question of aesthetic autonomy, which Rancière locates in the experiencing of art:

> Matters would be easy if we could merely say—naïvely—that the beauties of art must be subtracted from any politicization, or—knowingly—that the alleged autonomy of art disguises its dependence on domination. Unfortunately this is not the case. . . . The "autonomy of art" and the "promise of politics" are not counterpoised. The autonomy is the autonomy of the experience, not of the

> work of art. . . . So the original scene of aesthetics reveals a contradiction that is not the opposition of art versus politics, high art versus popular culture or art versus the aestheticization of life. All these oppositions are particular features and interpretations of a more basic contradiction. In the aesthetic regime of art, art is art to the extent that it is something else than art. It is always "aestheticized," meaning that it is always posited as a "form of life." The key formula of the aesthetic regime of art is that art is an autonomous form of life. This formula, however, can be read in two different ways: autonomy can [be] valorized over life, or life over autonomy—and these lines of intersection can be opposed or they can intersect.
>
> Such oppositions and intersections can be traced to the interplay between three major scenarios. Art can become life. Life can become art. And art and life can exchange their properties. These three scenarios . . . [are also] variant[s] of the politics of aesthetics, or what we should rather call its "metapolitics"—that is, its way of producing its own politics, proposing to politics re-arrangements of its space, re-configuring art as a political issue or asserting itself as true politics. (*Dissensus* 116–119)

Thus, aesthetic autonomy is "a form of legitimization which delegitimates at the same time" (Rancière, "The Method of Equality" 276). This aspect of art is fundamentally, even inescapably, discomfiting for any governmental effort to use artworks as a means of legitimating a political regime.

In considering this definition of aesthetic autonomy, we do well to remember Rockhill's caveat that "it would be a grave mistake to confuse Rancière's position . . . with the conception of art that affirms its innate political force as a form of resistance to the status quo" (Rockhill and Watts 199). We do even better to apply that warning to Adorno's position as well. If, for Rancière, "just as there is not always art (though there is always music, sculpture, dance, and so on), there is not always politics (though there are always forms of power and consent)," so, too, for Adorno, there is not always immanent critique ("Contemporary Art" 32). Likewise, we should not conflate the positions of these two thinkers, especially given the critical, if sympathetic, care with which Rancière has spelled out the differences between his view of the politics of aesthetics and Adorno's.[20] Even so, Rancière's interest in the work of art as a site for redrawing the field of politics, a site whose condition of possibility is the willingness of the artwork to address anyone whatsoever, chimes suggestively with Adorno's insistence on the politically critical power unleashed within the artwork in its disintegration over time. Both views point to the need for historical rather than historicist understandings of the artwork's political impact.

Identified by his teacher Siegfried Kracauer as an important component of Adorno's earliest forays into aesthetic theory, the proposition that "the truth-content of a work reveals itself only in its collapse" entails acknowledging that the "work's claim to totality, its systematic structure, as well as its superficial intentions, share the fate of everything transient; but as they pass away with time the work brings characteristics and configurations to the fore that are actually images of truth" (Adorno, *Kierkegaard* xv).[21] Appeals to a strictly linear understanding of this claim have been central to interpretive projects dedicated to revealing a work's political unconscious, projects chiefly taken to involve the detection and deciphering, within the work, of coded commentary on the social conditions of its moment of appearance. This encryption is an aspect of art, to be sure. It is not necessarily true, however, that such coded commentaries follow a narrative logic, nor is it certain that a political consciousness so unleashed only functions retrospectively as a shamed or regretful reading of history. In fact, bringing Adorno's interest in the artwork's dissolution into relation with Benjamin's similar observation that "history disintegrates into pictures, not stories" raises the possibility that the *images* of truth left standing in the rubble of the artwork's collapse might actively resist narration as much as they invite it. Such images may also invite proleptic or speculative readings of a future in which they might speak otherwise.[22] Adorno's claim for art's historical persistence in dissolution, then, does not require the critic to provide an economic or sociological narrativization of the artwork and related subordination of its sensuous quiddity. Rather, the critic needs to activate a particular and complex understanding of temporality as a register of art's autonomy. The work's claim *on* time is precisely its collapse *over* time, a claim that constitutes not only the time of its emergence but also the time before and the time after. Taking the full measure of this collapse is what allows for a historical understanding of art; it is also what allows us to understand art's heteronymous power to evoke the experience of autonomy.

For both Rancière and Adorno, art's ability to reconfigure the terms in which we experience and understand the world—its capacity to reread and rearticulate what counts as sayable, doable, seeable, knowable: in a word, what counts as politics—cannot be properly understood through programs of interpretation that limit a work's meaning and impact to its function as a narrative, however indirect, of the terms and conditions of its appearance. This enlarged understanding of art's metapolitical significance should not be mistaken for a reassertion of the power of art to do good. Like politics itself, which both Rancière and Adorno see as fundamentally concerned with the expansion of democracy, the metapolitics of art has no guarantees. Adorno claims that "art's *promesse de bonheur* means not only that hitherto praxis has blocked happiness but that happiness is beyond praxis" (*Aesthetic Theory,* 1997, 12), and Rancière observes that "the time of a 'democracy to come' is the time of a promise that has to be kept even though—and precisely because—it can never be fulfilled" (*Dissensus* 58–59). Thus, a final sympathetic resonance in their thought lies in the stress both place on the political importance of negation and dissensus in the artwork. Adorno's emphasis on negation as the signal feature of art in the age of cold war chimes with Rancière's stress on dissensus as not only the essence of politics but also the "connection *between* art and politics, . . . the very kernel of the aesthetic regime: artworks can produce effects of dissensus precisely because they neither give lessons nor have any definition"—because, to put it another way, they don't act (*Dissensus* 140).

For the scholar of cold war culture, this understanding of an artwork's tacit but potent capacity to produce dissensus raises the possibility that both government efforts to enlist art in the cold war and scholars' efforts to read the era's artworks for evidence of political complicity are driven by anxieties about the politically protean powers of art. In the light cast by Adorno and Rancière, both efforts emerge as attempts to contain and control those powers; both seek to set and thereby limit the parameters within which art circulates and has its political effects. Following Rancière, we might say that government uses of art during the cold war and the heretofore dominant mode of politically engaged reading that seeks to tie the art to those uses are practices not of politics but of the police: "discourses founded on the singularity of the other [that] . . . are ultimately predicated on keeping the other in its place" (Rockhill, "Translator's Introduction," 2).

For Isobel Armstrong, whose work on the gendering of the aesthetic owes a significant debt to Adorno, this anxiety of the police is, more than anything, a function of art's powers of metaphor. What she identifies as "the threat of metaphor," the fear of its ability to incite "the collapse and elision of categories as a permeable, dissolving meltdown of difference" (36) is, for Rancière, the estranging force of "the possibility that a metaphor or a play of light and shadow [may] be no more than a metaphor or a play of light and shadow *or* that it may be the power of a love or a testimony of a specific time and world. It is the possibility that a thing be a work *and* a commodity," the possibility for "*substitutability,* the thing that breaks with consensus" and sets dissensus free (*Dissensus* 213). Drawing this parallel between Rancière's broadly political interest in the power of metaphor and Armstrong's expressly feminist characterization of that power brings us closer to understanding why art so often is cast as the threatening other of society, especially in the United States. It also helps us begin to recognize those aspects of art's public life that resemble the public lives of others that are similarly subject to policing. In tracing this resemblance, we find a set of interpretive practices that, precisely because of their historical footing, link the theories of Adorno and Rancière with cold war cultural interpretation via feminism and queer theory.

Roughly two-thirds of the way through *Distinction,* Pierre Bourdieu elaborates on his definition of artistic cultural capital as "a dominated principle of domination," drawing an analogy between gender difference and class distinctions (291):

> Men [of the working class] especially are forbidden every sort of "pretension" in matters of culture, language, or clothing. This is not only because aesthetic refinement, particularly as regards clothing or cosmetics, is reserved for women by a representation, more strict than in any other class, of the sexual division of labor and sexual morality, or because it is more or less clearly associated with dispositions and manners seen as characteristic of the bourgeoisie ("airs and graces," "la-di-da," etc.) or of those who are willing to submit to bourgeois demands so as to win acceptance, of which the "toadies," "lick-spittles," and "pansies" of everyday invective represent the limit. It is also because a surrender to demands perceived as simultaneously feminine and bourgeois appears as the index of a dual repudiation of virility, a twofold submission which ordinary language, naturally conceiving all domination in the logic and lexicon of sexual domination, is predisposed to express. (382)

Bourdieu's "not only / but also" construction, usually a means of introducing two related but distinct points that shed light on a larger issue, here simply reiterates, by appeal to the operations of "ordinary language," precisely the terms of the "sexual division of labor and sexual morality" that beg for critical examination. Perhaps this is because he is discussing a collectively held compensatory fantasy that operates, as all fantasies do, within the logic of the trauma it means to overcome. The structures of modern capitalism force the proletariat into the economically dominated (that is, feminine) position, so the men of the working class maintain their dignity by ostentatiously rejecting the publicly signifying cultural trappings of those who get screwed. The claim is probably true enough, but the offhand fashion in which Bourdieu *naturalizes* this logic gives pause. Indeed, he barely moots the view that "all domination" is "naturally" analogous to sexual domination before he develops it along the lines all too clearly foretold by those characteristically submissive "airs and graces" of "bourgeois" "pansies."[23] His observation that "the whole set of socially constituted differences between the sexes tends to weaken as one moves up the social hierarchy" becomes, through a rhetorical sleight of hand that turns "differences between the sexes" into "deviations from the norm," a strategy for reading gender and sexuality as interchangeably femininized categories whose roles in structures of domination become increasingly attenuated (that is, symbolic) among the elites (382).[24] "The greater tolerance of deviations from the norm of the sexual division of labor no doubt partly explains why the proportion of homosexuals known and acknowledged as such rises strongly with position in the social hierarchy" (383).

In *The Rules of Art,* Bourdieu returns to this matrix of aesthetic refinement, gender, and class so as to clarify for readers his understanding of the isomorphic power structures of sexual relations between women and men, on the one hand, and the arts and society, on the other. "Designated by the opposition between work and leisure, money and art, the useful and the futile to concern themselves with art and taste, and with the domestic cult of moral and aesthetic refinement (which was, moreover, the major condition of success in the matrimonial market), women of the aristocracy and the bourgeoisie occupy in the field of domestic power a position homologous to that held by writers and artists, dominated among the dominants, at the heart of the field of power" (250). My point here is not to accuse Bourdieu of homophobia or sexism. Rather, by emphasizing both the flatly descriptive rhetoric and the wider analysis it serves, I aim to highlight what Rancière has diagnosed as a frustrating tendency in Bourdieu's sociology to confuse the arbitrary with the necessary (*The Philosopher and His Poor* 204). His reliance on frankly gendered oppositions—work, money, and the useful (the masculine dominants) standing against leisure, art, and the frivolous (the feminine dominated)—promulgate what Armstrong has identified as the "insistently denigrating Enlightenment connection of the aesthetic with the feminine" and the concomitantly sexualized—indeed, homosexualized—dismissal of the aesthetic as a realm of *passive* experience incapable of generating political "meaning and possibility" (29, 30).[25]

Armstrong's call for a radical rereading of the artwork as a "form of mediation, a transitive, interactive form" with a political charge irreducible to an individual artist's ideological investments or a particular socioeconomic or governmental regime is now more than a decade old (59). A blending of historical, formal, and feminist reading strategies bent toward reclaiming the aesthetic for radical politics, her claims have percolated into some quarters of contemporary cultural scholarship (the new lyric studies, for example), but have yet to make an impact on cold war cultural studies, where for the most part artworks continue to be read as soft manifestations of hard phenomena, and where the perceived formalist excesses of high modernism are ritualistically denounced.[26] Subordinated, feminized, and queered, the arts play rib to that Adamic first principle, political economy, in cold war cultural histories—an ironic development given the timing of the rise of both second-wave feminism and the gay and lesbian civil rights movement in the United States. They, too, are distinctly cold war phenomena that, no less than "parting the curtain," need to be understood in relation to the era's cultural front, the unanticipated side effects of government support of art despite its traditional connections to those denigrated, dominated classes: women and homosexuals.[27]

Histories of the NEA that emphasize the importance of the cultural cold war in overcoming resistance to government arts funding document how frequently that resistance was articulated in misogynistic and homophobic language, though these outbursts are less often analyzed than simply reproduced (often, one suspects, because they lend drama and spice to the longer, more sober narrative of governmental deliberation and action). Yet the widespread tendency of opponents of U.S. government arts funding to express contempt for the arts in gendered and sexualized terms is in itself highly meaningful, indexing an anxiety about those politically critical capacities of the artwork that are in some degree a function of art's marginalized, queerly feminine status. Of all the art forms sustained by government programs during the cold war, none is more connected in the American imagination to women and homosexuals than the dance—and it was the dance that was the most frequent target of conservative opponents of federal funding for the arts. In Livingston Biddle's narrative of the creation of the National Foundation on the Arts and Humanities, misogynistic and homophobic rhetoric characterized congressional opposition to government arts funding from the outset, and almost all of it expressed antipathy to the dance. This rhetoric has received no serious attention in cold war cultural studies, which tends to cast opponents to government arts funding as advocates of fiscal conservatism expressing libertarian fears of government control of culture. Yet Biddle's history brims with anecdotes in which opposition to government arts funding is expressed through mockery of or hostility to the dance, which is always understood as a euphemism for sex. In the months leading up to the passage of enabling legislation, Republican representatives Harold R. Gross and Durward Gorham Hall sought to scuttle the bill by amending its definition of dance to include "a precisely anatomical" description of a belly dancer (Biddle 176). After the amendment was read out, Gross observed that "he would have worn his 'tuxedo and dancing shoes' . . . had he realized the full extent of the federal giveaway" (176). Because the legislation called for federal aid for "professional practitioners" in the arts, he added, with broad insinuation, "Who else but a belly dancer" could be the bill's intended dance "professional" (177)?

Such dismissive rhetoric can be traced back as far as Eisenhower's failed 1954 effort to create a National Council on the Arts, which members of Congress derided as the "President's toe dance bill" (Taylor and Barresi 13). It continued into the early years of the NEA, when Roger Stevens, first head of the endowment, finessed anxious inquiries from the House Appropriations Subcommittee as to whether "most of the so-called male dancers in these companies . . . are homosexuals." "It may be true in a few instances," he replied. "But . . . if any male dancer happened by right now, he'd be strong enough to pick you up by the waist and put you over his head and throw you straight out that window" (Biddle 219). Unimpressed by this appeal to the brawn of "so-called male" dancers, Democratic representative George H. Mahon, the powerful chairman of the Committee on Appropriations, informed Stevens that the NEA would have his full support only if the agency would never fund dance. As it happened, the government's "first [NEA] check . . . issued . . . in direct support of the arts" was a 100,000-dollar emergency grant to the American Ballet Theatre, and the NEA had promised an additional 250,000 dollars in assistance to cover expenses for a proposed national tour. In Biddle's account, the plan to pacify Mahon involved claiming that the money was not being spent on dance but on theater. ("The American Ballet *Theatre.* It's wonderful theatre. It's unique.") Smaller grants for other dance troupes were redescribed as "technical assistance," "a marvelously enigmatic and ubiquitous phrase in government" (219–220).

Yet even as dance stood, in the minds of many Congressmen, as the perfect symbol of all they found objectionable in art, it remained the case that ballet had become the Sputnik of cold war cultural combat, the art form in which perceived Soviet dominance posed the most compelling challenge. After all, it was public reaction to the visits of the Moiseyev and the Bolshoi that had triggered the sense of governmental urgency that ultimately transformed desultory and amorphous musings about federal support for the arts into a presidential vision of national cultural greatness. Even though ballet, in particular, represented "everything America was against, . . . a lavish, aristocratic court art, a high—and hierarchical—elite art with no pretense to egalitarianism," the exigencies of cultural combat combined with the forces of a dedicated cadre of émigré Russian and European artists to produce an "astonishing explosion of ballet" in cold war America (Homans 448, 451). By fully acknowledging the degree to which theatrical dance was and is viewed as an intensely feminized art form uniquely hospitable to the talents of gay men, we move toward understanding this particular post-atomic cultural explosion as a consequence of cold war politics with a political consequence of its own. As the bureaucratic sleights of hand that Biddle describes gradually fell away, gay liberation entered the American political stage, thanks in no small part to the metapolitics of dance in the cold war.

4

Dancing

"Don't Act, Just Dance"

The metapolitics of cold war culture are linked to a perception of the aesthetic as a queerly feminine realm of experience. Clinging to this perception are several otherwise antithetical views of the arts and government arts patronage that, as I have shown, circulated widely in the United States during the cold war, from the confident assumption that propagandists can manipulate art to dismissals of art as a useless frivolity and denunciations of its fickle, subversive energies. Rather than study the origins and accuracy of modern perceptions of art's essential femininity and/or queerness, I want to explore how this view informed cold war culture and shaped its effects.[1] Such an exploration becomes possible, even necessary, once dance is accorded its rightful place at the center of the cold war cultural landscape.

The growing field of dance studies has produced much fine research on this extremely important period of its American history. For the most part, however, this scholarship has not gotten the attention it deserves in the larger fields of modernist studies, American studies, and cold war cultural studies.[2] Given that these academic fields are dedicated to furthering interdisciplinary approaches to cultural interpretation, this neglect makes little intellectual sense, but it is in some ways explicable. An art no less formally complex than music, cinema, literature, or painting, dance has its own specialized vocabulary and a history as rich and globally varied as those of its sister media. It places demands on the interpreter/critic no less rigorous than those of other art forms, but far fewer Americans study dance than learn to read, and dances do not live parallel lives as investment commodities in the manner of painting, sculpture, or cinema. Consequently, dance history enjoys nothing like the attention within the undergraduate liberal arts curriculum accorded to literature or art history (and however increasingly imperiled that attention may be today, it is at least recognized as imperiled). Then, too, dance puts the human body on display and under investigation with an intensity unmatched by the other arts, one that, even today and however unconsciously, can be seen as justifying its relegation to the margins of scholarly discourse. Dance's constitutive and disconcerting blend of the concrete with the abstract, the corporeal with the ephemeral, has kept it out of serious conversation about art and politics, which often follows the old, specious division between feminine being and masculine becoming that has long kept women and their feminized analogues in the American imaginary out of education and public life and obscured their claim on history. As W. H. Auden, no friend of the dance, said in 1954, "ballet time . . . is a continuous present; every experience which depends on historical time lies outside its capacities. . . . Ballets take place in . . . [a] world of pure being without becoming . . . a world without history and without seriousness" (393, 394).

Unquestionably, the formal concerns and aesthetic values of dance cannot be subsumed into those of other artistic media. Dance is not simply storytelling, music making, or picture drawing, though it can be narrative and musical as well as visual. Its difference is expressed in the spatial-temporal properties of the aesthetic worlds that it bodies forth, which do exist historically, despite the irreproducible singularity of an individual work and its performance. In what almost seems to be a deliberate response to Auden's airy dismissal, Mark Franko has described those worlds as a fundamentally political "reverse architecture."

> What the movements (spacings) of dance establish is . . . a space that intends to become. . . . Movement through space leaves the trace of place that would have made movement possible, architecturally inevitable. In other terms, dance is reverse architecture, taking down what was not there. This is its monumentality. The architectural fantasm of dance is impermanent but not unstable, under erasure but not as "non-sense." Movement both evokes and shapes a surviving social response as a physical environment. Dance, in other terms, calls social space into being.[3] ("Mimique" 211)

What Franko describes as the monumentality and sociality of dance should be understood, in Rancière's terms, as its metapolitics: its richly imagined, critically interrogative redistribution of the sensible world in formally unique terms that work to "disturb the clear-cut rules of representational logic" determining "who can have a share in what is common to the community based on what they do and on the time and space in which this activity is performed" (*The Politics of Aesthetics* 15, 12). In less theoretical terms, it is what Jennifer Homans has described as the central aesthetic effect of the most successful cold war ballets of George Balanchine: "When the curtain went up . . . one did not see a ballet; one witnessed a group of dancers making their way through a living, shifting labyrinth of split-second choices, calculations, mistakes, regrets, adjustments, and consequences. . . . Balanchine created ballets for dancers to live in, and when everything worked, they ran free" (500–501).

When she retired from the New York City Ballet in 2010, Darci Kistler was widely described as "the last of the Balanchine ballerinas" (Macauley, "A Long Goodbye from the Last of Balanchine's Ballerinas").[4] During an interview conducted at the height of her career, just a few years after Balanchine's death, she recalled being introduced to one of his central tenets during her struggle to learn the role of Odette: "Here you are in *Swan Lake.* You're supposed to be a swan queen; he would say, 'don't be a swan.' You're supposed to be in love with your partner; he would say, 'don't look at your partner.' Most people would think, well, you have to act dramatic; he would say, 'don't act.' But those were all things that I knew I didn't have. So what he ended up doing was always giving me myself. He would say, 'you know, dear, just dance'" (Belle, *Dancing for Mr. B*).

Like Kistler, nearly all of the dancers who worked with Balanchine entered into his aesthetic through a counterintuitive exercise in refusal ("don't be a swan," "don't look at your partner," "don't act"). To be sure, his rhetoric altered over the course of his long international career, which began in 1920s Saint Petersburg, ended in 1980s New York City, and included extended sojourns in Paris, Monte Carlo, and London. Moreover, different dancers understood his aesthetic differently. Those involved in Balanchine's earliest choreographic forays with Diaghilev's Ballets Russes in Paris and Monte Carlo and his short-lived American Ballet in 1930s New York City were urged to practice emotional restraint in their onstage affect. Felia Doubrovska, who created the role of the Siren in his 1929 *Prodigal Son,* recalled Balanchine telling her that "being modern is being cool. No feeling" (Tracy and DeLano 40).[5] Not until the cold war years, when the New York City Ballet was established as a major cultural institution, did his pursuit of modernist reticence solidify into the catchphrase "don't act, just dance," which scores of American dancers describe as his most common piece of advice. While some were confused, even angered, by this injunction, many report experiencing the same blend of autonomy and release that Kistler described: a sense of being freed (and also dared) to find the dance in themselves and themselves in the dance, especially when they were cast in a ballet that seemed to require acting like someone or something they were not.[6]

More than just a reassuring nostrum to be themselves, "don't act" was, for many dancers, shorthand for a fundamental aspect of the Balanchine aesthetic: a resistance to narrative teleology, to *action* prosaically understood. "You have great freedom to develop [a role] in your own way," recalled Merrill Ashley, a principle with the New York City Ballet during the 1970s and 1980s, "because there aren't any stories. . . . Stories can be confining." Melissa Hayden, a member of the company from its founding in 1948 to her retirement in 1973, added, "There was no point in asking Balanchine what the ballet was about. He'd just say, facetiously, 'Ten or fifteen minutes.' So you listened to the music and danced the choreography as it related to what you heard" (Tracy and DeLano 178, 116). Thus "don't act, just dance," a phrase meant primarily to clear a path for the individual dancer's full, uninhibited engagement with the choreography, amounted, for many of Balanchine's dancers, to something like a dance ethics: a belief in the transformative power of dance itself in its capacity to signify *as dance* (and not as mimed story or gestured psychology), to be meaningful and revelatory solely in terms of the human body negotiating both its physical limitations and the constraints of its environment as it travels through space. This is a philosophy of the dance—and a politics—that stresses its most fundamental materiality: dance is about what it takes to move bodies forward, to make progress.

Tempting as it may be to assimilate this view of the dance to the dogma of American midcentury modernist formal absolutism as articulated by, say, Clement Greenberg, we need to recall that, for Balanchine, the ontological terms of ballet were not only "abstract" (in dance terms, non-narrative): they were also gendered. It is not going too far to say that the phrases "don't act, just dance" and "ballet is woman" (the much more famous comment) define the entirety of the Balanchine aesthetic.[7]

In its particular instantiation of cold war modernism, then, Balanchine's choreography takes precisely those negations and refusals identified in Adorno's aesthetic theory and embodies them in an explicitly gendered mode of address: "don't act" describes the terms of a cold art for a cold war, a deliberately paradoxical filling of the negative space consigned to art with the blanks of affective deterrence and narrative nonproliferation. What might be the metapolitical effects of this refusal to tell the story of woman *in* ballet ("don't be a swan," "don't look at your partner") while insisting that woman is the story *of* ballet? To put the question another way: what happens to our understanding of cold war culture if we take the modernist choreography of George Balanchine and Merce Cunningham (to bring into the discussion another artist whose work is equally crucial to this study) as important not for how it can be made to serve a turn in a longstanding narrative about cultural advocates for America's growing cold war global hegemony but for what it has to say, through an art form at once abstract, gendered, and queerly sexualized, about making progress through—not only within but also against and beyond—that hegemony?

That the metapolitics of cold war dance emerge in modernist investigations of its non- or a-narrative formal properties, which are at once both concrete and abstract, embodied and ephemeral, and that the dance accordingly should be understood as a key cultural formation of the era: these claims are at the heart of *Don't Act, Just Act* and they accordingly are at the heart of part 2, which opens with a reading of the work of Balanchine and Cunningham in terms of their complex engagements—as choreographers, company directors, and citizens—with the U.S.-engineered cold war fortunes of Iran. For Balanchine this engagement took the form of a ballet; for Cunningham it involved dancing within the ruins of Persepolis.

An eye-catching spectacle premiering seven years after the CIA-orchestrated overthrow of Iran's democratically elected prime minister Mohammed Mosaddeq, Balanchine's *The Figure in the Carpet* (1960) took the rapid intensification of monarchical absolutism in the rule of Reza Shah Pahlavi as an opportunity to revisit the imperial origins of ballet. The work itself is lost beyond any hope of reconstruction; Balanchine himself abandoned it. But the passing of this *Figure* has left a path worth retracing. Although it could easily be dismissed as a particularly naked example of artwork as instrument of flattery and advancement, it may also be viewed as a work of immanent critique remarkable for its sly maneuvers in camp discourse, a dance virtually called into existence by Christopher Isherwood's 1954 assertion that "High Camp," a way of "expressing what's basically serious . . . in terms of artifice," constitutes "the whole emotional basis of the ballet." (110). Isherwood's understanding of ballet's queer method of speaking the past through the present is both more sympathetic and more shrewd than his friend Auden's, and my reading of *Figure* builds on that understanding. Unquestionably, the ballet was a cold war artwork of exceptional calculation: it was made at the instigation of the Barnum-like historian of Persian art (and Pahlavi sycophant) Arthur Upham Pope, and Lincoln Kirstein, keenly aware of the benefits to arts organizations of cultural diplomacy, hoped the work would help capture the shah's patronage for New York City Ballet (a hope that never materialized). Yet in the ballet itself, the double pressures of modernist formal rigor and orientalist exoticism combined to unexpected effect, rearticulating courtly obeisance in a manner that highlighted not only its glamour but also its superannuation and, correlatively, its contemporary implausibility. Revisiting the intimate connection between royalty and the ballet, *Figure* offered a discomfiting vision of the recent "restoration" of the Peacock Throne as itself a clever piece of choreography. The dance illustrates how the continuing modernist development of ballet during the cold war was giving rise, sometimes unexpectedly, to a quiet yet insistent interrogation of precisely those reverently hierarchical, courtly, and courting traditions in which the art had found its being.

A more radical articulation of modernist dance as immanent critique emerges in the ballet-infused, chance-based, recombinatory choreographic practice of Merce Cunningham, whose troupe's carefully calibrated participation in the 1972 Shiraz Arts Festival in Iran opens similar lines of analysis. Here, however, the medium/object of interrogation was not only modernist dance but the whole of the postwar avant-garde, an interrogation made possible by Cunningham's decision to presented disarticulated segments of his work in a site-specific event. In the established vein of historicist cold war cultural symptomatology, some have denounced Cunningham's aesthetic practice as an apolitical "aesthetic of indifference"—a politically "dangerous" "paralysis" and "extreme passivity" offering "no messages, no feelings and no ideas" (Roth and Katz, "Aesthetic of Indifference" 47, 34, 40, 41). But what emerges in the context of the shah's fantastically militarized ruins of Persepolis is an especially compelling example of precisely that coolly appraising "distance" from "society's structures, or social groups, their conflicts or identities" that Rancière identified as a profoundly political aspect of art.

These historically framed, theoretically informed close readings of Balanchine's and Cunningham's contributions to cold war culture uncover the political charge embedded in what many of their dancers have described as an aesthetic of revelation rather than explanation—of showing rather than telling.[8] Such an aesthetic is much less passive or decorative (that is, much less apolitical in senses both gendered and sexualized) than many commonly assume. For to speak *with* the body is perforce to speak *of* the sexed, raced, gendered, and/or aging body; of its abilities and its limitations (innate or imposed, defied, internalized, or worked around); its mutability and its facticity; its social positioning and its accompanying political power or lack thereof. To understand this is also to understand how much dance meaning goes missing when the only meaning that counts politically is narrative: Balanchine's and Cunningham's lack of interest in telling stories has often wrongly been taken as a signal of their lack of interest in making meaning. Yet as Cunningham dancer Carolyn Brown has asserted, "it's impossible for human bodies placed together in time and space not to reek with secret and not-so-secret meaning, be it spiritual, psychological, sociological, physical, chemical, emotional—whatever.... Yes, of course, the meaning *is* in the dancing, but dancing can never be merely the sum and substance of mechanically executed steps" (273–274).[9] Truly, how could such an art *not* be political?

In taking as its title Balanchine's pithy articulation of the terms of modernist dance's appraising "distance," then, *Don't Act, Just Dance* moves dance from the margins to the center of our understanding of the politics of cold war culture. Casting modernist dance practice as itself as much a part of that understanding as the government's use of dance companies in cultural diplomacy makes clear how the current wisdom about what could be called the political affects of cold war modernism (which both are and are not the same as political effects) needs to be rethought. In their shared commitment to an aesthetics of showing (rather than narrating) the potentialities and limitations of human movement in space and time through differently conceived but similarly rigorous constraint-based poetics of extreme physicality, Cunningham's and Balanchine's modernist dance interventions into the body politics of the cold war U.S. body politic signify not only internationally (as evidenced by their specific engagements with U.S.-Iranian relations) but also domestically, placing sex, sexuality, gender, race, and age simultaneously on display and in question. Translated into dance terms, Rancière's understanding of the aesthetic regime of literary production as emerging at the moment of language's democratizing coming-to-consciousness of itself as the "secret" "constitutive contradiction" of literature offers a way of reading the cold war efflorescence of U.S. dance modernism as a similarly democratizing coming-to-consciousness of the human body as the doubled subject/object of art and politics (*The Flesh of Words* 92). For Rancière, "art does not do politics by reaching the real" but by "inventing fictions that challenge the existing distribution of the real and the fictional" ("Contemporary Art" 49). Since inventing fictions "does not mean telling stories" but "undoing and rearticulating the connections between signs and images, images and times, or signs and space that frame the existing sense of reality," Rancière's thought sets the terms for understanding the supremely unrealistic worlds of Balanchine's and Cunningham's dances as landscapes bodying forth a liberated "people to come" ("The Method of Equality" 286).

The line of analysis begun here carries over into the chapter on Spartacus. A central figure of the cold war cultural imaginaries of both the United States and the Soviet Union, Spartacus presided over the period's most popular and fiercely contested narrative of freedom and justice. Between 1951 and 1968, the revolt of the gladiators was the subject of a best-selling novel (by Howard Fast), a film (Stanley Kubrick's second for Kirk Douglas's Bryna Productions), and several Soviet ballets, culminating in Yuri Grigorovich's stunning 1968 Bolshoi Ballet realization of Aram Khachaturian's score. In 1970, the first commercially successful series of vacation travel guides targeting gay tourists was released under the name of Spartacus. If Balanchine's and Cunningham's Persian engagements ask us to reconsider assumptions about the "apolitical" nature of non- or a-narrative aesthetic practices, the protean narrative capacities of Spartacus invite a parallel reckoning of the ways in which art and sex were energized and radicalized as related means of imagining and enacting freedom during the cold war. Tracking the engagements with Spartacus as both figure and narrative of anti-statist dissensus on both sides of the Iron Curtain over more than twenty years of cold war exposes several lines of dialectical tension in the relationship between art and politics during the era, tensions that fueled the forceful emergence of new understandings of sex, sexuality, and gender as political categories.

Don't Act, Just Dance closes on a reading of the 1987 opera *Nixon in China,* a late cold war work whose formal and thematic engagements with modernist aesthetic practices and government involvements in culture are strikingly multifaceted. Readings of the opera that focus on the accuracy of its representation of Richard M. Nixon's 1972 trip to China or on its putative sympathy for the disgraced president—or that sidestep these questions by emphasizing its indebtedness to nineteenth-century predecessors such as Verdi's *Don Carlo* or Mussorgsky's *Boris Godunov*—miss the degree to which cold war *cultural* politics, no less than the "pure" political event of its title, constitute the opera's subject. Indeed, the key scene in the opera's second act—a rarely discussed, complexly layered episode structured around the command performance during Nixon's visit of Jiang Qing's favorite ballet, *The Red Detachment of Women*—raises important questions about the purposes and effects of politically instrumentalized artwork. Like Moore's "Combat Cultural," *Nixon in China* is a cold war work of art about the cold war use of art—though the opera's meta-political energies are complemented and intensified by what we could term its meta-aesthetic commentary on the likely future shape of the relationship between art and politics. Created by artists native to the age (composer John Adams was born in 1947, choreographer Mark Morris in 1956, director Peter Sellars in 1957, and librettist Alice Goodman in 1958), *Nixon in China* offers a reading of cold war culture that—in its prefigurations of a certain globalized, post–cold war relation between aesthetics and politics, "high" art and popular culture—brings calculation and sincerity into uncanny relation.

The readings in part 2 show how cold war artworks and cultural productions should be understood as more than discrete articulations of specific political circumstances. They are also historically specific crystallizations of a set of abiding aesthetic concerns within a still-evolving modernist project, concerns whose constantly shifting terms of association unfold in relation to a similarly mutable political landscape. Though impossible to capture fully, it is precisely this sense of *movement* within the work of cold war cultural production and interpretation—movement at once political and aesthetic—that I aim to represent not only through my interest in dance but also in my reading practice. It is this effort to put to the test my own sense of what (again following Rancière) I want to call the metapolitics of interpretation that leads me to center my readings on artists, forms, and practices (Balanchine and Cunningham; ballet, Hollywood cinema, and opera; modernism) usually seen as paradigmatically representative of establishment U.S. cultural and political values during the cold war. This is not to say that I am unaware of or uninterested in the work of more clearly resistant artists (for example, Katherine Dunham and Alvin Ailey) or those popular cultural forms (comic books, science fiction novels, rock-and-roll) that might seem to speak more directly to a cold war cultural studies project bent on interrogating received understandings of the period's cultural politics and traditional modes of cultural interpretation.[10] Rather, I explore the formal complexities and constitutive contradictions of exactly those genres and modes of cultural production whose relationship to cold war politics has come to be treated as an entirely settled question within contemporary critical discourse. In other words, I aspire to an interpretive practice operating along the lines of Rancière's aesthetic regime of production: one aiming to reconfigure the terms of our understanding, opening established works and modes of analysis to new forms of intelligibility and meaning making; new ways of thinking about the relationship between history and theory, art and politics; new ways of remembering cold war culture.

Finally, in selecting works for analysis in a cold war cultural studies project centered on, but not limited to, the dance, I address three loosely related concerns: first, what lost or lesser works created by canonical cold war artists might be able to tell us about the unique formal challenges of the era (*The Figure in the Carpet*); second, how works by a highly regarded artist whose practice is rarely described as crucial to an understanding of cold war culture might be seen once they are reframed as creations central to the period (Cunningham's dance Events); and, third, what a series of contestatory takes on a single thematic subject (Spartacus) might reveal not only about organized efforts to yoke art to a particular ideology or political formation but also about art's capacities for slipping that yoke. This last concern also informs my interest in the growth of cultural diplomacy. Thus, I focus on the work of artists who, at some point in their careers, were touched by this particular form of cold war government arts patronage.

Given the critical stance I adopt here towards traditional historicist cold war cultural studies, I should make clear that it is not my aim to dismiss or diminish the important contributions of this scholarship to our understanding of the history of government efforts to enlist the arts and individual artists in the cold war. Useful as it is, however, historicist contextualizing is no substitute for an engagement with the works themselves, one that seeks to account for the still-unsettling claims they have on our attention—which is to say, it is probably never a good idea to take the state's view of the meaning and function of art as the final word. Among other things, the works I examine reveal how certain aspects of the famed cold war consensus were more willed than real, including the characterization of the period as an age of consensus. Thus, efforts to understand the near-simultaneous unfolding within the United States of modernism and government patronage of the arts are not well served by narratives reducing this extraordinarily complex interplay of various forms of representation to a bad romance of power and beauty. Nor does the oppositional logic that pushes one to choose between understandings of art as either a sacramental practice cloistered within "cathedrals of culture" or a "spontaneous and natural manifestation of the élan" of a people leave much room for an appreciation of the artwork as a mode of interrogation, a way of thinking otherwise (Saab 4; McDonald 8). It is possible that the dialectical understanding of art as simultaneously engaged and distanced might be the cold war era's most important contribution to the modernist project. To take this possibility seriously is, I argue, to take our first steps toward recognizing the role artworks play in enlivening and staging dissent, even when dissent speaks *sotto voce.* "Don't act" does not mean "do nothing." As John Cage's masterpiece *4′33″* (1952) tried to teach us during the coldest years of the cold war, there is no such thing as total silence.

Part II

Rereading Cold War Culture

5

Figures in the Carpet

Balanchine, Cunningham, "Persia"

William Faulkner was not the only difficult American novelist whose stock enjoyed high valuation during the cold war. The story of Henry James's elevation to literary canonization, however, bears little resemblance to Faulkner's dramatic, rags-to-riches narrative of critical redemption, following instead the same slow path that characterized the rise of government arts patronage in the 1930s.[1] James's full accession to the title of "The Master" of American letters was accomplished in the early 1950s with the publication of the first installment of Leon Edel's five-volume biography, but Ross Posnock traces of the start of James's canonization to the 1934 publication of R.P. Blackmur's "The Critical Prefaces of Henry James"—a sign that Edel's biography is better understood as the crowning achievement of a decades-long process than as a cold war cultural symptom.[2] Posnock asserts, with reason, that the essay played a key role in establishing James as "one of the most prestigious, indeed, sacred cultural icons on the altar of American high culture" (345). Nonetheless, his claim for the uniquely transformative effect of this *particular* essay is less convincing, and not only because there were earlier, equally impassioned arguments for James's greatness. For Blackmur's paean was part of a team effort, one of fourteen tributes to James published in a special issue of the literary journal *Hound & Horn*. Included in that chorus of praise were contributions by Marianne Moore, Stephen Spender, Edna Kenton, Glenway Wescott,

Robert Cantwell, and others; the chorus was orchestrated not Blackmur but the journal's founder and editor, Lincoln Kirstein.[3] It was Kirstein who had conceived the notion of producing a "significant symposium on the then-underappreciated Henry James," soliciting and editing the contributions and writing the preface to the volume (Duberman 214). And while Blackmur's essay does identify aspects of the novelist's art that continue to draw thoughtful attention (the subordinate elaborations and syntactical challenges of the late style, the "tight and contained" narrative form), another essay in the issue, Edmund Wilson's louche foray into "The Ambiguity of James," heralded the arrival of the interpretive challenge that governed nearly every significant critical approach to James during the astonishingly fertile "high theory" years of mid- to late cold war literary scholarship—from Shoshana Felman's Lacanian intervention to Tzvetan Todorov's structuralist poetics, J. Hillis Miller's deconstructive hermeneutics, and Eve Kosofsky Sedgwick's epistemology of the closet (Blackmur 20, 44).[4]

Many readers see Jamesian ambiguity as a kind of hermeneutic paradox, but Kirstein was likely to appreciate it differently. He was well positioned to grasp the centrality of what today's scholars, working in the wake of Sedgwick, reframe as something less ambiguous: James's queerly telling (or tellingly queer) silences and obliquities.[5] Not that *Kirstein's* queerness was all that oblique: wealthy, well connected, and devoted to the arts, he was quite aware of and, for his time, remarkably unconflicted about his own homosexuality. Although he dutifully fulfilled the era's normative demands (in 1941 he married Fidelma Cadmus, sister of the gay painter Paul Cadmus), he did not live a wholly closeted life, as Martin Duberman's recent biography has made clear.[6]

Kirstein founded *Hound & Horn* in 1927 during his sophomore year at Harvard. Initially conceived as a forum for student work, the quarterly rapidly broadened its scope and gained respect in the world of modernist "little magazines," publishing literary criticism as well as significant fiction and poetry by contributors such as Katherine Ann Porter, Gertrude Stein, and Elizabeth Bishop. However, the spring 1934 "Homage to Henry James" was the journal's last number. Its demise was due less to economic issues (though its finances were never robust) than to the rapid evolution of its founder's interests. In 1933, Kirstein, an aesthetic polymath and dabbler, had taken the first steps toward transforming one of his many passions, the dance, into a lifetime vocation: the creation and management of an American ballet company. The Russian choreographer George Balanchine had arrived in the United States in October 1933 entirely at Kirstein's invitation, and maintaining the commitment to *Hound & Horn* while simultaneously working to build, virtually from the ground up, a performing troupe and allied training school proved beyond the capacities of even a manic multitasker like Kirstein. Always a writer, often an editor, sometimes a poet, he folded the journal and devoted his fortune and talents entirely to developing what eventually became the New York City Ballet, a decision that had far-reaching consequences for the postwar development of American dance. Kirstein's departure from the world of literary publishing was hardly perfunctory, however; he lavished considerable care on the Henry James issue of *Hound & Horn*, which he correctly considered his "masterpiece" (Duberman 214). Nor should it be assumed that Kirstein's admiration for James and love of ballet had nothing in common, or that moving on to the world of dance meant abandoning modes of aesthetic engagement cultivated and honed by years of appreciative encounters with The Master. Sixteen years after folding his magazine Kirstein would offer another salute to Jamesian ambiguity via the title of one of the most enigmatic productions in the history of the New York City Ballet, the company that he and Balanchine built together on the ruins of *Hound & Horn*.

Premiering on April 13, 1960, *The Figure in the Carpet* was the company's most expensive production since its extravagant 1954 version of *The Nutcracker*. *The Nutcracker* had proven to be a sound investment. A dependable box-office draw, it minimized deficits incurred during the rest of the year, when Balanchine's more astringently abstract, neoclassically modernist ballets comprised much of the repertoire. It seems that Balanchine and Kirstein designed *Figure* with the aim of producing another money-making hit. A long but less than evening-length ballet in five scenes, *The Figure in the Carpet* was conceived as a spectacular, crowd-pleasing closer. The work was set to Handel's popular *Royal Fireworks* and *Water Music,* and its costumes and decor departed dramatically from the austere "lights and tights" aesthetic that by 1960 had become something of a Balanchine trademark. Designed by Spanish painter Esteban Francés, the costumes were inspired by the engravings of Jean Bérain, the seventeenth-century draftsman and designer who flourished during the reign of Louis XIV, the "Sun King," whose love of dance infused court ballet with political import. In realizing those designs, costumer Barbara Karinska made lavish use of brocade, gold braid, embroidery, feathers, and jewels. *Figure*'s final scenes evoked an orientalist vision of a Persian palace surrounded by elegant gardens; its concluding "Apotheosis" featured a working fountain. Described by the *New York Times* as a "sumptuous" *pièce d'occasion* "sponsored by Mohammad Reza Pahlevi [*sic*], Shah of Iran, and produced . . . in honor of the Fourth Congress of the International Association for Iranian Art and Archaeology," *The Figure in the Carpet* employed virtually the entire company of dancers and cost the New York City Ballet at least 120,000 dollars—almost 950,000 dollars in today's currency and more than double the price tag of *The Nutcracker* (Martin "The Dance: Iranian").[7]

Figure received a cool review from the *Times*'s John Martin, but other critics admired the ballet. The *Herald Tribune*'s influential Walter Terry called it "one of George Balanchine's most splendid works, . . . not to be missed" ("'Figure in

Carpet' Featured by the City Ballet" 8). Likewise, the *Saturday Review's* Irving Kolodin called it "a major addition to [the] repertory, . . . destined to outlast by far the occasion which brought it into being" (34). To accommodate demand, the company had to add an additional performance.[8] The ballet was so successful that portions appeared eight months later in a WNBC-TV *Omnibus* broadcast promoting the development of Lincoln Center. Along with a scene from Shakespeare's *King John,* a segment showing Metropolitan Opera members and Juilliard School students singing arias from Mozart's *Don Giovanni,* and a New York Philharmonic performance of William Schuman's *American Festival Overture* (conducted by Leonard Bernstein), *Figure* was offered as an example of the high-caliber, highbrow work that New Yorkers could expect to see in the proposed deluxe performing arts complex (Graham, "A Midwinter Night's Dream").

The obscure nature of the shah's involvement notwithstanding, Balanchine's and Kirstein's gamble appeared to have paid off: *Figure* seemed poised to join *The Nutcracker* as one of the company's dependable cash cows. Yet, almost unaccountably, the work quickly vanished from the company's repertoire. After a second run of performances in 1961, it went unproduced until 1964, when Balanchine considered reviving it for the company's first season in the New York State Theatre at Lincoln Center—a sensible move given the ballet's prominence in the *Omnibus* broadcast. Unfortunately, neither he nor any of *Figure*'s original principals, which included celebrated dancers such as Violette Verdy, Melissa Hayden, Jacques d'Amboise, Patricia McBride, Suki Schorer, Edward Villella, Arthur Mitchell, and Diana Adams, could remember enough of the ballet to remount it. Despite a considerable investment in costumes and scenery, Balanchine decided he wasn't interested in crafting new steps to fit the existing musical and scenic frame (though such choreographic revision and recycling was common throughout his career), and *Figure* was abandoned.[9]

Because it is a work from what is regarded as Balanchine's golden age in America—the period extending from the late 1940s into the 1960s that saw the creation of ballets as brilliant and various as *The Four Temperaments, Symphony in C, Orpheus, Agon, Square Dance, Episodes,* and *A Midsummer Night's Dream* (not to mention *The Nutcracker*)—and because it is irretrievably lost, *The Figure in the Carpet* has become, in the words of Barbara Horgan of the Balanchine Trust, "a ballet with a great mystique." Well before the ballet's disappearance, Kirstein had linked it to a world of mystery by way of its allusive title, which, he later wrote, was intended to serve as a "resonant metaphor, . . . a possible rallying cry for a demonstration of the mystery of design" (*Thirty Years* 155). Indeed, not long after the ballet had vanished from the stage, James's 1896 novella did come to serve as a kind of rallying cry for cold war literary scholars eager to demonstrate that an appreciation for the techniques of narrative mystification (that is, understanding how manipulations of point of view, syntax, diction, plot, and voice can conspire to create effects of ambiguous import) was far preferable to the deluded quest for total interpretive command so painfully pursued by the hapless narrator of James's tale. Of course, Balanchine's ballet has never received anything approaching this sort of critical intensity, partly because it is lost but also partly because it is ballet, which, as I have discussed, has yet to receive the broadly sanctioned, institutionally sustained, popular and scholarly attention that Americans have devoted to literature. Still, today's relative neglect of the art form is an improvement over the actively hostile reactions typical of the mid-twentieth century. The source of that hostility was no mystery to Kirstein. "The dancer's career is not viewed kindly by that American family who is depicted as the core of our country, backbone of TV, supermarkets, automobiles and eaters of mass-media," he wrote in 1959. "Ballets, such as those enlivening the first famous extravaganzas that were shown in this country (*The Black Crook,* 1866; *The White Faun,* 1868) gave our great-grandfathers and their young sons a serious trauma. The women were painted hussies to be sure, but those boy-things were straight from Sodom" (*Ballet* 398–399).[10] As had been the case in the 1930s with the work of Henry James (and, Kirstein probably intuited, for similar reasons), ballet was an underappreciated art form in postwar America. So as he had with James, Kirstein went to work, tackling Americans' fear of ballet's mysteriously and/or ambiguously designing figures on two fronts.

Publicly, Kirstein seized every opportunity to present ballet in general, and male dancers especially, in wholesome, all-American terms. There was nothing particularly new in this approach; he was following a path blazed years before by Ted Shawn (though Shawn disdained ballet and sought to cast modern dance as the embodiment of manly American dancing). But during the cold war, ballet enjoyed high public esteem and heavy government subsidy in the rapidly heightening cultural competition between the United States and the Soviet Union. Thus, Kirstein was able to emphasize the true-blue patriotic manliness of male dancers in ways that furthered important public relations work and related institutional growth for the New York City Ballet. In 1941, he gained experience in contact building and networking during Ballet Caravan's five-month tour through South America, sponsored by Nelson Rockefeller's Office of the Coordinator of Inter-American Affairs when Kirstein and Balanchine were struggling to get their own company off the ground.[11] After the New York City Ballet was founded in 1948, Kirstein immediately began pursuing international touring and cultural diplomacy as a means of strengthening the troupe. Between 1950 and 1958, the company made five tours of Europe and one of the Pacific rim; three were government-sponsored, and Kirstein never missed a chance to trumpet the troupe's service as "cultural ambassadors . . . appearing in State Department tours to impress our hoped-for allies with our spiritual superiority" (*Ballet* 371, 399). This superiority was evidenced in part by the unaffected, breezy, masculine athleticism of dancers such as Jacques d'Amboise and Edward Villella.[12]

Privately, as he hinted in his arch remark about the "boy-things . . . straight from Sodom," Kirstein relished the many ways in which ballet, like the Jamesian narrative, is an art of preterition, simultaneously invoking and obscuring the sex at its heart.[13] With the body as its medium of expression, all dance draws considerable signifying power from an underlying sexual tension. Arguably, however, it is in the ballet—where a distancing armature of tradition and technique presents the body as something to be both gloried in and transcended—that this tension operates most powerfully as a kind of open secret. This is especially the case in Balanchine's neoclassical style of modernist ballet in which streamlined abstract dances emphasizing clear lines, extreme athleticism, and utmost visibility are typically presented in skintight leotards that simultaneously cover and flaunt crotch, breasts, and buttocks in a fashion at once de- and hyper-sexualizing. Like the ambiguity of James's prose, modernist ballet bodies both are and are not about sex; and as in James's work, this mode of discourse—not exactly reticent, not entirely frank—summons affective worlds usually relegated to the wings of "normal" sexual feeling.

Not unlike the Master, then, Kirstein had designs on his audience that worked in several registers at once. His public posture toward homophobic ballet bashing contained little defensive denial. A favorite tactic involved acknowledging ballet's "effete smell" before launching into a disquisition on its virtues as the flower of public diplomacy, the art form most perfectly suited for cultural combat with a ballet-loving Soviet Union (*Ballet* 398). And his personal delight in that "effete smell" was consequential. Though he was not a choreographer, Kirstein's aesthetic predilections carried weight at the New York City Ballet. Far from conflicting, his public and private approaches to ballet's connection with homosexuality functioned in tandem to help effect two important transformations in American life, which are among the most enduring domestic cultural and political legacies of the cold war era: the establishment of theatrical dance, especially the ballet, as a respected art form, and the emergence of a gay and lesbian civil rights movement.

Recent scholarship has amply demonstrated how the needs of cold war cultural diplomacy led to the rapid, dramatic development of dance as a viable American art form, helping dance companies achieve greater institutional stability and creating conditions in which dance artists could produce work of increasing political relevance and sometimes radical urgency.[14] However, the abstract (that is, formalist) non-narrative dances of the sort made by Balanchine and the even more austere Merce Cunningham are generally not seen as likely candidates for politically unsettling choreography, and the possibility that government support of such work might have had unintended yet profound effects on cold war cultural politics—sexual politics, in particular—is rarely entertained.[15] Yet as Mark Franko notes, dance's political impact is less a function of a given work's subject than an effect of how its formal properties make manifest the "kinesthetic and visual means by which individual identities are called or hailed to larger group formations"—an observation that admits the largest possible construction of what counts as political activism in dance and demands a rethinking of the commonplace notion that abstract work is perforce nonpolitical. In making his point, he largely accepts the notion of a "great divide between modernism and the postmodern" wherein the modern is the realm of "compromises," the postmodern the world of "critical self-reflexivity" ("Dance and the Political" 6). However, a paired reading of Balanchine's and Cunningham's choreographic explorations of Iran disrupts that neat distinction.

Iran became a strategic client state of the United States after the CIA-engineered overthrow of Prime Minister Mohammed Mosaddeq in 1953, and the nations remained linked until the 1979 Islamic revolution. Twelve years after the premiere of the New York City Ballet's Iranian-themed *The Figure in the Carpet,* the Merce Cunningham Dance Company was a featured guest at the Shiraz Arts Festival in Persepolis, the extraordinarily lavish showcase of the international avant-garde launched in 1967. Pairing Cunningham's and Balanchine's cold war engagements with "Persia" reveals how they produced critically self-reflexive work through their formal engagements with a particular cold war geopolitical formation, engagements that put several ironies into productive play precisely because of their commitments to an abstract, non- or a-narrative idiom. As Franko acknowledges, "dance can absorb and retain the effects of political power as well as resist the very effects it appears to incorporate within the same gesture. This is what makes dance a potent form of political expression: it can encode norms as well as deviation from the norms in structures of parody, irony, and pastiche that appear and disappear quickly, often leaving no trace" ("Dance and the Political" 6).

Balanchine's *Figure* appeared when the New York City Ballet was in a frenzy of international touring and the company was reaping the benefits, tangible and intangible, of its participation in cold war cultural diplomacy. Both the State Department and the USIA were delighted with the troupe's performances under sometimes grueling traveling conditions in uncertain political climates. Its first government-sponsored tour in 1953 (Italy, Germany, and Belgium) was followed by a much larger European tour in 1955 (Monte Carlo, France, Italy, Portugal, Switzerland, Germany, the Netherlands). In 1958 it toured Japan, Australia, and the Philippines; and in 1962 the troupe embarked on the famous tour of the Soviet Union that put it in Moscow in the midst of the Cuban missile crisis.[16] Clearly, Kirstein and Balanchine knew how to please a state sponsor. Yet contrary to the *New York Times* report, the shah of Iran contributed nothing to the creation of *Figure;* indeed, it's not clear that he even saw it.

Unlike Balanchine, Cunningham had tremendous difficulty getting U.S. government sponsorship for his company's foreign tours. Members of the Dance Panel of the American National Theater and Academy (until 1963 the consulting agency that vetted performers for State Department and USIA-sponsored appearances abroad) repeatedly rebuffed his requests for support, turning down appeals for assistance with his Asian (1955) and European (1960) tours and condemning both his choreography and the music of his lover and artistic collaborator John Cage. The work was too "confusing and abstract," they claimed, so "way out on the fringes of American dance" as to do little more than "stir up a lot of controversy" (Prevots 54, 57). Even after the Merce Cunningham Dance Company took Europe and Asia by storm in its unsponsored but diplomatically significant 1964 tour—reviewers rarely failed to note that the company's set designer, Robert Rauschenberg, had received the Grand Prize in that year's Venice Biennale, the first American ever to do so—State Department officials remained reluctant to support the troupe, rejecting requests for assistance with summer 1966 appearances in Spain, France, and Germany.

The company's participation in the 1968 Cultural Olympics in Mexico City marked its first federally supported appearance abroad, fifteen years after its founding and more than a decade after its initial requests for government assistance. But if the State Department believed that this long-sought largesse would transform troupe members into grateful, tractable cultural ambassadors, those hopes were quickly dashed. During an interview in Mexico, Cage bluntly criticized the "'don't talk against the government' clause of the State Department contract," and relations were often strained between the company and U.S. embassy cultural attachés during the ensuing State-sponsored tour to Brazil, Argentina, and Venezuela. According to company dancer Carolyn Brown, the U.S. embassy in Buenos Aires "sabotaged" the troupe's appearances there (*Chance and Circumstance* 515, 517).

One might expect that such a politically independent and headstrong group of artists would be unwelcome at an event sponsored by the autocratic Pahlavi regime, but the Cunningham troupe appeared in the 1972 edition of the Shiraz Arts Festival by Iranian invitation and traveled to Persepolis without U.S. government assistance. Interestingly, and importantly, Cunningham's contribution to the shah's event was not an ambitious, specially created work, as was the case with the productions of many of the festival's other participants (Karlheinz Stockhausen and Robert Wilson among them). Rather, it was an "Event" of his own: a performance in which the company presented passages of choreography lifted from several different dances. Cunningham had adopted this practice during the 1964 world tour in response to performance invitations from museums in Vienna and Stockholm, where the company danced in the galleries. But while widely noted in the criticism, the Events have yet to receive their fair share of recognition and analysis as a politically charged component of his modernist dance aesthetic.

In her study of cold war modern dance, Rebekah J. Kowal argues that dance "possesses an inherent potential to disrupt and destabilize on levels both personal and social," a claim that resembles Penny Von Eschen's insistence, in her study of the political effects of the State–sponsored tours of Louis Armstrong, Dizzy Gillespie, and others, on the uniquely interrogatory and liberatory powers of jazz (Kowal 185).[17] Like Von Eschen's assertion, Kowal's brief for the body's "inherent power to counteract forces of normalization and . . . to stand for change," articulated as it is in the context of dance modernism, is, I think, better understood less as an essentialist or ahistorical claim about the political power of the dance than as an invitation to consider how certain approaches to art making and, correlatively, certain kinds of aesthetic experience (approaches and experiences available in a wide variety of artistic media, as Kirstein's twinned passions for Henry James and the ballet indicate) can create critical consciousness precisely through their formal strategies (253, emphasis added). In the middle years of the cold war, from the end of the Red Scare to the beginnings of détente, the modernist dance practices of Balanchine and Cunningham frequently did exactly that.

Like the story of postwar cultural diplomacy, the story of the cold war rearticulation of the history and culture of ancient Persia is, to a significant degree, a story about a government's hubristic confidence in its ability to manipulate history and culture to its own ends. Balanchine's *Figure* and Cunningham's Persepolis Event add important complicating chapters to those stories. The choreographers' shared awareness of the limitations of storytelling and a related aesthetics of expression in dance underpins the metapolitical terms of their modernist dance autonomy. By extension, such an appreciation opens a space for reconsidering the dance as a cold war cultural practice that frequently (certainly as often as literature, music, and cinema) helped launch into flight figures long kept underfoot.

The key role played by the CIA in fomenting the August 1953 Iranian coup overthrowing Prime Minister Mosaddeq and returning the shah to greatly expanded power has long been known, but the agency's claim to have destroyed most of the records related to the operation and its refusal to declassify others had for some time left the full extent and nature of that involvement shrouded in mystery. That changed in April 2000, when the *New York Times* published James Risen's analysis of CIA operative Donald N. Wilber's leaked report ("How a Plot Convulsed Iran in '53 [and in '79]," 1).[18] Written in March 1954 and originally titled "Clandestine Service History: Overthrow of Premier Mossadeq of Iran, November 1952–August 1953," the report is commonly abbreviated as the "Secret History." Eventually, the *Times* published it as a redacted pdf file on its website, and even in that abridged form it has proven to be a highly informative and influential document.[19] Among other things, it reveals that the plot to overthrow Mosaddeq was hatched in 1952 by Great Britain, which saw in the Iranian parliament's 1951 decision to nationalize the oil industry the alarming prospect of losing its virtually colonialist control of the country's oil fields, control it had enjoyed since the 1908 creation of the Anglo-Persian Oil Company.[20] Noting the rising influence of Tudeh (Iran's communist political party), MI6 proposed to a rabidly anti-communist United States a joint Anglo-American destabilization project. Although Truman declined the invitation, Eisenhower authorized the plan, code named TP AJAX, shortly after taking office, and CIA director Allen W. Dulles rapidly approved 1 million dollars (8.7 million in current dollars) "to be used 'in any way that would bring about the fall' [of Mosaddeq]" (Risen A14). The "Secret History" makes clear that the primary motive was Washington's and London's shared "interest in maintaining the West's control over Iranian oil"; American concerns about communist influence in Iranian politics, while not insignificant, were mostly useful as a cover story for managing the shah's deep suspicion of Great Britain (A1, A14).

In some ways, the "Secret History" puzzles as much as it illuminates. Wilber presents the coup as a meticulously plotted operation that drew on the expertise of both U.S. and British intelligence. Yet for all its expense and careful planning, it very nearly failed. The report describes the operation's success as "mostly a matter of chance," and recent histories of the coup disagree on core reasons for Mosaddeq's downfall (Risen A1).[21] Still, the official agency narrative, which rapidly took hold in Washington, made no mention of luck: "The CIA took full credit inside the government. The following year it overthrew the government of Guatemala, and a myth developed that the agency could topple governments anywhere in the world" (A15). Predictably, many aspects of TP AJAX—such as placing agency-authored anti-Mosaddeq cartoons and editorials in the local press and whipping up anti-communist public sentiment by hiring Iranian operatives posing as Tudeh members to orchestrate bombings and threats against religious leaders—became the blueprint for all subsequent CIA interventions (A1).

The "Secret History" is also striking for its disdainful and contemptuous attitude toward the shah, whom it portrays as a "vacillating coward" (Risen A1). The report describes "tortured efforts" on the part of American operatives and their Iranian contacts to "seduce and cajole" him into participating in the coup, efforts that included pressure from his "forceful and scheming" twin sister Princess Ashraf and multiple meetings with Kermit Roosevelt, Jr., chief of the CIA's Near East and Africa division (and Theodore Roosevelt's grandson), who had been sent to Iran to oversee the operation (A14). The CIA wrote the two royal decrees dismissing Mosaddeq and installing General Fazlollah

Zahedi as the new prime minister; according to the report, the shah put off signing them as long as he could, capitulating only after American advisors (among them General H. Norman Schwarzkopf, father of the commander of coalition forces in the 1991 Gulf War) assured him that he would have the support of the Iranian military. The shah who emerges in the pages of the "Secret History" is not simply a client of the United States. He is its creation.

Little of this was widely known in the United States in the years immediately following the coup, years that set the mood for the reception of Balanchine's Persian-themed ballet. Several Iranian and Soviet news reports claimed CIA involvement in Mosaddeq's overthrow, but they received perfunctory attention in American media, which had long tended to portray the shah as a cross between a charmingly old-school monarch and a dashing young jetsetter. (A United Press International dispatch describing the February 1949 assassination attempt against the shah, for instance, reported that he "told visitors at his bedside that 'a few shots won't deter my duties to my beloved country' " and described Fawzia Fuad, the first wife of the "curly-haired, darkly handsome . . . tall and slender" monarch, as "one of the world's most beautiful women.") Oddly, but in retrospect unsurprisingly, this tendency leaked into coverage of the coup itself. Consider, for example, *New York Times* Middle East correspondent Kennett Love's dispatch describing the shah's return to Tehran following the arrest of Mosaddeq:

> The Shah's private twin-engine plane flew straight in from the west and touched the earth at 11:17 A.M. It taxied briskly to a stop in front of stiff ranks of the Imperial Palace Guard.
>
> General Zahedi half-entered the plane and kissed the Shah's knee, then backed from the door to allow the 34-year-old Emperor to descend. The Shah wore the gold-braided blue gray uniform of the Air Force Commander in Chief that had been specially flown to Baghdad for his return. His eyes were moist and his mouth was set in an effort to control his emotions. (Love, "Shah, Back in Iran, Wildly Acclaimed")

This emphasis on Persian passion and glamour, and a related tendency to present Iranian events of state chiefly as exercises in pomp, is characteristic of the way in which many midcentury Americans thought of the nation and its people. Both European and American understandings of the region were suffused with orientalist imaginings of ancient, exotic lands. For most Americans, those imaginings remained entirely in the realm of *Arabian Nights* fantasies. However, the upper-crust folk who tended to fill the ranks of foreign correspondents and CIA operatives were able to indulge those fantasies through travel, study, and, not least, the delectation of rare and precious Middle Eastern artifacts, especially Persian carpets. In fact, Wilber, the author of the "Secret

History," had received a Princeton Ph.D. in Middle Eastern architecture and was for years a "leading figure" in the Princeton Rug Society. Among his published works is a study of Persian gardens ("Donald Newton Wilber, '29").[22] In the years before the 1953 coup, few Americans had made a greater name for themselves in this rarefied world, one that mingled club ties and political intrigue with a taste for the exotic and an appreciation for Middle Eastern antiquities, than Arthur Upham Pope, former philosophy professor, self-styled expert on ancient Persia, longtime Pahlavi sycophant, and organizer of the April 1960 Congress of the International Association for Iranian Art and Archaeology that was the occasion for the premiere of Balanchine's *Figure.*

Viewed today as "a Barnum-like showman who accomplished what he did through immense personal charm and drive," Pope, to the extent that he is remembered at all, has gone down in scholarly history as someone who did play an important role in advancing study of the arts of ancient Persia (his massive, multivolume *A Survey of Persian Art*, first published by Oxford University Press in the late 1930s, remains a useful resource) but also as someone who sold Persian antiquities on commission to private collectors and museums, and whose discoveries included more than a few fakes (Bloom 102).[23] In his heyday, however, he was both known and admired, as Robert Lewis Taylor's lengthy, two-part profile testifies. Published in *The New Yorker* in 1945 during a period that, in retrospect, would constitute the height of Pope's unorthodox (in some ways even unsavory) career, the light-hearted profile portrays him as equal parts scholar, aesthete, and cheerleader, a relentless promoter of all things Persian and, not incidentally, of himself ("Profiles: I" 28-32; "Profiles: II" 22–29). Pope's reputation as an expert in Persian art was launched in the early 1900s when he began dealing rugs while still an undergraduate at Brown University. He made his first trip to Iran in 1925, a year before organizing his first international congress on Persian art and four years after Pahlavi's father, Reza Khan, came to power through a military coup deposing the Qajar monarchy. Taylor claims that Pope "unveiled the wonders of Persia" to Pahlavi when the men met in 1932, two years after Pope's incorporation of the American Institute for Persian Art and Archaeology in New York (later called the Iranian Institute and eventually the Asia Institute). Then eleven years into his reign, Reza Khan "was thoroughly ignorant of what he had taken over"; Taylor writes that it was Pope's passion and enthusiasm that led the leader to arrange for the restoration and "all-around national rehabilitation" of the country's patrimony, a project his son continued on his ascent to the throne in 1941 ("Profiles: I" 28) It seems unlikely that Reza Khan was as ignorant of ancient Persia as Taylor claims, but it is true that Pope enjoyed a special relationship with both shahs, who appreciated his tendency to describe the ancient city of Persepolis as "that fabulous capital of the greatest civilization in history" (32). As Jonathan M. Bloom observes, Pope's orientalist but politically grandiose "vision of Persia as the unrecognized cradle of all civilization . . . accorded well with the aspirations of the new Persian monarchy" (101). Although he had never learned Farsi and had no true academic credentials in the field (his 1904 doctorate was in philosophy), he enjoyed the younger shah's special favor all of his life. Indeed, in 1964 the shah plucked Pope and his wife Phyllis Ackerman (like Pope, a specialist in Persian art whose doctoral degree was in philosophy) from the straitened circumstances in which they were living after Pope's retirement, inviting them to reestablish their institute in Shiraz through an affiliation with what was then called Pahlavi University (Bloom 100).[24] Pope died in Iran in 1969; his remains (and those of Ackerman, who died in 1977) are interred in a mausoleum in Isfahan.

Pope's skill at employing an elite type of cultural capital in the context of studied political opportunism responds well to one well-established mode of cultural critique, which would emphasize how the shah's support of Pope's campaign for the recognition of ancient Persia as "the greatest civilization in history" drew American attention away from the less civilized aspects of the Pahlavi regime. Such an analysis does not, however, tell the whole story of Pope, whose explicitly political activities unfolded in more leftward direction. In 1949 both his name and his photo appeared in *Life*'s now-infamous list of fifty "dupes and fellow travelers," a group of politicians, writers, artists, and scholars (among them Langston Hughes, Albert Einstein, and Dorothy Parker) derided for their participation in the Scientific and Cultural Conference for World Peace held in March at the Waldorf-Astoria Hotel in New York City ("Dupes and Fellow Travelers Dress Up Communist Fronts" 42–43). Sponsored by Cominform and the U.S. Communist party, the Waldorf Conference is remembered for the near-riotous anti-communist pickets thrown up around the hotel; the appearance within the Russian delegation of composer Dmitri Shostakovich, sent to the United States fourteen months after he had been denounced by the Central Committee for writing music indulging in the "formalist perversions" of "atonalism, dissonance, and disharmony"; and its role in sparking the creation, a year later, of a parallel, explicitly anti-communist organization, the CIA-funded Congress for Cultural Freedom (Werth 29).[25]

Pope's appearance in *Life* had consequences. The flow of donor funding to his institute shrank to a trickle, and by 1952 he and Ackerman found themselves forced to retire in "genteel poverty" to the small town in rural Connecticut from which the shah "rescued" them eight years later (Bloom 100). The fact that he was included in the list just four years after the publication of Taylor's easygoing profile indicates how speedily his fortunes had changed in the immediate postwar period, but in many ways the change had been long in the making. Even after censoring, Pope's FBI file is more than three inches thick. Its earliest document dates from 1922, when William J. Burns, then director of the Justice Department's Bureau of Investigators (the FBI's predecessor agency), received a letter from a contact in the rightwing National Security League denouncing Pope as a Soviet agent.[26] This letter launched the surveillance but hardly predicted its trajectory: the file's first twenty or so years' worth of memoranda and correspondence show an agency bemusedly searching for a common ideological thread or political purpose linking the various leagues, committees, councils, institutes, and congresses that Pope organized or with which he affiliated himself, all the while maintaining his primary occupation as an expert and dealer in Persian antiquities.

The file also reveals that Pope was bizarrely determined to attract as much FBI attention as possible. In 1941 the Committee for National Morale (an organization that Pope directed and probably also founded) published a bibliographic survey of German psychological warfare techniques, and in July he sent a copy to FBI director J. Edgar Hoover, along with a letter promising future committee publications on "the Russian psychological front" and "fifth column techniques." Pope describes the latter as a "comprehensive and systematic manual" containing "instructions for spies that were smuggled out on microfilm." "You probably have the same documents," he writes. "If not, they are available to anyone in your office at any time" (FBI, Pope file, July 24, 1941).[27] The Committee for National Morale did do some useful work, helping several German scholars of ancient Middle Eastern art and archaeology who had fled the Nazi regime find employment in the United States (Bloom 102). But Pope's eagerness to promote the committee's work to no less a figure than Hoover points to the root of his eventual undoing: his heedless "Barnum-like" tendency to oversell, overpromote, and overreach, often, as many suspected, with the chief aim of self-enrichment.[28]

A thirteen-page memorandum dated less than three months after the letter to Hoover details an informant's misgivings that Pope, "who poses as an art expert of Iranian art and archaeology, was, in fact, unethical due to the fact that many of the objects of Iranian art which he was supposed to be an authority on were owned by him. . . . He appraised their value as being great in some instances when it actually was not, merely to sell the objects to his own pecuniary advantage." Furthermore, "Pope was in ill-repute with the Iranian Government due to the fact that he had smuggled many pieces of ancient art objects out of Iran. . . . Although the Iranian Government knew of this . . . they preferred not to take any decisive steps to stop it due to the fact that they felt it was worth money to their country since Pope advertised their art." The Committee for National Morale was a front, this informant continued, though not for any program in political subversion: "Pope had organized the Committee . . . in order to forward his own financial interests. . . . In all of the organizations which Pope organized or had an interest he usually had persons of very high standing in various phases of national life on the

Board of Directors, or used their names to front for the organization." The report concludes by stressing that "although Pope was interested in his own financial advancement . . . [the informant] did not feel he would actually do anything to the detriment of the United States in favor of any foreign power" (FBI, Pope file, October 15, 1941).

Unluckily for Pope, the distinction between relentless self-promotion and the promotion of revolution blurred into invisibility after the war, as U.S. anti-communism rose to a fever pitch and behavior once deemed grating or eccentric (if also professionally unethical) came to be seen as politically threatening or subversive. Pope had lent his name or his presence to nearly all of the organizations that, in the late 1940s and early 1950s, became the favorite hunting grounds of McCarthyists: the Committee for the Protection of the Foreign Born, the Joint Anti-Fascist Refugee Committee, the National Council of American-Soviet Friendship, the National Federation for Constitutional Liberties, the Veterans of the Abraham Lincoln Brigade, and the Independent Citizens Committee of the Arts, Sciences and Professions. This made his chances of slipping unnoticed through the Red Scare even more unlikely. As was the case for many, his advocacy of the Russian cause in the face of Nazi aggression did not sit well with the FBI; and when, in 1943, he published a biography of the Soviet diplomat Maxim Litvinov, his fate was sealed.[29] This biography is played for laughs in Taylor's *New Yorker* profile: "Pope's story starts out with a discussion of the Russian revolution, switches to Persia, and then goes back to the revolution. Litvinoff [*sic*] comes in for several remarks at the end" ("Profiles: I" 28). However, the FBI took it seriously, and Pope's Security Index card was drawn up in July 1944. Two years later, he crossed swords with anti-communist intellectual Sidney Hook in the *New York Times*' "Letters to the Editor" section. The exchange was copied into Pope's file even as internal memoranda admitted difficulty in "obtaining admissible evidence which will prove directly or circumstantially [Pope's] membership in or affiliation with the Communist Party" (FBI, Pope file, December 23, 1946). At the time, that difficulty apparently was tough to overcome: a year later, a memorandum recommended that Pope be deleted from the agency's Key Figure List (FBI, Pope file, March 22, 1947).

It was the publication of his name and photograph in *Life*'s list of "dupes and fellow travelers" that finally produced the long-sought evidence: a statement from the former managing editor of the *Daily Worker* that Pope "was under Communist discipline" (FBI, Pope file, n.d.).[30] A letter, allegedly written by a student at the Asia Institute and dutifully citing the *Life* list, denounced Pope and his wife for their "vicious and shocking . . . Russian-Communist activities," which included being "publicly associated with the efforts of the notorious 'Peace Information Center' and its head, Dr. W.E.B. Du Bois" (FBI, Pope file, May 7, 1951). The writer claimed that twenty-two of the institute's one hundred students were veterans whose tuition was being paid through the G.I. Bill of Rights: "the income from the government for these G.I. students represents the foundation of funds which keeps the school running." This prompted Hoover to fire off a letter to the Veterans Administration announcing that Pope had been the subject of a security investigation. Hoover did not demand that the VA reconsider its approval of the tuition payments; he didn't need to. Though Pope had always hobnobbed with the wealthy and well connected (his own education was top flight), he suffered from a "perennial lack of funds" (Bloom 101). The almost certain loss of tuition from Hoover's meddling was compounded by the withering away of support from the rich patrons on whom he had so steadily relied. A 1954 memorandum in the FBI file notes that "the Asia Institute went out of existence in the fall of 1953." But even though Pope was dropped from the Security Index in 1955, agency surveillance continued until his death.

In 1959, Pope's resurrection as organizer of a fourth international congress on Iranian art and archaeology prompted a fresh flurry of memos as the agency followed up on queries from several individuals invited to sponsor the event. A copy of the three-page announcement of the 1960 congress is included in Pope's file. It provides a list of the event's supposed officers, trustees, and sponsors (in typical Pope fashion, lengthy, heterogeneous, and highly improbable) as well as its organizing committee. Most of the names would have been meaningful only to those well versed in New York's social register, though there are a few celebrities, such as Bernard Berenson, Lewis Mumford, Kenneth Clark, Will Durant, and the Aga Khan. The congress's two putative patrons were "Dwight D. Eisenhower, President of the United States, [and] H.I.M. Mohammed Reza Pahlavi, Shahanshah of Iran." Here was the old windy, overreaching Pope again, bloodied but unbowed, blithely playing every conceivable political angle against a broad middle in which Persian art and personal enrichment lived in awkward congress.

In a brief memoir she calls "a footnote to ballet history," Rosanne Klass claims credit for coming up with "the idea of a ballet based on the aesthetics of Persian art—specifically, Persian carpet art," suggesting it first to Pope and then to Kirstein (39). An employee in the office of the chancellor of the Jewish Theological Seminary, Klass had no ballet training nor any substantive dance knowledge. But she had volunteered to help the increasingly infirm Pope organize his conference, and at their first meeting in the fall of 1959 she succeeded in talking him out of his original "un-do-able" plan for a "big, splashy public event to draw widespread attention" by suggesting instead that a Balanchine ballet might ably "express the abstract linear movement of Persian carpet art" (41).[31] Pope liked the idea, and a few days later Klass called the offices of the New York City Ballet and asked to speak with Balanchine. Unsurprisingly, she was put through to Robert Cornell, Kirstein's assistant, who asked for her name, telephone number, and reason for calling. Klass described her work with Pope and explained her idea for a ballet transposing the principles of Persian carpet art into dance, and Cornell duly promised to pass along her message. After hanging up, Klass writes, "I . . . [realized] just how naïve and, well, dopey I had been, and abashed and rather embarrassed to have been so foolish . . . went back to work" (43). Fifteen minutes later, Kirstein called her back.

Over lunch the next day, Klass outlined her idea for a ballet, and Kirstein responded with typical impetuosity: "'I like it. George will like it. We'll do it. Now I have to find the money for it.'" In Klass' recollection, "Lincoln then began sketching out how he wanted to do it—all very abstract. . . . Movement, line, pure aesthetics—and told me something about the horrendous economics involved in producing a ballet: costumes, sets, meeting union requirements. For this one, he would use slide projections as backdrops to cut costs, and stick to simple abstract costumes, maybe just leotards" (44). While the emphasis on abstraction maintained what, by 1960, had become the signature Balanchine aesthetic, it also complemented Pope's longstanding insistence that Islamic art's "abstractness, [its] detachment from a specific ideational content or emotional entanglement" was its chief "source of tranquil power" (Pope, *An Introduction to Persian Art* 2). For the moment, Kirstein anticipated no problem in finding sufficient financial backing to cover those "horrendous" costs: Pope had personally assured him that deep-pocketed congress backers, including members of the Iranian royal family, would eagerly fund the work. Initially, then, this pairing of ancient Persian and cold war abstractions seemed promising.

During the next several months Klass acted as Pope's and Kirstein's go-between, sitting in on discussions in which they compared the histories and aesthetics of modern ballet and ancient Persian art and feeding Kirstein a steady stream of Pope's writings.[32] She did eventually meet Balanchine, who told her that he "had a special affinity for Oriental carpets, that when he was a child in Georgia his home was filled with them. 'I was a very naughty little boy,' he said. 'I took my penknife and cut one of the flowers out of the carpet'" (Klass 45). The anecdote of the mutilated carpet was telling, for by the time of Klass's discussion with Balanchine, "the concept of the ballet was changing."

> Instead of the purely abstract work that Lincoln had proposed, Balanchine had decided to do a court ballet. I don't know just when this happened or why, but . . . I recall being told in late January [1960, less than three months before *Figure*'s premiere,] that *Panamerica,* the recent evening of ballets based on Latin American themes, had been a financial fiasco and that Balanchine, Kirstein, or both felt they couldn't risk another financial flop; so they decided they had better do something colorful, theatrical, more surefire for the spring season. . . .

> Eventually—possibly taking their cue from Pope's analogy between Persian and baroque aesthetics—either Lincoln or Mr. B or both together hit on Handel's *Royal Fireworks Music* and *Water Music* and the idea of the court ballet, though which came first I don't know. (45–46)

The lackluster box office of *Panamerica* may well have been a factor in Balanchine's and Kirstein's decision to make *Figure* a more accessible ballet. But, as Klass points out, Pope's failure to produce the promised funding was a primary consideration:

> The première was scheduled to coincide with the opening of the Congress, and Pope had made assorted vague references to the Shah of Iran and his sister, to their very great interest in it all—very airy, very bland, never really specific but always very sure sounding. . . . In fact, Pope had very little funding at all. His allusions to money coming from the Shah were apparently pure fancy. Pope had no serious intention of paying any part of the costs of the ballet—or, if he ever did have any such intention, it was a pipedream that soon vanished. He was the worst administrator I ever met, very lofty, grandiose, given to airy vagueness about any sort of practical details, concrete commitments, paying bills, keeping promises, etc., and was highly manipulative. But neither Lincoln nor I knew that in the beginning. (46–47)

Klass's interpretation is sensible. The decision to make a "surefire" popular ballet must have seemed inevitable once Kirstein realized that the shah would never deliver the money; and as we will see, *Figure* engages issues of royal patronage and cultural diplomacy in a fashion that this funding backstory helps explain. But the move from abstract neoclassical modernism to historicist quasi-narrative court ballet was not entirely direct, as an undated four-page carbon typescript scenario in the Kirstein papers indicates. Though unsigned, the scenario is almost certainly Kirstein's work, and it offers a narrative treatment of the Persian carpet theme that, like the final version of *The Figure in the Carpet*, also revisits important ballet history—just not the seventeenth- and eighteenth-century rise of the European *ballet de cour*.

Divided into two acts that neatly contrast the honest peasant labor of carpet weavers with the decadent and imperiled leisure of the royals for whom the carpets are woven, the draft scenario of *Figure* hearkens back to the early twentieth-century emergence of ballet modernism via the erotic orientalism of the Ballets Russes as expressed in one of its most celebrated works, Michel Fokine's *Schéhérazade* (1910). This and other Fokine ballets for Diaghilev's path-breaking company had received considerable scorn in Kirstein's dance writings during the late 1930s and early 1940s, when he was laboring to create an audience for Balanchine's decidedly less voluptuous work and the productions of Fokine's ballets offered by the two touring American epigones of the original Ballets Russes were presenting serious box-office competition for his own ventures. In his 1937 pamphlet "Blast at Ballet: A Corrective for the American Audience," Kirstein mocked the "indiscriminate, pot-flung color" of Léon Bakst, the painter and scenarist who created the opulent harem setting of *Schéhérazade,* while also deriding the "caramel orchestrations of Rimsky-Korsakov, Glazounov, or Tcherepnin" and "the old dancers' galvanic, drugging physicality" (*Ballet* 170). He launched his attack at a time when most Americans' understanding of ballet was almost entirely limited to productions of this sort, and his polemic did do some important cultural work—not only for ballet but also for modern dance and other American ballet choreographers, such as Agnes de Mille, who shared Kirstein's impatience with the dominance of the old Russian style.

Still, as the draft scenario for *Figure* indicates, the "orgiastic simulacra" of these ballets, which had provided the original setting for the "sinewy vitality" and "mysterious personal charm" of Vaslav Nijinsky, had been important early influences in the development of Kirstein's dance aesthetic, and he never really renounced them or their distinctly homoerotic allure (*Ballet* 6, 7).[33] What Kevin Kopelson has termed the "queer afterlife" of Nijinsky—integral to the Ballets Russes classics that shaped the popular American conception of ballet during the interwar period—is fundamental to the perceived relationship between homosexuality and the ballet in the United States. Both Kopelson and Peter Stoneley have described how U.S. journalists reviewing the 1916 American tour of the Ballets Russes remarked on the "effeminate" "lack of manliness" in Nijinsky's dancing, particularly in his role as the Golden Slave of *Schéhérazade.*[34] In 1934, just three years before "Blast at Ballet," Kirstein had published a largely favorable study of Fokine's work. That same year also saw the publication of Romola de Pulszky Nijinsky's biography of her husband, written with Kirstein's considerable assistance.[35] And in 1975, when Balanchine's neoclassical ballet modernism had achieved canonical status, Kirstein wrote the text for a lavishly produced, large-format book of Nijinsky photographs in which he positions the New York City Ballet not as the enemy of the Ballets Russes but as its heir (*Nijinsky Dancing* 13).[36]

The "queer afterlife" of the early twentieth-century Ballets Russes creations that made Nijinsky a gay cultural icon found several outlets in the draft scenario of *The Figure in the Carpet,* which is something of an aesthetic way station between Kirstein's impatient denunciations of the late 1930s and the fond reassessment of the 1970s. The scenario has no Golden Slave; but its first scene, set in a carpet-weaving studio, opens on the entrance of a group of "lithe, dark young men in ragged apparel," dye workers who carry "huge hanks of wool . . . damp from the vats" that "fall with a thud on the stage" and prompt "a brief dance-movement of the thumping of the wet hanks" (Kirstein, "Figure in the Carpet" 1).[37] An ensuing ensemble dance for these men and a group of women carpet workers ends with a touch of the same erotic cruelty infusing *Schéhérazade* when "a severe, savage, high-cheekboned overseer" enters with a "long, springy switch" and orders everyone back to work. "As each man passes before him, he gives a sharp whack to the butt of the men [*sic*], which sets each off into a series of increasing pirouettes as they exit off stage" (2). Moving from the studio to the palace, the second scene opens onto "a luxurious atmosphere, as shown in the miniatures of the XVth and XVIth century illustrating the poems of Firdauzi, Nizami, Hafiz, etc." Servants bring yellow and orange melons to dancers dressed as Persian royalty. In a moment clearly inspired by Jean-Léon Gérôme's orientalist and queerly erotic *The Snake Charmer* (1870), "an almost naked small boy brings [a] tray with fruit and silver knife [and] kneels before the principle personage." This sentence concludes with a parenthetical query—"(Shah??)"—that shows an author mindful of the usefulness of making some gesture toward the contemporary political context even as he seeks to evoke an early twentieth-century orientalist fantasy (3).

This languorous, titillating atmosphere is abruptly dispelled by the entry of a messenger bearing unspecified "disastrous news." Quick defensive action follows:

> Everyone begins to remove outer clothing, jewels. Rough burlap or heavy cotton . . . outer garments are put on. Swords and some breastplates, gleaming in the light, round shields, spears, helmets, are brought to the men.
>
> The court ladies, previously gloriously rich in brocade, rub ashes on their faces and tousle their hair, letting it fall untidily. Before the whole audience, the entire court, except for one forgotten bright jeweled and enameled nightingale's cage, is now transformed into bleak, drab, colorless poverty. The women now take [the] ordinary-sized carpets, which . . . covered the stage at the commencement of the scene, [and] lift them from the stage floor, exposing the dull reverse of the brilliant flowered patterns. Into the carpets they throw their scarves, jewels, all precious possessions, [and] roll them up. The rolled carpets are placed on the women-dancers heads and shoulders and they slink away in dance formation. (Kirstein, "Figure in the Carpet" 3–4)

One woman, however, has stuffed too much into her carpet and has difficulty keeping her loot hidden; her appeals for assistance are ignored by the exiting courtiers. Left alone onstage, unable to bring herself to flee without her treasures, she is trapped by "three enormous Central Asian or Mongol warriors" described in the scenario as "men of bronze with terrible mask-like faces of cruel power" (4). Kicking the birdcage out of their way, the warriors move in on the captive woman. In its near-telegraphic rush to a conclusion, the scenario climaxes with a "*pas de quatre* of woman, pleading for her life and [the] three brutes finally killing her with spectacular acrobatics."

> After she is killed (either with Grand Guignol bloody severed head trick, or by other means), the barbarians slash the things keeping the carpet rolled, and there spills out a wealth of jewels, scarves, etc., also revealing the beauty of the carpet itself (symbolically), because there now glows out [of] the backdrop lighting the luminous and palpitating beauty of the great Ardabil rug. The barbarian Central Asians at first adore the jewels, but as they notice the carpet, they become even more fascinated with the glory of its design. Symbolically they spurn the woman and her jewels, and bow before the great backdrop carpet as if conquered by this garden of man's handicraft and civilization, unknown to the barbarian Central Asia (4).

Very little in this draft scenario holds promise for a commercially successful, "surefire" ballet, and it is not surprising that Balanchine never chose it as the narrative framework for his *Figure* (assuming he ever saw it). Yet it is noteworthy for its attempted recasting of signal aspects Fokine's orientalist classic (the "Grand Guignol" execution of the Persian courtesan, for example, hearkens back to the sultan's violent frenzy at the end of *Schéhérazade*) in a manner that would yoke broadly-drawn narrative spectacle to a claim for the power of abstract design, and something of this effort to weld narrative and abstraction made itself felt in the final version of the ballet. Here, and despite (or because of) its obvious clumsiness, the move invites consideration, however "symbolically" (a word the scenario emphatically repeats), of the ways in which a "dull reverse"—a ballet without action or story, say (or, to take a step further, a life without heterosexual interest, one "spurn[ing] . . . woman and her jewels")—might unfold to reveal a "luminous and palpitating beauty" that needs no narrative justification. Kirstein's draft of a never-realized scenario is, of course, little more than a window into a transitory moment in the development of *Figure* and should not be overinterpreted. Understood as an effort to link abstraction and narrative, however, the draft can be seen as an attempt to make manifest the signifying power of modernist ballet's hidden abstract figures, emphasizing their connection to an undying "queer afterlife" by revisiting the hyperbolic narrative terms in which that power was first articulated.[38]

The Figure in the Carpet that was unveiled in April 1960 is a ballet in five scenes that follows a trajectory leading from figural abstraction to loosely narrative representation, from a nomadic life in the desert to a royal entertainment in a courtyard garden. It preserves the producer-to-consumer trajectory of the *Schéhérazade*-inspired draft—first we see the carpet makers, then the carpet owners—while employing a more traditional formal structure. In *Repertory in Review,* Nancy Reynolds quotes a narrative abstract of the ballet (almost certainly written by Kirstein):

> [*Figure* is] a theatrical spectacle which has as its subject the history, construction, and philosophy of the Persian carpet, one of the greatest concepts in the history of world art. In form, it is a court ballet of the early eighteenth-century, when Persian patterns first affected the West. The music was composed at the same moment when the greatest Persian carpets were being woven, and it echoes the same principles of interlacing counterpoint and harmony visually apparent in the arabesques of their intricate design. (203–204)

Of course, this cross-cultural emphasis on a common interest in the abstract arabesques of ballet, music, and carpet design sets aside the significant geographic and cultural differences mediating that interest; but it does serve, however subtly, to highlight the common circumstance of royal (or state) patronage in the development of those art forms. And though by opening night Kirstein and Balanchine knew that not a single Iranian *rial* would make its way into the New York City Ballet's coffers, they chose to maintain the fiction that the ballet was being sponsored by the shah.

As Reynolds points out, the somewhat academic concerns outlined in the narrative abstract of the ballet were "fascinating . . . but excessively literary for an instinctual creator such as Balanchine." Citing a review of *Figure* that appeared in the May 1960 issue of *Dance News,* she declares that Balanchine "disposed of the problem" of choreographically elucidating a shared approach to counterpoint and harmony in ballet, baroque music, and Persian carpet design "by ignoring it. This left him free to allow everything that belongs to Persia to be contained in the scenery while he had a lot of fun devising a court ballet in eighteenth-century style with all the additions that his twentieth-century ingenuity could devise" (204). Still, there was a relationship between the elaborate Persian scenery and Balanchine's equally elaborate choreography. *Figure* incorporated not only outré costumes and flamboyant sets (recall the fountain) but also regal music and bravura choreographic touches (tricky lifts, gigantic leaps, hops *en pointe*). Even the location of its premiere was spectacular: the neo-Moorish City Center of Music and Drama, built in 1923 as the Mecca Temple of the Ancient Arabic Order of the Nobles of the Mystic Shrine. Everything about the ballet was set at the highest possible pitch of fabulousness. An over-the-top execution of an already-improbable subject—an eighteenth-century court ballet set in the shadow of Persepolis—*Figure* presented itself as a tribute not only to the ballet's imperial Persian "sponsor" but also to the contemporary practice of cultural diplomacy itself. What else, after all, is the eighteen-century *ballet de cour* if not one of modernity's earliest explorations into the utility of blending art with statecraft?[39] In the hyperbolic

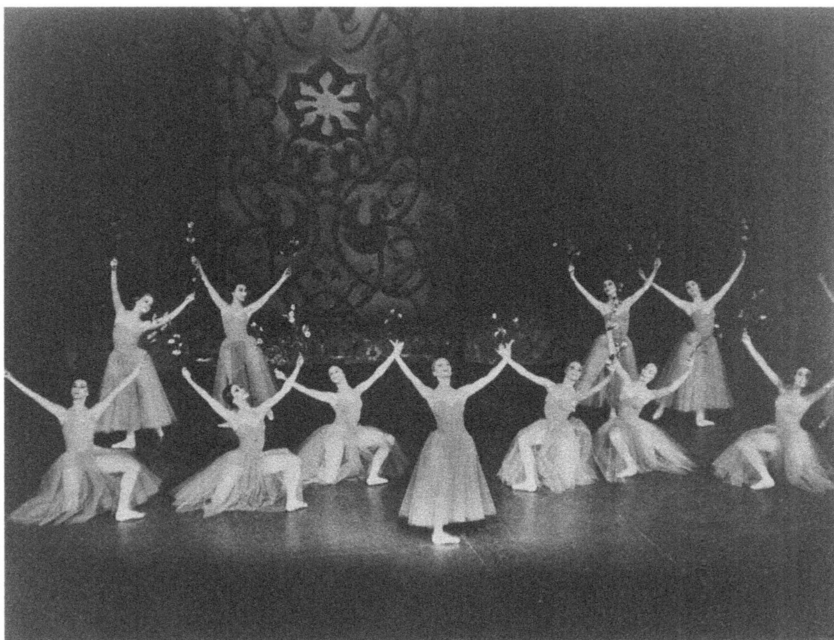

FIGURE 1 Violette Verdy flanked by female members of the *corps de ballet* in the New York City Ballet production of *The Figure in the Carpet,* 1960. *Source:* Choreography by George Balanchine © The George Balanchine Trust. Photograph by Martha Swope © Jerome Robbins Dance Division, The New York Public Library for the Performing Arts.

execution of its tribute to royal patronage and cultural diplomacy, *Figure* adopted the histrionic approach to historicism that Philip Core has identified as the very essence of camp.[40] And like any good piece of camp, the ballet is best understood not as a tribute but as a "tribute," a double-voiced take on its subject that simultaneously celebrates and mocks the terms of its articulation.

The ballet begins in "The Sands of the Desert" (figure 1). Featuring Violette Verdy and eighteen women, this section has been universally described, by both reviewers and the dancers themselves, as "*Serenade* . . . in beige.".[41] A ballet without narrative, though not without drama, set to Tchaikovsky's C major *Serenade for Strings,* Balanchine's *Serenade* is a half-hour work for a mostly female ensemble in simple, pale-blue gowns performing on a bare stage whose dappled lighting scheme evokes a Romantic, moonlit landscape. By 1960 it was well established as an iconic work, so comparing "The Sands of the Desert" to *Serenade* is high praise.

This opening section was followed by "The Weaving of the Carpet," a *pas d'action* that added Conrad Ludlow and six nomad tribesmen to Verdy and the female corps, the dancers manipulating long varicolored ribbons to indicate the patterns of Persian carpet design. Though *pas d'action* denotes a scene in a story ballet that moves the plot along through passages emphasizing mime over dance, the evidence of photographs and dancer recollections indicate that both "The Sands of the Desert" and "The Weaving of the Carpet" were more abstract than narrative and offered much dance interest. In Reynolds's judgment, "the most sophisticated choreography was in these sections" (204). Verdy, remembering her part years later, agreed. She said to me in an interview, "Without being as lengthy or important or romantic in feeling as *Serenade* was, it was very much the same thing because he attempted to really give us something, the so-called abstract, which means pure dancing to pure music."

With the third scene, "The Building of the Palace," abstract evocations of artistic creation give way to a representation of royal entertainment as diplomatic exchange. Dancers in the ornate costumes of visiting ambassadors enter in *défilé* as delegates from France, Spain, America (represented by the West Indies), China, Africa, and Scotland join corps members dressed as Iranian courtiers (figures 2–8). All briefly dance together before the entrance of the Prince and Princess of Persia inaugurates "The Reception of the Foreign Ambassadors." While the choreography for "The Sands of the Desert" and "The Weaving of the Carpet" is entirely lost, a portion of "The Reception of the Foreign Ambassadors" is preserved in the film of the January 1, 1961, *Omnibus* broadcast. Most striking about this section is its heavy reliance on one of the hoariest plot devices of nineteenth-century narrative ballet: the royal ball in which a series of *divertissements,* frequently in the style of national dances, constitute the chief entertainment. A favorite pretext of Marius Petipa, the royal ball plays a central role in *Swan Lake, The Sleeping Beauty,* and *The Nutcracker,* providing plausible narrative cover for many minutes of choreographic invention. The ball also is the setting for the climactic dance encounter of the ballet's central romantic couple—whether their love be doomed, as in *Swan Lake;* a hard-won accomplishment, as in *The Sleeping Beauty;* or a projection, as in *The Nutcracker.* Though it has no story to tell about the course of romantic love, *Figure* nevertheless presents the Prince and Princess of Persia as its central couple. And despite the ballet's stated focus on a modernist, formal exploration of the common arabesques of dance, music, and carpet design, "The Reception of the Foreign Ambassadors" climaxes in nineteenth-century narrative style with a grand *pas de deux* for the Prince and Princess that places heterosexual romantic love at center stage (figures 9–11).

The first two scenes of *Figure,* then, engaged the audience largely through the dramatic play of formal devices without recourse to storytelling. To be more precise, the tale they told was the modernist story of technique in service to form: of how a given design takes shape, how art is made. Insofar as these scenes addressed the ballet's Persian theme, they did so by drawing attention to the dynamic use of space, the shaping and articulation of the choreographic line, and the play of light on moving fabric, with the interweavings of musical phrase and dance phrase miming a carpet's structuring warp and woof. Though there were soloists, the uniformity of the costumes in both scenes and the emphasis, in "The Weaving of the Carpet," on the creative importance of the ensemble served a democratizing function. As is often the case in Balanchine's abstract ballets, there was little distinction between soloist and corps in technical challenge or aesthetic impact of the steps.[42]

By all accounts, the ballet's shift from this abstract evocation of a world of art making and democratic collectivity to a realm of art consumption, political hierarchy, and heterosexual romance was disconcertingly abrupt in a way that prompted critical reflection. "The first part was completely different from the second part," Verdy told me. "The Sands of the Desert" and "The Weaving of the Carpet" comprised "a world apart," a meditation on art making and community that engaged "history without . . . burden of epoch." By contrast, the second half of the ballet was "the traditional type of celebration that you would have if you go to court and are an ambassador." In a concurring observation, Reynolds notes that "the format of the second part," with its embrace of nineteenth-century narrative ballet convention, "did not allow for much variety in tone or pacing" (204). Rather, it obsessively sounded a single note of regal self-satisfaction. Despite the spectacular effects of the concluding "Apotheosis" (chiefly the fountain, which, as Patricia McBride recalled in an interview, "leaked all over the stage"), "by the end of the evening, there was . . . a certain sameness" as one fabulously outfitted couple or small ensemble of dancers after another performed their obeisance before the Persian monarchs (Reynolds 204).

The swoony, orientalist aesthetic of the early twentieth-century Ballets Russes had served as its own type of "rallying cry for the mystery of design," providing a celebratory camp vehicle for sexual minoritarian identification and community building while laying the foundations for the emergence of ballet modernism. In contrast, *The Figure in the Carpet*'s evocation of an earlier era in the history of ballet tapped into camp's slyly mocking, ironic edge, its second half emphasizing ballet's regal, elitist origins even as U.S. efforts in cultural diplomacy aimed to promote America as a country possessed of a uniquely democratic high culture reflecting the nation's deepest values. Indeed, the awkward suturing of the opening scenes of the ballet and their abstract evocation of art-making as a communal enterprise to a second half seemingly at pains to naturalize the trappings of monarchical absolutism disconcertingly implied that, in the spreading cold war U.S. imperium, the democratic project was useful chiefly for producing decorative cover—a way to cushion the footfalls of the genuine powers-that-be.

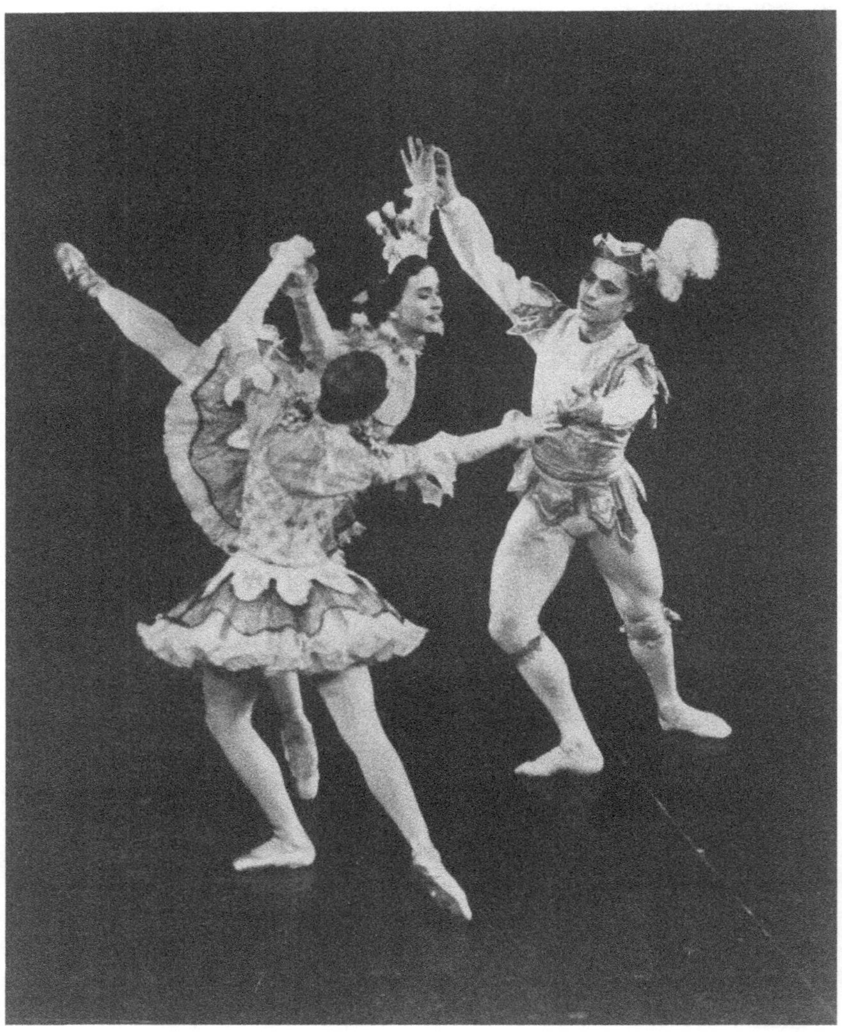

FIGURE 2 Suki Schorer and Edward Villella supporting Susan Borree in arabesque as the Princesses and Prince of Lorraine in the New York City Ballet production of *The Figure in the Carpet,* 1960. *Source:* Choreography by George Balanchine © The George Balanchine Trust. Photograph by Martha Swope © Jerome Robbins Dance Division, The New York Public Library for the Performing Arts.

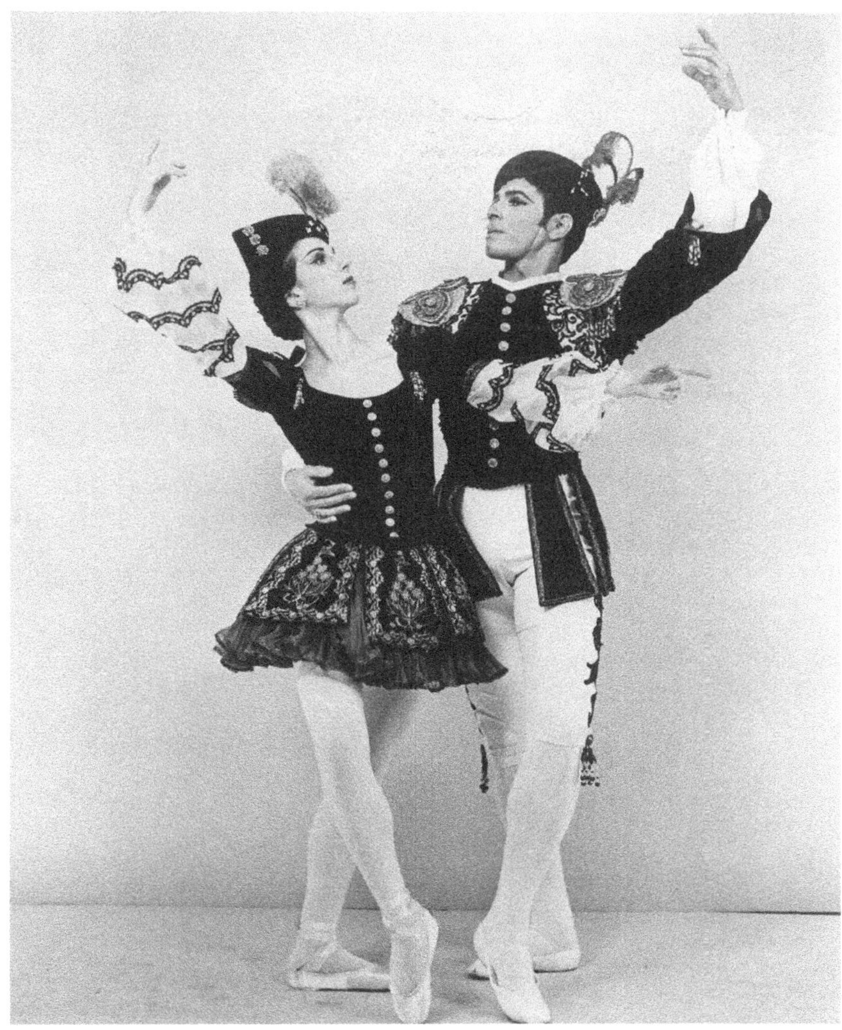

FIGURE 3 Judith Greene and Francisco Moncion as the Duke and Duchess of Granada in the New York City Ballet production of *The Figure in the Carpet,* 1960. *Source:* Choreography by George Balanchine © The George Balanchine Trust. Photograph by Martha Swope © Jerome Robbins Dance Division, The New York Public Library for the Performing Arts.

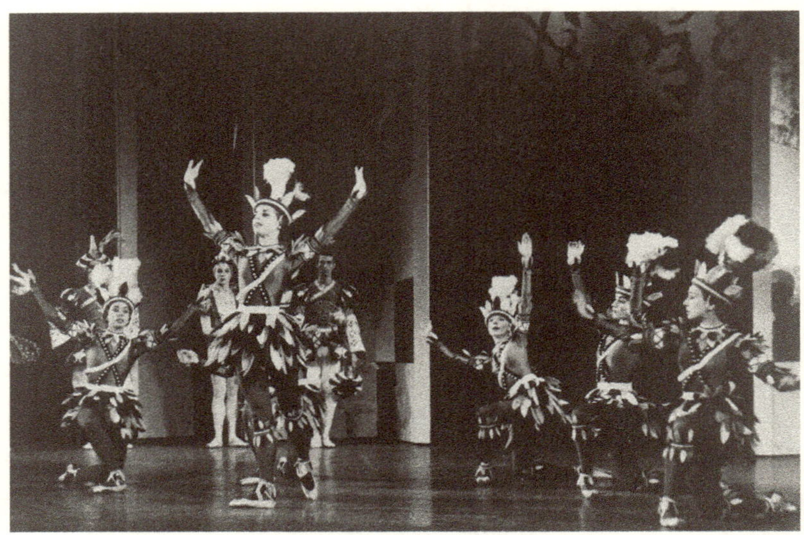

FIGURE 4 Francia Russell as the Princess of the West Indies with female members of the *corps de ballet* in the New York City Ballet production of *The Figure in the Carpet,* 1960. *Source:* Choreography by George Balanchine © The George Balanchine Trust. Photograph by Martha Swope © Jerome Robbins Dance Division, The New York Public Library for the Performing Arts.

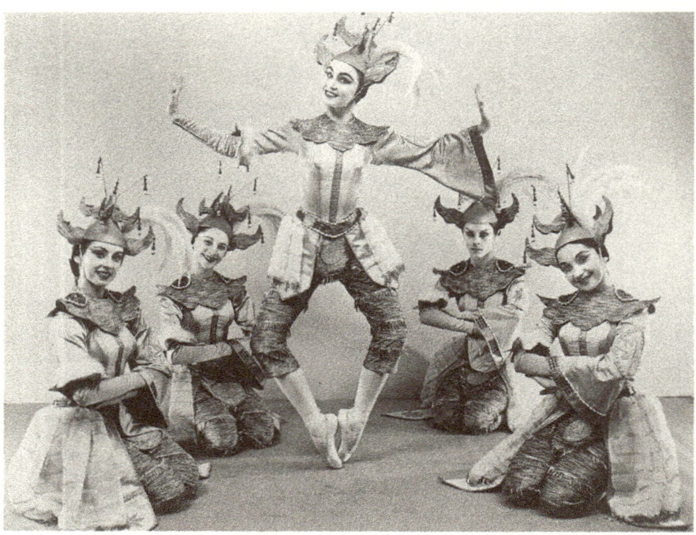

FIGURE 5 Patricia McBride as the Duchess of L'an L'ing flanked by Joyce Feldman, Nancy Reynolds, Lois Bewley, and Judith Friedman in the New York City Ballet production of *The Figure in the Carpet,* 1960. *Source:* Choreography by George Balanchine © The George Balanchine Trust. Photograph by Martha Swope © Jerome Robbins Dance Division, The New York Public Library for the Performing Arts.

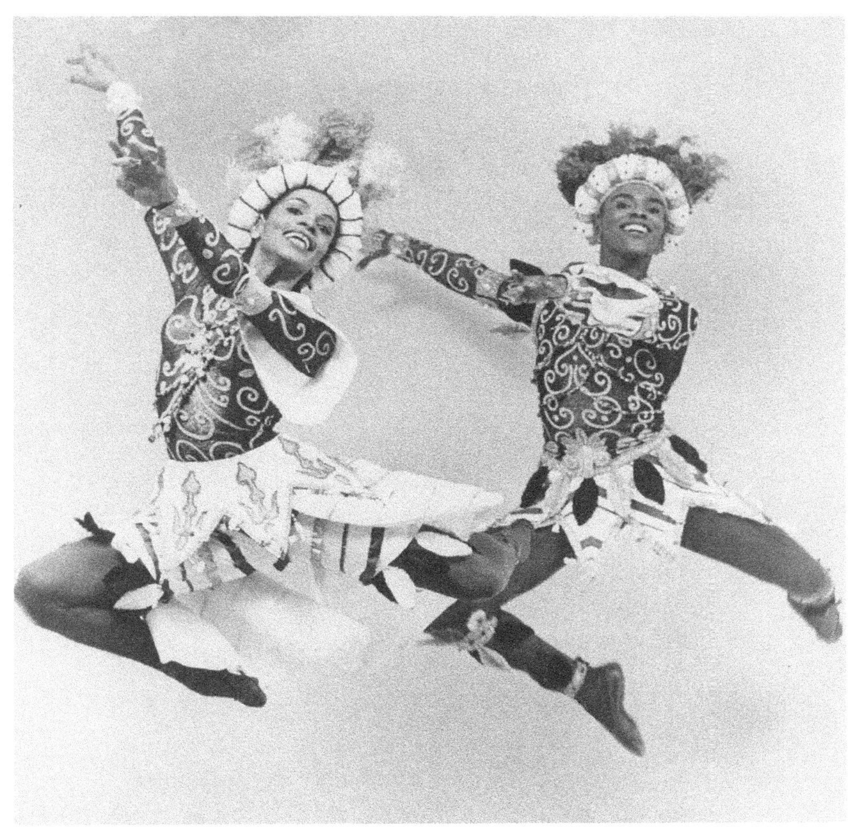

FIGURE 6 Mary Hinkson and Arthur Mitchell as the Oni of Ife and His Consort in the New York City Ballet production of *The Figure in the Carpet,* 1960. *Source:* Choreography by George Balanchine © The George Balanchine Trust. Photograph by Martha Swope © Jerome Robbins Dance Division, The New York Public Library for the Performing Arts.

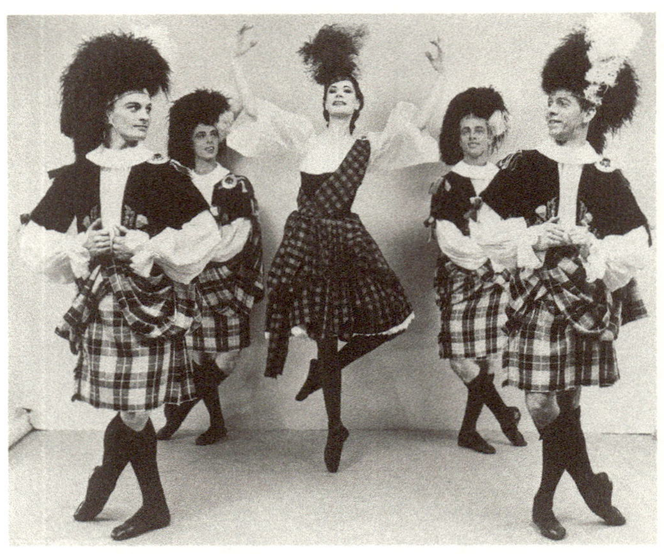

FIGURE 7 Diana Adams flanked by Michael Lland, Deni Lamont, Richard Rapp, and Roy Tobias as the Lairds of the Isles and Their Lady in the New York City Ballet production of *The Figure in the Carpet,* 1960. *Source:* Choreography by George Balanchine © The George Balanchine Trust. Photograph by Martha Swope © Jerome Robbins Dance Division, The New York Public Library for the Performing Arts.

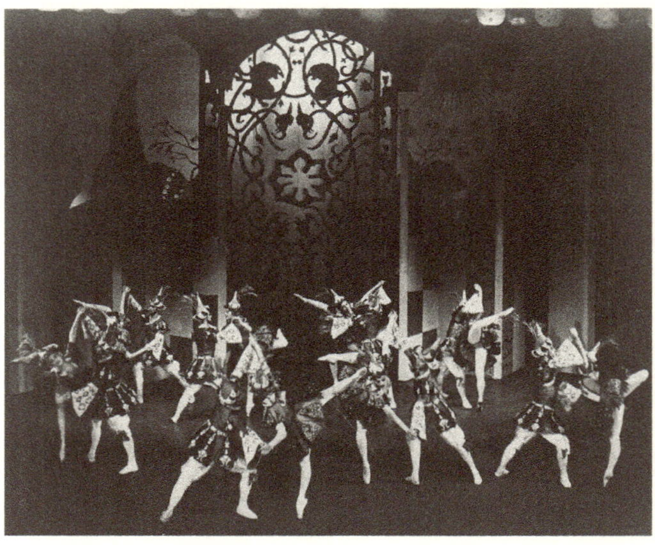

FIGURE 8 Members of the *corps de ballet* as Iranian courtiers in the New York City Ballet production of *The Figure in the Carpet,* 1960. *Source:* Choreography by George Balanchine © The George Balanchine Trust. Photograph by Martha Swope © Jerome Robbins Dance Division, The New York Public Library for the Performing Arts.

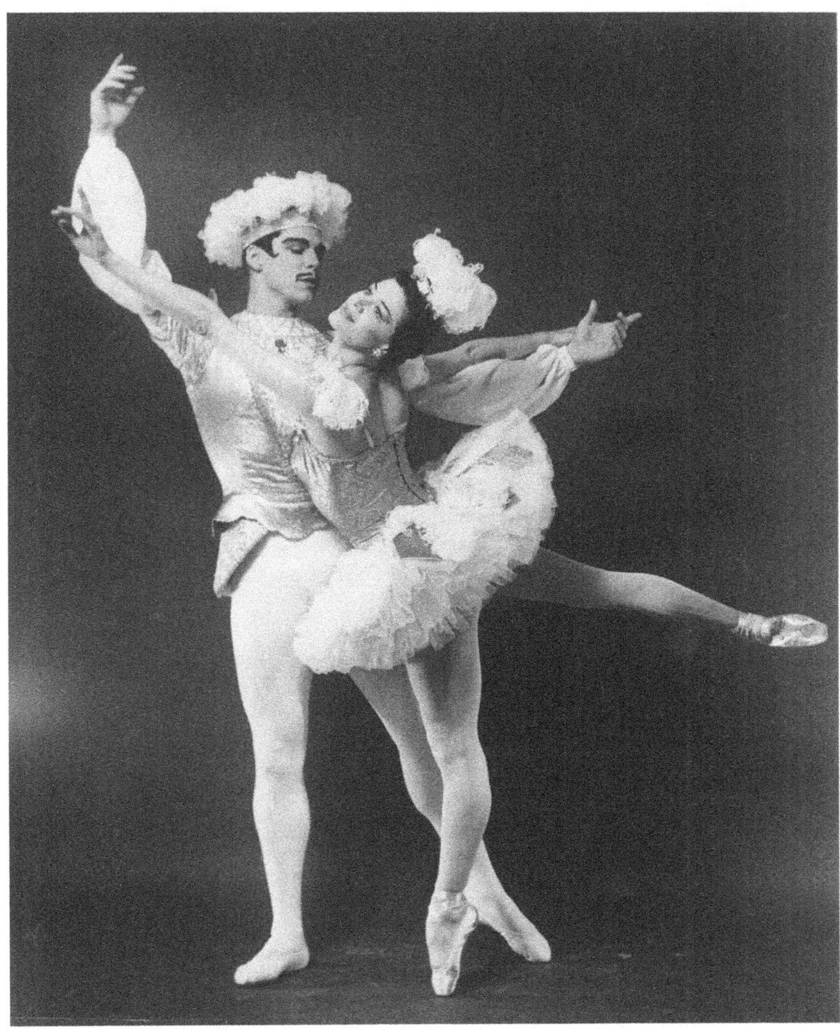

FIGURE 9 Jacques d'Amboise supporting Melissa Hayden in an arabesque as the Prince and Princess of Persia in the New York City Ballet production of *The Figure in the Carpet*, 1960. *Source:* Choreography by George Balanchine © The George Balanchine Trust. Photograph by Martha Swope © Jerome Robbins Dance Division, The New York Public Library for the Performing Arts.

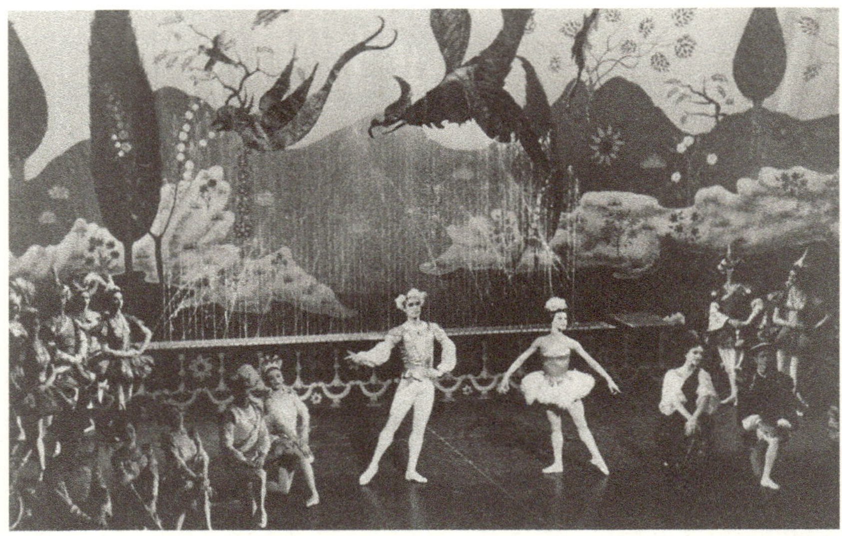

FIGURE 10 Company pose with Jacques d'Amboise and Melissa Hayden as the Prince and Princess of Persia in the New York City Ballet production of *The Figure in the Carpet,* 1960. *Source:* Choreography by George Balanchine © The George Balanchine Trust. Photograph by Martha Swope © Jerome Robbins Dance Division, The New York Public Library for the Performing Arts.

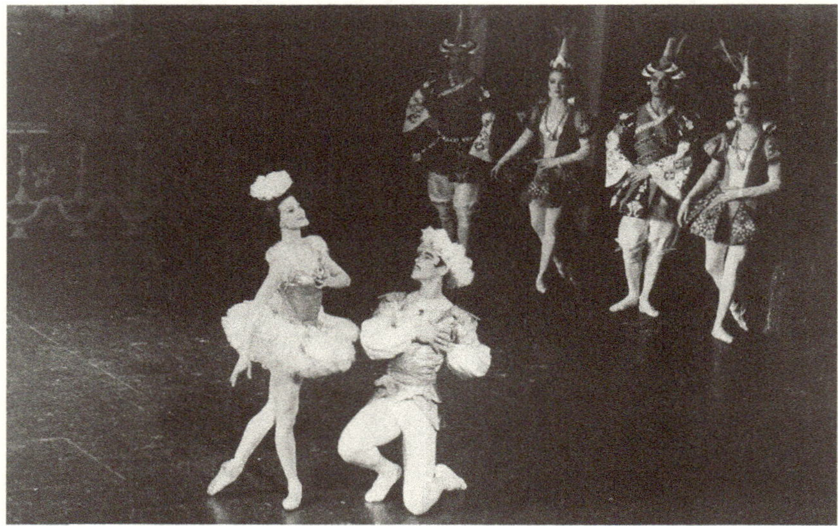

FIGURE 11 Jacques d'Amboise and Melissa Hayden as the Prince and Princess of Persia with the *corps de ballet* in scene 3, "The Building of the Palace," in the New York City Ballet production of *The Figure in the Carpet,* 1960. *Source:* Choreography by George Balanchine © The George Balanchine Trust. Photograph by Fred Fehl courtesy of Gabriel Pinski and Jerome Robbins Dance Division, The New York Public Library for the Performing Arts.

Both the evidence of the *Omnibus* footage and the dancers' recollections indicate that the second half of the ballet was quite inconsistent choreographically. Melissa Hayden, who performed the role of the Princess of Persia, rhapsodized in an interview about her "gorgeous" *pas de deux.* McBride, seventeen at the time and dancing her first major role with the company (as the Duchess of L'an L'ing), told me that she "loved" her variation. Francia Russell, however, had mostly unpleasant memories of her turn as the Princess of the West Indies, in which she executed undistinguished choreography while battling a headdress with "enormous plumes."[43] Other dancers also remembered the ballet more for its challenges than its satisfactions. Mary Hinkson, a dancer with the Martha Graham Dance Company who was recruited into the ballet as a partner for Arthur Mitchell in the African variation ("The Oni of Ife and His Consort"), said in an interview that she was terrified that she would be ask to dance *en pointe.* Suki Schorer, one of two Princesses of Lorraine, told me about performances in which applause drowned out her music during a particularly tricky bit of counting. For the most part, the dancers tended to see the work as a kind of curio, a ballet memorable only as a synecdoche for a particular moment in New York City Ballet history. Hinkson told me that she saw her invitation to appear in *Figure* as an echo of *Episodes,* the 1959 Balanchine-Graham collaboration. In interviews McBride recalled it as one of the company's last major ballets staged at City Center, while Russell remembered it as one of the first she did after being promoted to soloist.

Given the fate of the shah and the current state of U.S. relations with Iran, we might be tempted to put an allegorical spin on Kirstein's observation that *Figure* was abandoned because it proved "too unwieldy to maintain," both in its scenic properties and in its disconcerting approach to its subject (*Thirty Years* 156). Indeed, it's a temptation Kirstein himself may have indulged: his postmortem on the ballet was written in the 1970s, when protests against the Pahlavi regime had become impossible to ignore. The reality is probably more prosaic: the premise of the ballet simply failed to fire Balanchine's imagination to the pitch necessary to inspire creative reengagement and revision. It's also possible, however, that *Figure* was deemed "unwieldy" chiefly because its ironic take on its themes of royal patronage and cultural diplomacy had a limited shelf life. In 1963, a year after New York City Ballet's tour of the Soviet Union, the Ford Foundation awarded a ten-year, 2 million–dollar grant to the company and two additional grants, totaling almost 4 million dollars, to its allied School of American Ballet. More than 45 million dollars in current funds, the grants were a both a remarkable gesture of confidence in the future of Balanchine's enterprise and an indication that City Ballet's days of State Department dependence were drawing to a close (Hughes A1, 42). As the need for government patronage lessened, the intensity of Balanchine's critical engagement with its terms and conditions probably lessened as well.

Peter Stoneley's claim that Balanchine's "stripped down phrase 'ballet is woman' " amounted to "a perfect response to earlier accusations that ballet was effeminate" and that "the slow triumph" of Balanchinian "neoclassicism" would entail the obscuring of "more obviously queer possibilities" for modernist ballet does have a certain limited utility (102). However, Stoneley himself admits that such a reading prematurely forecloses a "more diverse and complex response to neoclassicism, . . . a response that can be related to homosexuality but that does not conform to a monolithic notion of 'the homosexual response'" (119). An analysis of *The Figure in the Carpet* that emphasizes the camp aspects of its representation of both the shah's regime and cold war cultural diplomacy is just such a response, drawing out a deeply contextual critical self-reflexivity too seldom acknowledged in cold war modernist dance. Evidence that Balanchine himself saw *Figure* as a mostly ironic creature of its particular historical moment can be discerned not only in his refusal to remount the ballet in 1964 but also in his chosen setting for the one piece of choreography he did decide to salvage. In 1976, parts of *Figure*'s Scottish variation found new life in the Royal Canadian Air Force section of *Union Jack,* a "tribute" to the American Bicentennial that ends with the entire *corps de ballet* spelling out "God Save the Queen" in semaphore.

The ambiguous, seemingly paradoxical practice of scripted indeterminacy lies at the heart of Merce Cunningham's aesthetic. He engaged it across the full range of his choreographic activity, from its first tentative appearance in *16 Dances for Soloist and Company* (1951), which launched his lifelong exploration of chance operations in dance making, to its confident, metacompositional use in the recombined extracts he called Events (Harris 58). The practice emphasized an understanding of the dance as an art of perpetual de- and reformation, as process rather than artifact—or, to put it more accurately, process *as* artifact. It is founded on a similarly ambiguous approach to movement, one setting the aerial verticality of ballet tradition within the grounded torque of modern dance innovation.[44] Most famously, it insists on the mutually dependent independence of every aspect of the choreographic spectacle. Not only the Events but also the larger compositions from which they were derived were composed with the bare minimum of conceptual information: Cunningham's collaborators rarely knew little more than a work's proposed duration and number of dancers. Costume, music, and decor were never conceived simply as accompaniments to or enhancements of the steps. All were equal partners in a single theatrical experience. At once arbitrary and calculated, Cunningham's dances are rooted in the multimedia ambitions of the *Gesamtkunstwerk* even as their welcoming acceptance of dissonance, fortuitousness, and individuality slyly gives the lie to the totalizing politics of the total work of art.

Dance has been comparatively invisible in not only cold war cultural history and histories of modernism but also theories of the politics of spectacle. Cunningham's work could never be said to enjoy anything approaching the mass appeal that analyses of the politics of spectacle strive to explain, nor does it offer the narcotic reassurances that Bertolt Brecht, Theodor Adorno, Antonin Artaud, Guy Debord, and others have identified as constitutive of spectacle within capitalist regimes of production. That Cunningham's dances nevertheless incorporate many of those aspects of spectacle said to be most conducive to this politically narcotizing effect—in refusing intuitive modes of art making, for example, Cunningham's compositional practice springs from exactly that knowing "separation" of experience and expression so emphatically denounced by Debord—indicates that raising the visibility of dance within the history of modernism, as well as cold war cultural studies, may significantly complicate our understanding of the politics of twentieth-century spectacle. Rancière's recent analysis of the dominant theories of the politics of spectatorship is useful for understanding the politics of Cunningham's Events.

Debord's critique of spectacle resembles both Benjamin's concern about the fascistic potential of cinema and Adorno's dissection of culture industry, but his categorical denunciation of spectacle for producing existential separation does not proceed directly from these earlier Marxist critiques. For while both Benjamin and Adorno entertained the politically radical potential of the gap between experience and its representation, Debord countenanced no such disjunction. His denunciation of spectacle amounts to a denunciation of mediation and an assertion that a world in which "authenticity and transcendence are both present and everywhere" is not only desirable but possible, blocked only by a capitalist economy productive of alienation and abstraction (Stewart 23). For Debord, "genuine experience and genuine dialogue can exist only when each person has access to a direct experience of reality" (Jappe 39). He rejected psychoanalytic or philosophical investigations into the problem of unmediated access to the real as politically impotent contemplation serving chiefly to magnify a separation that by rights should be overcome. Instead, he sought to create a political and cultural program that, as it transformed the social order, would usher in unmediated experiences of reality. The cultural aim of revolution, for Debord, was the creation of a world in which aesthetic mediation would be liquidated through the creation of situations of direct experience enabling a transparent relationship between the world and its representation.

Debord's oddly Platonist and, in many ways, Lukácsian situationist critique of spectacle operates within this theory of revolutionary action through its diagnosis of the insidious way in which spectacle, as the agent of separation and mediation *par excellence,* obstructs the drive to unify art and life.[45] It does this by recognizing the human desire for the plenitude of direct experience. In fact, in Debord's formulation, spectacle is capitalism's response to this longing, this nostalgia, but it works to amplify rather than abolish the alienation that gives rise to this desire. Spectacle responds to human longing by capitalizing it. What is striking about Debord's analysis is how an insistence on an eventual unity of experience and expression, such that reality is not mediated by art but rather is infused with it, is paired with a denunciation of spectacle as an especially powerful unified and coherent aesthetic experience. In thesis 219 of *The Society of the Spectacle,* he attacks spectacle for its ability to "erase the dividing line between self and world" (153). His point, of course, is that this erasure comes prematurely, before proper revolutionary action and in the service of capital, but we should not forget that such an erasure is exactly what his own cultural program is meant to achieve. Unsurprisingly, cinema was the prime target of Debord's critique and the signal form of his own artistic practice. In truth, his critique arises less from his suspicion of spectacle than from his faith in its promise: the realization of the dream world of the nostalgic wherein alienation, separation, and loss are banished and we are restored to the enveloping comfort of what Susan Stewart has described as the "walled city of the maternal" (23). Debord was absolutely correct when he wrote that "the origin of the spectacle lies in the world's loss of unity" (Stewart 22). What remained to be discovered was the degree to which spectacle might function not simply as a bad-faith effort to reconstruct that imagined unity but also as a means of investigating that postulated loss, assessing its consequences and interrogating its various political effects. Intended as a subversion of spectacle, Debord's own cinematic project stalls in a denunciatory mimeticism: "the film is unsatisfying because the world is unsatisfying; the incoherence of the film reflects that of reality; the poverty of the film's materials serves to emphasize the poverty of its subject, and so on" (Levin 90). What Debord struggled to articulate—what in many ways remained beyond him—was the possibility and form of spectacle's immanent critique.

Such a possibility can be found in Cunningham's Events, which, like Debord's critique of spectacle, were a product of the politically turbulent mid-1960s.[46] The name *Event* itself embodies the tensions these works put into play. Insofar as they were performances accommodating the needs of specific audiences and sites (museums, art galleries, parks, school gymnasiums, ancient ruins, public plazas, technologically challenged university art center stages, and conventional theatrical venues), they embodied a certain egalitarian unpretentiousness. Insofar as they were irreproducible and individual, however, they also trafficked in the rarity and singularity central to economies of aesthetic distinction. Described by Jack Anderson as "seemingly unapproachable" "great hunks of theater" that managed to "intimidate" precisely to the extent that they were "legitimized as major endeavors by the Cunningham company," Events raised "fearful questions, not only about the nature of Cunningham's art, but about art in general" (97, 96). For Anderson those questions grew from a friend's "shocked exclamation"—"He's dismantling his repertoire!' " (96)—into the recognition that an Event's principle effect is to bring the knowing dance viewer (one who has already seen and confidently interpreted the individual works whose disarticulated and recombined parts make up the dance Event) into an awareness of the myriad ways a given dance phrase or set of gestures may signify. "One starts to realize how movements which have a certain character in one context may assume a totally different character in a new context," Anderson observes, noting how "movements which look so horrific in *Winterbranch* [1964] . . . seem tame or game-like in some of the Events" (98). Phrases whose aesthetic and/or political meaning and impact had been assessed and categorized according to a postulated essential or expressive quality of movement (lyrical, menacing, anxious, even abstract) are discovered to have previously unsuspected powers of signification; they convey, even contradict, meanings well beyond their initial implications. In freeing dance phrases from their original contexts, then, Events make manifest hitherto unrecognized possibilities of action, reorganizing the spectator's understanding of what is before her and prompting her to consider how the inconceivable might, in fact, be brought to life.

Rancière has made clear that this ability to make visible what had been invisible, to reorder our understanding of the sensible world, is a quintessentially political aspect of all art, no matter how seemingly abstract. Cunningham's Events thus should be understood as spectacles whose aim is not political anesthesia but social emancipation, works whose de- and refocusing of emphasis and attention strategically blur what had been taken to be the clear aesthetic, affective, formal, or psychological impact of a movement. In that blurring, different possibilities come to light. As Rancière observes, "what the word 'emancipation' means [is] the blurring of the boundary between those who act and those who look, . . . a reconfiguration of the here and now of the distribution of space and time" (*The Emancipated Spectator* 19). He respectfully draws attention to the limits of the dominant leftist critique of spectacle mounted by Debord and, before him, Brecht and Artaud, which casts viewing and acting as utterly opposed activities and which condemns theatrical, cinematic, operatic, or choreographic spectacle as the parasitic re-presentation to spectators of "the activity they have been robbed of, . . . their own essence become alien, turned against them, organizing a collective world whose reality is that dispossession" (7). This can be an aspect of the politics of spectacle, to be sure; but as Rancière matter-of-factly notes, "being a spectator is not some passive condition that we should transform into activity. It is our normal situation," with its own activist properties (17).

While they differ in many respects, the dominant leftist critique of spectacle and the traditional Marxist condemnation of modernism actually harmonize quite well, and they have worked together to encourage a view of Cunningham's Events as fundamentally apolitical. The best-known and most influential articulation of this view appeared in 1977, when Moira Roth's essay "The Aesthetic of Indifference" identified Cunningham as a "key exponent" of an "aesthetic of indifference" whose practitioners (including Cage, Rauschenberg, and Johns, Cunningham's chief collaborators in the 1950s and 1960s) produced work marked by a "cool intelligence" that "advocated neutrality of feeling and denial of commitment in a period that otherwise might have produced art of passion and commitment" (Roth and Katz 39, 47).[47] She laments the mid-1950s decline of the engaged, emotionally heated style of the "politically concerned abstract expressionists" and its replacement by the cool, "extreme passivity" of works such as Cage's *4'33"* and Rauschenberg's *White Paintings* (37, 40). Though she has nothing to say about Cunningham's choreography, Roth chides him and the "slender, cerebral, philosophical, iconoclastic" artists of his circle for producing "trivial," "beguiling," and "playful" work that amounts to a deliberate and regrettable renunciation of the politically engaged aesthetic of their predecessors in the immediate postwar period (45–46). As her admiration of abstract expressionism indicates, she is no enemy of modernist abstraction; yet her assertion that the "silent, empty," "blank" works produced by the artists of the Cunningham circle contain "no messages, no feelings, and no ideas" closely resembles Lukács's critique of modernism as an introspective, politically irresponsible refusal of the artist's duty to speak clearly and directly to the social problems of the day.[48] For Roth, the art of Cunningham and his colleagues similarly shirks this responsibility. Whatever political interest such work may be said to possess lies only in its symptomatic status as "an unconscious tragic acknowledgment of [the] total [political] paralysis" brought on by the Red Scare persecutions of Joseph McCarthy and the House Committee on Un-American Activities (41).

Roth's claim that, thanks to the rise of the aesthetic of indifference, "there was virtually no politically radical art in the 1960s" (Roth and Katz 46) is certainly up for discussion. For the purposes of my argument here, however, I am less interested in judging the accuracy of that claim than in highlighting the odd moment in her essay when Roth acknowledges the sexual politics at work within the shift from "the machismo attitudes proudly displayed by the abstract expressionists" to the affiliation with "homosexuality and bisexuality . . . [within] the new aesthetic group" of the Cunningham circle (37). Concerned throughout the essay to emphasize the importance of Marcel Duchamp in the formation of the aesthetic of indifference, Roth grants that Duchamp's embrace of drag in the creation of his "female alter ego" Rrose Sèlavy must have unsettled many Abstract Expressionist champions of a crusading, *soi disant* "ballsy" aesthetic of political engagement and direct personal expression and may even have served as an inspirational call to gay artists—like Cage, Cunningham, Rauschenberg, and Johns—who found such views objectionable (37). But despite the sly testimony of Johns's brilliant AbEx sendup, *Painting with Two Balls* (1960), Roth finds no evidence that the artists of the Cunningham circle produced any work that addressed cold war sexual politics. On the contrary: "but for the Aesthetic of Indifference, Rrose Sèlavy might well have served as a symbol of new sexual and artistic freedoms and flexibilities" (37).

This is a strange and contradictory moment, with Marcel Duchamp/Rrose Sèlavy being praised as an agent of subversion even as the aesthetic practices he/she inspires are denounced as the essence of passive accommodation. It points to the central weakness of Roth's analysis, which is her failure to consider how a shift in aesthetics might signal a call for a fundamental rethinking of what actually *counts* as politics and political action. Roth accepts with little question notions of the political that, by her admission, are thoroughly saturated with heterosexist assumptions about masculinity, power, and action. Indeed, her own diction reflects those assumptions to a discomfiting degree. The "new artist" of the aesthetic of indifference, she notes, "had a dandylike elegance of body build and a manner which delighted in cool and elegant plays of mind"—and she does not intend this as a compliment (Roth and Katz 37).

Roth's argument about the lamentably apolitical cast of the so-called aesthetic of indifference has not gone unchallenged. In a 1998 reply to Roth's essay, Jonathan D. Katz's "Identification" asserts that what she saw as passive silence in the face of injustice was, on the contrary, a politically charged "*performance* of silence," an immanent critique not only of the Red Scare but especially of the closet to which these gay artists found themselves consigned in cold war America (Roth and Katz 53). Hardly apolitical, Katz writes, the artistic strategies Roth ascribes to an aesthetic of indifference constitute "a particular species of politics, . . . a strategy of queer resistance to a social context of control and constraint within a culture that offered little room to maneuver, especially for gay men" (51). Far from the dandy scourge of political action, Duchamp emerges in his analysis as "the antimasculinist patriarch of what would turn out to be a most queer family" of artists whose politics centered on the development of new strategies enabling refusal and interrogation of the status quo (54). Duchamp's subtle but insistent approach showed these artists how to create work that would open a space for critique while also permitting survival in the ferociously hostile world in which they were forced to live. Duchamp, Katz writes, "was an artist who didn't care *and* he was a powerfully rebellious presence in the art world of his time. Seamlessly, [he] inhabited a paradox: he combined indifference with resistance" (54).

Katz's link between Duchamp and paradox brings us back to the similarly ambiguous energies informing Cunningham's artistic practice, where innovative approaches to movement, sound, and stage design unfolded within the context of a fairly traditional theatricality. Katz invokes performativity not to spotlight Cunningham's work but to indicate his theoretical and methodological debts to contemporary queer theory. Like Roth, he foregoes analysis of the choreography, focusing instead on the art of Cage, Duchamp, and Rauschenberg, but to a considerable degree, this mirroring omission is a function of his point-by-point response to Roth's essay. Katz's essay appeared six years after the death of Cage; by then the romantic relationship between composer and choreographer was widely acknowledged, and though Katz's critique has enjoyed nothing like the reception granted Roth's essay (first published in *Artforum* and reprinted many times since), it would not be surprising to see his turn to identity politics and queer theory finding its counterpart within dance studies.[49]

In many ways, Susan Leigh Foster's reading of Cunningham's aesthetic as a "closet" is that counterpart (174). For Foster, Cunningham's rejection of "the gynocentrically marked concerns of feeling and psychological intensity" that characterized the "feminine" modern dance tradition in which he began his career in favor of a "masculine rationality" focusing on "overt action rather than interior identity" amounted to a choreographic "version of chasteness" that "deflected any inquiries into his sexual orientation and provided a safe haven for his homosexuality" (169, 177, 175). Like Katz, Foster sees cold war homophobia as the determining cultural factor in Cunningham's aesthetic. Indeed, the one thing Roth, Katz, and Foster have in common is the impulse to read the work of Cunningham and his colleagues as entirely symptomatic. For Roth, the aesthetic of indifference is a protective response to the Red Scare, while for Katz and Foster, Cage's performance of silence and Cunningham's "determination to cultivate the body as a neutral field of possibilities" are defensive reactions to a dangerously homophobic culture (Foster 175).

Foster contextualizes Cunningham's objective approach to movement by aligning it with Alfred Kinsey's contemporaneous and similarly dispassionate approach to human sexuality (*Sexual Behavior in the Adult Male* was published in 1948, four years after Cage and Cunningham's first joint concert). In doing so, Foster acknowledges, even if indirectly, the subversive potential of Cunningham's aesthetic. However, her reading of his choreography serves a larger argument that gives the palm for gay liberation in dance to the 1970s emergence of contact improvisation and its embodiment in the work of the all-male San Francisco troupe Mangrove. Thus, she chooses to emphasize the "increased fear and condemnation of homosexuality" that was the immediate reaction to Kinsey's research rather than the gradual acceptance of the range and variety of human sexuality that was the longer-term and more consequential response. Her reading of Cunningham's choreography takes a similarly narrow view, limiting the discussion to immediate questions of technique and persona. The incorporation of ballet movements within the modern dance idiom, she claims, "allied his dances with the more masculine ballet tradition than with the feminine modern dance," while in the roles he created for himself "within this masculine environment, Cunningham circulated as the odd man out" (Foster 177). In this way, she portrays his work as a wholly defensive "personal and aesthetic negotiation of white matriarchal modern dance on the one hand and vicious homosexual prejudice on the other" (178).

Foster's reading has been criticized recently by Rebekah J. Kowal, who convincingly sees Cunningham's solos within his group dances as "emphasiz[ing] his departure from normative constructions of masculinity by posing himself against the norm embodied by the others" (174). In this dispute over the nature and legibility of the sexual politics of his choreography, however, neither Foster nor Kowal tackles the meta-choreographic questions raised by the Events. Then, too, this focus on the issue of whether or not Cunningham's dance practice was closeted ignores the elephant in the room of cold war U.S. cultural discourse, in which the simple fact of being a male dancer was taken as prima facie evidence of homosexuality. The question is not *whether* Cunningham's work made legible the political realities of life in homophobic cold war America but *how* it did so—and, as important, how that work may have resonated beyond the realm of identity politics.

Late in his essay, Katz asserts that Duchamp's paradoxical, passively active aesthetic laid the foundation for "a politics of negation" within the artistic practices of the Cunningham circle (Roth and Katz 63). While the overall thrust of his approach is more aligned with the Derridean impulses of contemporary queer theory than with Adorno's understanding of modernism as immanent social critique, Katz's subtle acknowledgment of the political charge of refusal does indicate how his insights might support a more thorough analysis of the politics of Cunningham's art. As a move in that direction, Seth McCormick's recent brilliant reading of Jasper Johns's *Star* (1954) works with the cluster of terms and concepts (misidentification, disagreement, dissensus) that Rancière used to develop a framework for articulating the relationship between art and politics and formulating a ground for political action beyond identity politics.

Commissioned as a painting by the performance artist Rachel Rosenthal and executed by Johns as a "peculiarly hybrid" construction of wood, housepaint, newspaper, canvas, beeswax, tinted glass, nails, and fabric tape, *Star* emerges in McCormick's analysis as an extraordinary meditation on the midcentury relationship between art and politics that simultaneously evokes and critiques the identity politics that Roth, Katz, Foster, and Kowal all construe as the epitome of activism as such. In 1950, Mattachine Society founder Harry Hay, likening gay life in America to Jewish life in Nazi Germany, had called for the creation of a homosexual rights organization. Four years later,

Star re-presented the six-pointed Star of David as "a partially lidded, partially glassed-in space like that of a locked display case in a department store, a space in which privacy and concealment are not to be distinguished from incarceration and enforced visibility" (McCormick 259). The work's facture, which combines collage, construction, and painting, clearly identifies it as a product of the American neo-Dada movement, whose influences included not only the coolly rational Duchamp but, just as importantly, Kurt Schwitters, whose Merz collages appeared in the infamous 1937 Nazi exhibition *Entartete Kunst* (Degenerate Art). "It was through an engagement with the work of . . . Schwitters, whose death in 1948 occasioned renewed and widespread attention to his work and art, that Johns and his fellow artists Robert Rauschenberg and Cy Twombly were able to broach the relationship between McCarthyist persecution [of homosexuals] and a longer history of totalitarian constructions of identity" (McCormick 251).

Johns's *Star* shows how that engagement rapidly moved beyond a queer identification with Dadaism via Schwitters's work—an identification that aligned the political persecutions of Jews and homosexuals and linked both to an aesthetics of degeneracy and decadence—to a "performative *mis*identification" that, in revealing the "hidden continuity of McCarthyism with totalitarianism . . . demonstrated the necessity of breaking with that double bind of invisibility and exposure, secrecy and confession" that set the terms of persecution and identificatory resistance alike (McCormick 242).

> If *Star* implicitly opposes two models of artistic practice or aesthetic politics, they are not the ones Moira Roth had in mind when she contrasted the aesthetic of indifference with a politics of self-represented identity. Far from being simply indifferent to contemporary politics, the recuperation of a totalitarian paradigm of degenerate art aimed to reoccupy and reclaim persecutory modes of identification, transforming the aesthetic codes of degeneracy and subversion into practices of opposition. In doing so, however, it risked reinforcing the very structures of persecution that foreclosed the possibility of its own political subjectivation.
>
> To this model is opposed a second, the model of misidentification, in which a particular political identity is figured, but not for its own sake and not in order to arrogate for itself the status of persecuted minority (a claim that would merely rehearse the risks attendant upon the first model). In *Star* . . . the figuration of a particularized Jewish identity serves primarily as a means to refuse totalizing structures of persecutory identification and domination. This refusal involves the staging of a disagreement, an event that becomes political, as Jacques Rancière has theorized, not due to the nature of the competing interests or claims at stake, but only insofar as the very identities of the two parties, and their acceptance or refusal of a common language, becomes the object of dispute. (259–260)

Thus, for McCormick, "the supposedly repressive blanks and anti-expressive silences of the works" of the Cunningham circle "did not conform to the imperatives of homosexual closeting and political censorship; rather, their highly determinate content reveals the limitations of these concepts' applicability to the economy of homosexual visibility in the United States of the 1950s" (240).

Like Johns's *Star,* a Cunningham Event is a "site of disputation" (McCormick 239). As is well known, Cunningham turned to chance methods of composition to get beyond the limitations of his own imagination and experience. What began as an expedient method for getting around blocks in the creative process rapidly became a technology for precisely disputing notions of modern dance as uniquely revelatory of psychology (anchored in Graham's famous claim that "movement never lies"), of dance as an *expression* of hidden mental or emotional states. A dance, for Cunningham, was not about saying something; it was about doing something so that the action was understood "exactly . . . in its time and place, and not in its having actual or symbolic reference to other things":

> A thing is just that thing. It is good that each thing be accorded this recognition and this love. Of course, the world being what it is . . . we know that each thing is every other thing, either actually or potentially. So we don't, it seems to me, have to worry ourselves about providing relationships and continuities and order and structures—they cannot be avoided. . . .
>
> The body shooting into space is not an idea of man's freedom but is the body shooting into space. And that very action is all other actions, and is man's freedom, and at the same instant his non-freedom. You see how it is no trouble at all to get profound about dance. It seems to be a natural double for metaphysical paradox. ("The Impermanent Art" 86)

Cunningham's sly reading of propulsive movement as signifying both freedom and non-freedom and his comment about dance as a metaphysical paradox align suggestively with Franko's assertion that the politics of dance are found in its ability to "absorb and retain the effects of political power as well as resist the very effects it appears to incorporate *within the same gesture*" ("Dance and the Political" 6, emphasis added). Of course, one can, with Foster, read Cunningham's disagreement with the view of dance as an inherently and uniquely confessional art form as entirely symptomatic of his life as a gay man in cold war America, where confessing the truth of one's inner emotional self was dangerous and a masculinist rejection of a "gynocentrically marked" tradition linking dance with psychological release might offer safer footing. However, doing so risks losing sight of what, for Cunningham, is the fundamental and thoroughly political goal of his disagreement: to increase our capacity for extending to *all* "things" the "recognition and love" that they deserve—Kirstein's "boy-things," to be sure, but others, too, regardless of their place or seeming lack of place in the larger structure.

Cunningham's insistence that his dances are not interested in "saying something" but in "doing something," that the dance presents "no stories and no psychological problems" but is "simply an activity of movement"—with everything that the word *movement* implies—is indeed a kind of refusal, but it is not a refusal of politics (Cage 10).[50] Rather, in refusing an expressive, symptomatic understanding of the dance, Cunningham's work refuses an expressive, symptomatic view of art as a reflection or representation of the political conditions of its emergence, the view that, as we've seen, was foundational to cold war programs of cultural diplomacy. As Anderson's interlocutor understood, the Events were the *ne plus ultra* of this aesthetic, refusals of both the notion of dance movement as psychologically revealing as well as of a dance work as an organic expression of an individual choreographer's personal vision. Indeed, the Events were an extension at the meta-choreographic level of precisely that interrogation of expression that Cunningham sought when he turned to chance compositional procedures.

Moreover, in presenting movement, dance, and décor as full and independent partners, the Events insisted on a distribution of the sensible that emphasized the total equality of all aspects of the spectacle. The claim that dance, in particular, was the equal of music and painting had a special charge in midcentury America, where, as we have seen, ballet and modern dance were viewed with contempt largely because of their connection to homosexuality. By insisting that the internal connections of the dance phrases were as fortuitous as the links among gesture, sound, and décor, Events questioned related notions of power, authority, and control. Thus, they went beyond creating situations and opportunities for extending recognition and love to things: they insisted on the right of things disdained as insignificant or meaningless to recognition and love. As Anderson explains, the Events "not only [provide] us with different kinds of things to see, [but they also remind] us that the same things may be seen in different ways" (100). For cold war America, this was a radically democratic politics of the dance. Small wonder that the adjective most commonly used to describe Cunningham's work, then and now, is *challenging*.

The Shiraz Arts Festival was founded in the same year that Pahlavi crowned himself and his third wife emperor and empress of Iran. An unusual hybrid, it was both a showcase for the most advanced work of the European-American avant-garde and a forum for introducing little-known traditional Eastern art to an international audience. The festival was a particular interest of the shahbanu, Farah Diba Pahlavi, whose taste and cultural interests had been deeply influenced by her education in France. In addition to the Merce Cunningham

Dance Company, the 1972 festival featured performances by a Kathakali troupe from India's Kerala Kalamandalam, an evening of traditional Persian music, screenings of recent Iranian films, concerts of music by Karlheinz Stockhausen and John Cage, and, most spectacularly, Robert Wilson's *Ka Mountain and GUARDenia Terrace,* a nonstop theatrical event staged at various locations in and around Shiraz during the festival's eight-day run. With the shahbanu's encouragement, organizers made a point of eschewing mainstream art. The result, as poet John Ashbery said in the *Saturday Review,* was an "uncompromising" mixture, "not for dilettanti."

> The real purpose of the festival is to confront Iranians with the art of the past from countries close to them both geographically and culturally and with the new art from the West. To a country without significant modern traditions, still under the spell of its own great past, where a production of Shaw or Ibsen would count as a novelty, such an effort might seem quixotic. In fact, the festival has been bitterly attacked by Iranians, not all of them Philistines by any means. Perhaps the consensus was expressed by a writer to the Tehran newspaper *Kayhan:* "What justification is there for subjecting the inhabitants of Shiraz . . . to Stockhausen before, say, Bach's Mass in B Minor, Mozart's *Requiem,* or Beethoven's Ninth Symphony? Why should those who have never seen a good production of Shakespeare, Chekhov, Corneille, or Molière have to go through the agony of incomprehension during a performance of *Orghast?*"[51] (Ashbery and Sorouchian-Kermani 60)

While not the view of a philistine, the *Kayhan* quotation does express a culturally conservative position and points to a problem that dogged the Shiraz festival over the course of its ten-year existence. Though it intended "to elevate 'the standard of culture in the country'" by bringing to Iran "the best, the newest, and most avant-garde art of the world" while promoting an "appreciation for traditional Iranian art forms," it also highlighted rapidly growing divisions in the country, not only between the monarchy and the nation but also within the Iranian people (Afkhami 404). Ashbery had it right. However inadvertently, the Shiraz Arts Festival fostered confrontation between tradition and the avant-garde, European and Asian cultural forms, and monarchical, Islamic, leftist, and so-called commonsense notions of the proper relationship between art and politics.

Despite its stated mission to showcase Iranian art while developing a more cosmopolitan appreciation within Iran for foreign art forms, both ancient and contemporary, festival organizers made little effort to show how Western avant-garde and Eastern classicism might speak to each other. Rather, the main concern of National Iranian Radio and Television executives charged with overseeing the festival was to create the biggest possible international splash, and domestic reaction was predictable.[52] Perhaps thinking of the theatrical productions of Peter Brook and the musical compositions of Shiraz regular Iannis Xenakis, *Kayhan*'s letter writer saw the programming as a problem of putting too many atonal carts before too few diatonic horses, but the Ayatollah Ruhollah Khomeini (almost certainly provoked by the scandal of the 1977 festival, *Pig, Child, Fire!*), condemned the entire enterprise as a scene of "indecent acts."[53] Years after the collapse of the Pahlavi dynasty, Queen Noor of Jordan described the festival as an attempt "to spark a cross-pollination between Iran and the rest of the world" that "backfired badly" (Gluck 27). This backfiring was partly a function of an artistic agenda that was as formally ambitious as it was politically tone deaf, but as composer Robert Gluck has observed, it can also be attributed to the festival's lavish production values, which the regime's Islamic and leftist oppositions viewed as the symptomatic excesses of an oppressive government (27). This was particularly true of the 1972 festival, held ten months after the October 1971 Anniversary Celebration. Outrageous by any standard, the four-day observation of 2,500 years of Persian monarchy unfolded within and around a 160-acre Maison Jansen–designed "tent city" of deluxe temporary housing built for the sole purpose of accommodating the nearly seventy heads of state who attended the festivities at Persepolis. Included in those festivities were ceremonies at the tomb of Cyrus the Great and a state banquet catered by Maxim's of Paris.[54] In his highly sympathetic biography of the shah, Gholam Reza Afkhami characterizes both the 1971 Anniversary Celebration and the 1967–1977 Shiraz Arts Festival as intended "affirmation[s] of Iran's progress under the Pahlavis" that instead "did much damage to the shah and the regime" (412). He attributes the damage to Islamist and leftist misrepresentations (with assistance from Western journalists sympathetic to the shah's critics in the National Front and Tudeh), but even in his analysis we glimpse an auto-intoxicated regime almost willfully blind to the probable political fallout of such ostentatious public displays of wealth.

The Cunningham company's appearance at the 1972 festival was the first stop of a ten-city tour that included performances in Venice, Belgrade, Warsaw, London, Köln, Düsseldorf, Grenoble, Milan, and Paris. The tour was studded with performances at the many government-sponsored arts festivals that flourished in the atmosphere of cold war cultural combat: the troupe appeared at the Venice Biennale, the Belgrade International Theater Festival (like the Shiraz, founded in 1967), the Warsaw Autumn (a celebration of contemporary music founded in 1956), and the Festival d'Automne à Paris (in its inaugural year). As the history of cold war cultural diplomacy shows, international arts festivals, particularly those held in politically strategic locations such as Warsaw or Belgrade, were a favorite target of U.S. cultural export. In fact, the Cunningham company did receive 9,000 dollars from the State Department for its performances in Poland and Yugoslavia (slightly less than 50,000 dollars in current funds).

In Belgrade the company received a festival award for its performance of *Canfield* (1969), chosen for the Yugoslavian dates because composer Pauline Oliveros had dedicated the score to Serbian-born engineer Nikola Tesla. A report from the embassy to State Department officials in Washington described the company's performances as "among the most important experiences . . . audiences have been exposed to since the [founding of the festival]" (Cultural Affairs Collection, box 59, file 24). Acknowledging a "wide cross-section of opinion among critics," the report insists that "the most thoughtful were completely captured by the performances." It approvingly quotes a review in *Borba*—"the essential goal of Cunningham's conception of modern dance . . . [is] to stimulate the spectator to observe more sharply, listen more carefully, and think more deeply"—to support the claim that the Cunningham appearances constituted "a triumph for the entire ensemble, and for American cultural achievement in general" (Cultural Affairs Collection, box 59, file 24).[55] However, as the translated reviews in the file indicate, few, if any, reviewers saw Cunningham's choreography as a uniquely American cultural achievement. In fact, "the most thoughtful" reviewers took an internationalist, cosmopolitan perspective on the work, exploring connections between his aesthetic principles and those of Brecht and Jerzy Grotowski.[56] The tendency of government cultural officials to over-estimate the likely political effects of sponsored productions was discussed in general terms in chapter 2; this particular example is interesting for the way it reveals a strikingly different view of the Cunningham company within State from what had prevailed in 1968, when the troupe undertook its first government-sponsored tour.

That tour opened in Mexico City, where the company appeared as part of the International Festival of the Arts offered to complement the nineteenth Olympic Summer Games, and the troupe received 5,000 dollars from the State Department to offset travel costs (Brown, *Chance and Circumstance* 515).[57] For most Americans today, the most memorable choreography of the 1968 Mexico City games was the silent gesture of U.S. track champions Tommie Smith and John Carlos, the African American gold and bronze medalists in the two-hundred-meter race. Shoeless, they stepped onto the awards podium and raised their fists in a black power salute during the playing of "The Star-Spangled Banner." Official reaction was harsh and swift: condemned by International Olympic Committee chairman Avery Brundage for politicizing the games, both were suspended from the American track team and banned from the Olympic village. Although Brundage and much of the U.S. press sought to portray them as isolated malcontents, contemporary scholarship has largely validated their action, placing it the context of not only the American civil rights struggle but also democratic activism unfolding globally during that year, from the May protests in Paris to the Prague Spring, the Democratic National Convention in Chicago, and the bloody

Tlatelolco demonstration in Mexico City itself, which occurred less than two weeks before the opening of the games.[58]

Though billed as part of the Olympic festivities, the Cunningham company's performances at the Palacio de Bellas Artes took place in mid-July, three months before the opening of the games themselves, when the possibility that an athletic or cultural event might become the scene of political protest seemed remote. Indeed, the embassy airgram describing Mexican reaction to the troupe's appearances sounds by turns bemused, derisive, and condescending, even as it unwittingly admits the company's potential to spark political reaction. Granting that "no [other] American attraction appearing in the 'Cultural Olympics' has aroused so much interest among Mexican 'avant-garde' dancers, musicians, artists, and intellectuals," it attributes that interest chiefly to "social and intellectual snobbery. . . . As the extremely wide coverage of Cunningham on the 'society pages' of the capital reveals," there were "no packed houses" during any of the company's seven performances. The airgram notes, by contrast, the "hordes" who saw the "dull, conformist, and very square" Bolshoi Ballet, whose dates at the "cavernous" Auditorio Nacional coincided with the Cunningham company's engagement at Bellas Artes. In typical self-congratulatory fashion, the report attributes the troupe's lack of broad appeal as proof "once again . . . that America is the most 'contemporary' culture in the world, the most daring, the most iconoclastic, the most totally and anarchistically free. [Cunningham and Cage] hit a significant Mexican minority right in the solar plexus." Almost as an afterthought, the attaché describes that "significant Mexican minority" as "the rebellious young." Written on September 4, 1968, a month before these "rebellious young" would find themselves the target of government forces in Plaza de las Tres Culturas (in what today is known as the Tlatelolco massacre), the report obviously meant to describe nothing more rebellious than a fashionable eagerness to embrace a "shocking" "modern sensibility" (Cultural Affairs Collection, box 59, file 23).[59] Yet the possibility that Cunningham's work could be seen as a call to rebel in directly political ways would soon become a reality—in fact, as soon as the troupe's next stop on its South American tour, Rio de Janeiro.

The Merce Cunningham Dance Company arrived in Brazil four months after the death of Edson Luís de Lima Souto, a teenager shot by military police while they were breaking up a student demonstration against high prices at the Calabouço restaurant of the Instituto Cooperativa de Ensino, and a month after the June 26 March of the One Hundred Thousand, a protest held largely in response to that murder. The march was one of the most significant demonstrations against the Brazilian military since 1964, the year it had seized power following the U.S.-backed overthrow of leftist president João Goulart. In 1968, General Artur da Costa e Silva was one year into the presidency handed to him by the military-dominated National Renewal Alliance Party; in December he would respond to the increasing protests against his regime with the infamous Ato Institutional Número Cinco, known as the AI-5 decree. AI-5 arrogated extraordinary powers to the president, allowing legislative rulings by decree, the summary suspension of political rights of any individual or organization he deemed subversive, the ability to dismiss the National Congress, and comprehensive censorship of film, music, theatrical works, and television.

Although AI-5 had not yet passed when the Cunningham company arrived for their five performances at the Teatro Nôvo, theater officials informed company manager Lewis Lloyd that the troupe would not be allowed to perform until "police censors" had previewed its repertoire. When Cage and Cunningham "categorically refused" to submit to the request, the cultural attaché at the American embassy in Rio was contacted. According to Carolyn Brown, "[the attaché said that] if we refused the censorship evaluation, the police could force cancellation of the entire presentation, but if the censors were convinced that there was no text in the choreography, they could waive the pre-performance requirement, and then the Cunningham company would have established an important precedent for freedom of performance and artistic activities in Brazil." Because Lloyd, Cage, and Cunningham stoutly refused to preview the work, the censors instead attended the opening-night performance of *Suite for Five, Rainforest,* and *Place* with the rest of the public. Then "we waited to see what would happen. Nothing did" (*Chance and Circumstance* 514).

The government's lack of response was probably due to the press attention surrounding the company's refusal to comply with the censors. While the reportage was relatively cautious, news of Cunningham's defiance did leak out. Articles in *Jornal do Brasil, Diário de Notícias,* and other papers show that he was questioned directly about the situation during a lively July 25 press conference at the theater. A July 28, 1968, newspaper clipping in State Department files describes a "storm of questions" at the conference and Cunningham's patient, genial, but uncompromising response: "It's great to know that people approve, disapprove, cheer, and boo the show. I like the censorship of the public; I do not accept government censorship" (Cultural Affairs Collection, box 59, file 23).[60] This clipping, which the State Department's Bureau of Educational and Cultural Affairs preserved in a thick sheaf of preview pieces, profiles, and reviews documenting Brazilian reaction to the company's engagement, is not the only piece to quote Cunningham's remarks about censorship. One mentions the subject in its headline, while another declares, "There Is Protest in Merce Cunningham's Art" (Cultural Affairs Collection, box 59, file 23).[61]

The ensuing reviews of the company's performances were remarkably thoughtful and open-minded, with little of the crotchety head scratching that Cunningham's work sometimes provoked. Critical discussion of his choreography has long explored its engagement with notions of freedom and independence, and the censorship flap led many Brazilian reviewers to emphasize this aspect of the work. "There is nothing in art—or in life, for that matter—that is as beautiful as freedom," wrote the reviewer for the daily *Correio da Manhã,* who went on to observe, in describing *How to Pass, Kick, Fall, and Run,* that "the verb 'to kick,' besides kicking or tapping with the feet, also means, in the U.S.A., to object, to complain, to protest, to criticize" (Cultural Affairs Collection, box 59, file 23).[62] In her memoir, Brown describes an engaged and supportive embassy staff in Brazil, yet nothing in the official record indicates that government censorship was an issue during this particular foray into cultural diplomacy. The files contain no translations of these reviews, nor is there any assessment report from the cultural attaché.

Tellingly silent on the Cunningham company's encounter with Brazilian censors, State Department records of the South American tour also provide indirect support for Brown's claim that the troupe's appearance in Buenos Aires, its next engagement after Rio, was "sabotaged."

> [In Argentina] there was no pre-publicity. The Teatro Municipal General San Martín staff claimed that no photographs ever reached their press office, and even though they admitted that our posters had arrived, they could not explain why none had been posted. Union stage crews at the San Martín refused to unload our scenery and costumes. It wasn't until we women dancers began to do the work that they were shamed into doing their job. The theater management appeared unprepared for our arrival and astounded by the size and complexity of our scenic effects, and they gave the impression of wishing we'd never come. . . . When the assistant cultural attaché phoned to request free tickets, Lew Lloyd told him the embassy should follow its own policies to their logical conclusion and stay away, or at the least buy their own tickets. Why, Lew asked this man, hadn't the embassy done anything for us? His answer: a decision higher up had been made that the company was to be ignored. (*Chance and Circumstance* 517)

According to Brown, Lloyd was told by an executive at Pepsi-Cola, which had expressed some interesting in sponsoring the troupe's tour, that government opposition grew from reports that the company "show[ed] sex play on stage"—an utterly implausible explanation given what State Department cultural officials undoubtedly knew about Cunningham's work (*Chance and Circumstance* 517). Were one to trust the evidence of the government archive, one would conclude that the Merce Cunningham Dance Company had never appeared in Buenos Aires in August 1968. It has no press clippings, no photographs, no attaché report; nothing exists in the files to document the company's performances. This lack of evidence makes it difficult to draw a direct connection between the troupe's defiance of Brazilian censors and its suppression in Argentina. Even so, the blankness of the archive is itself a kind of testimony (Cunningham Archive, box 51, folder 4).[63]

As previously noted, embassy reports of the company's 1972 appearances in Yugoslavia and Poland have quite a different tone. In part, this reflects officials' acknowledgment of the troupe's increased global stature (and probably a certain degree of shoulder-shrugging, as well, on the part of baffled cultural attachés willing to accept the assurances of others as to the artistic merit of the work). However, and much more importantly, that altered tone also reflects the aims and ambition of U.S. cold war cultural diplomacy itself, revealing the degree to which government willingness to sponsor work was a function of where, exactly, that work was going to be seen. Dances that could be construed as calls for political freedom and protest were shunned as awkward reminders of the yawning gap between democratic theory and practice that characterized U.S. relations with the rightwing regimes of South America, yet these same dances were lauded as avatars of American values when performed behind the Iron Curtain. The company, however, danced the works it had always danced (*Rainforest* was included in both tours) in the manner it had always danced them.

Despite its strategic location, the Shiraz Arts Festival apparently did not enjoy any special attention from the State Department. Even though the performances in Iran kicked off a tour that included State-sponsored visits to Belgrade and Warsaw, the troupe's dancers and musicians appeared in Shiraz without benefit of government support. The company offered three performances at the 1972 festival: a September 5 Event that, according to the program, featured the reproduction of Duchamp's *The Large Glass* created by Johns for *Walkaround Time;* a September 7 concert focusing on the music of Cage, David Tudor, and Gordon Mumma; and, on September 8, the concluding "Persepolis Event" incorporating the helium-filled Mylar pillows Andy Warhol had designed for *Rainforest* ("Program, Sixth Festival of the Arts, Shiraz-Persepolis," Cunningham Archive, box 52, folder 4). Printed in Farsi and English, the program notes for these performances open with a Cunningham quotation: "Dancing has a continuity of its own that need not be dependent on the rise and fall of sound (music) or the pitch and cry of words (literary ideas). Its force of feeling lies in the physical image, fleeting or static. It can and does evoke all sorts of individual responses in the single spectator. These dances may be seen in this light." While emphasizing that this description constituted "the only explanation" that Cunningham had provided for his work, the notes do offer brief descriptive passages of *Walkaround Time* and *Rainforest* that emphasize the free and unscripted relationship between the music, the décor, and the choreography: "Cunningham will very often say no more to his collaborators than how long he plans [the piece] to be." The notes also explain the Events as an "idea . . . originally prompted by being presented with an unusual performing area, . . . an open room with the audience on three sides (space); a situation where an intermission would have been awkward or uncomfortable (time); and a 'stage' not equipped nor allowing for conventional arrangements of musicians, lighting, exits and entrances, etc." From this humble beginning, the notes continue, the Events grew into a meditation on Western traditions of spectacularized performance: "If we want to be flexible, then we must not preclude the theatre as it has been known and is still commonly used—a playing space in front of spectators. Now, as a consequence, these *Events* are sometimes given in regular performance situations also. Each *Event* is arranged for the particular stage where it will be given." By treating traditional theatrical venues as if they, too, are unconventional or uncongenial performance spaces, the Events interrogate received understandings of the "proper" use of space, calling for new conditions of flexibility and making visible previously unimagined opportunities for human action and reaction (Cunningham Archive, box 52, folder 4).

The company's first Event was staged in a recently constructed open-air theater in Shiraz (Brown, *Chance and Circumstance* 577). Its second was held in the ruins of Persepolis itself, long claimed by the Pahlavis as a symbol of the monarchy and a monumental ratification of their right to power (figure 12). Company members were not blind to the nature of the shah's regime. At the Persepolis Event, Brown recalls being shadowed by a "'guide'—a euphemism for the male uniformed guard with a lethal-looking gun who guarded our trips to the toilet, to the stage, to where ever we might need to go" (577–578). One such guide forbade Mumma from photographing the view from the stage of the Shiraz auditorium in which he, Tudor, and Cage would perform. During the performance itself, Brown says, Mumma realized that "half of the audience" consisted of these armed guides. At the Persepolis Event, "the military was everywhere. The Shahbanu arrived by helicopter. A red carpet—literally!—was rolled out . . . for her entrance to the stadium-like amphitheater" (578). For Brown, the performance in Persepolis was a "major" Event chiefly insofar as it supplied the antidote to the "lavish, ostentatious, . . . wildly extravagant" Anniversary Celebration staged in the ruins the year before (577). It included material from *Field Dances, Suite for Five, Scramble, Signals,* and *Landrover*, but Brown writes, "before a move was made, a step taken, *Rainforest* silver pillows were let loose from their hidden moorings and floated free above the jagged pillared skyline into the atmosphere. A gorgeous, thrilling moment with—I thought—a not-so-subtle political message! The performance had begun" (578). The pillows had been secured to the ancient pillars to prevent their floating off into the desert, but company manager Jean Rigg recalled that "the winds came up and many simply snapped their lines and floated off"—untethered, released, and free (Gluck 23).

The Shiraz Arts Festival would continue for another five years. While many artists became festival regulars, Cage and Cunningham were not among them. Although they had agreed to a return engagement in the 1976 festival, they

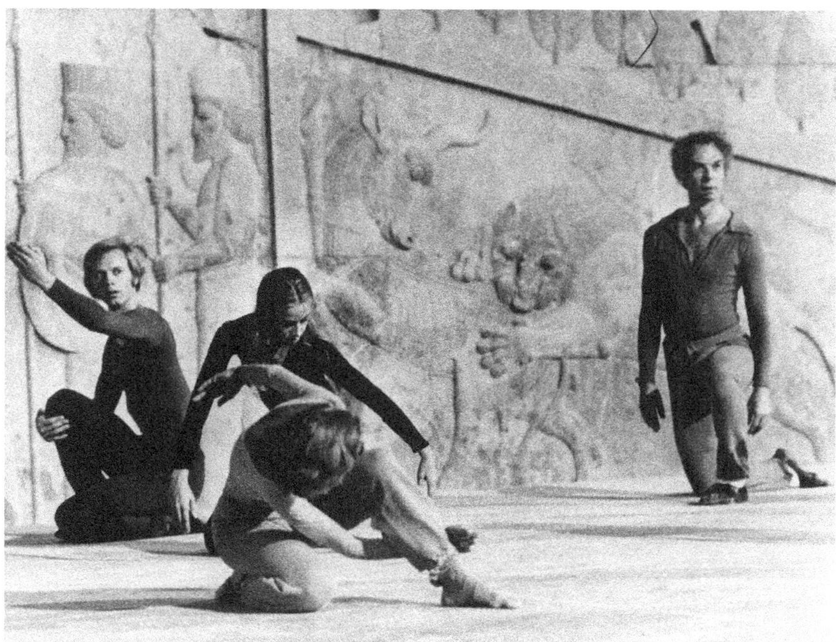

FIGURE 12 Douglas Dunn, Susana Hayman-Chaffey, and Merce Cunningham. Event, Persepolis, Iran, 1972. *Source:* Photographer unknown. Courtesy of The Merce Cunningham Trust and The New York Public Library for the Performing Arts Dorothy and Lewis B. Cullman Center.

reconsidered their decision following a discussion with a dissident Iranian poet (Gluck 26). "Merce decided to put the question to the dancers," Rigg remembered. "I was charged to gather information for the meeting. I recall a trip to Amnesty International's office at 72nd and Broadway." Composer David Behrman, who created the music for *Walkaround Time* but did not travel to the 1972 festival, recalled "a controversy about the politics, [with] several members of the company at that time, including me, [saying] we didn't want to go, because the invitation was from the Shah's inner circle" (Gluck 26). Following a particularly impassioned speech by Meg Harper, a dancer who had traveled to Iran in 1972, the dancers voted to refuse the invitation.

Cage and Mumma made it clear that they did not support this decision. In Mumma's view, "refusing the invitation would go unmentioned and unnoticed in Iran; [be] quickly forgotten in the United States, and nothing would be accomplished" (Gluck 27). Apparently Cunningham also disagreed with the dancers' vote. According to Brown, the decision to decline the invitation was "a political decision on the dancers' part but Merce would have gone, believing one should present one's work wherever [one was asked so that] the work itself might change people's minds—that is, to open them" (Gluck 26). Though the three most powerful figures of the Merce Cunningham Dance Company disagreed with the dancers' vote, that vote was honored: it was that kind of operation. The troupe did not return to Iran.

Frustrated by his long inability to discover the "secret" of Hugh Vereker's literary art, the narrator of James's "The Figure in the Carpet" lashes out at Gwendolen Erme—like Vereker a novelist, and a keeper of his secret—declaring that there was, after all, "nothing" there to be discovered (James 601). As we have seen, such invidious fits of pique in the face of challenging art are not confined to the world of fiction. The State Department's effort to treat Cunningham's 1968 South American tour as if it were nothing—in the case of the Buenos Aires dates, going so far as to make it look as if literally nothing had happened at all—takes this attitude to its logical conclusion. Yet in one of his most famous comments about dance, Cunningham, too, acknowledged that his life's work was a kind of nothing. Dance, he wrote, was an activity that "gives you nothing back." The dancer has "no manuscripts to store away, no paintings to show on walls and maybe hang in museums, no poems to be printed and sold—nothing but that single fleeting moment when you feel alive" (Cunningham, *Changes n.p.*). All "the impermanent art" can offer, these fleeting moments nevertheless have, for Cunningham, the heft of compendia—"if the dancer dances, *everything* is there" ("The Impermanent Art," 86; emphasis added). Balanchine held a similar view. "A ballet is a movement in time and space, a living moment," he observed in a 1961 interview. "A ballet is life. It is not architecture or a column that stands forever, or a painting, but something which belongs to the people who execute it, to their bodies" (Nabokov and Carmichael 48). When, later in this interview, he comments on the career of the expatriate African American dancer and singer Josephine Baker—"an American Negro from Harlem—people said, Who the hell is she, who does she think she is? And she really was wonderful: a wonderful woman, a wonderful singer, a beautiful voice, really talented, but she couldn't do anything" in pre-civil rights America, which saw her talent as a threat to the racial order (49)—he reveals his understanding of the political implications of a dancer's sure ownership of movement. As Balanchine and Cunningham both knew, silent gestures may leave nothing behind, but they make claims that are hard to ignore.

6

Spartacus

Despite disagreements about the political motivations and effects of cold war culture, most scholars concede that American dance, literature, and visual art came into their own after World War II largely thanks to a reinvigorated exploration of modernist principles of form and style. This was not the case, however, for cold war U.S. cinema. Although the postwar years saw the emergence of a group of artists whose film practice had clear formal allegiances to modernism and the European avant-garde (for example, Maya Deren, Kenneth Anger, Stan Brakhage, and Jonas Mekas), their explorations of visual abstraction and figuration in purely cinematic terms had little impact on the bulk of cold war American film production, which remained narrative and commercial, turning out the hugely successful movies that Theodor Adorno and Max Horkheimer famously denounced as the anodyne, disposable products of a capitalist culture industry.

Still, as the French New Wave revaluation of Hollywood films demonstrated practically and much subsequent writing about film has enlarged on theoretically, distinguishing between abstraction and narrative is no simple thing. Nor is it easy to use that distinction as a means of assessing the aesthetic and/or political progressiveness of individual films or filmmakers. The medium itself complicates the distinction between image and story, an aspect of cinema that makes it a tempting yet slippery object of ideology critique. Literally stills in motion, film operates through an intermeshing of contrastive systems of meaning (image/sound, narrative/figure, lyric/epic) that are not interchangeable, and a surface appearance of smooth interconnectedness often reveals, on closer inspection, suggestive gaps in the chain of signification—gaps that themselves signify. Thus, certain films (perhaps especially those with unabashedly commercial aims) can be powerful precisely insofar as they fail to form a coherent, unified whole. In such films, what matters most is how they make visible internal struggles over the shape of signification itself.

This is the case for Stanley Kubrick's *Spartacus.* In describing it as a film engaged in a struggle over signification, however, I do not ascribe to it the sort of heightened self-awareness constitutive of the modernist work of art as defined by Adorno. Nor is it a film whose form and subject connect in any straightforward way to the issues of cold war cultural diplomacy and government arts patronage taken up by Balanchine's *The Figure in the Carpet* and the Merce Cunningham Dance Company's "Persepolis Event" at the Shiraz Arts Festival. And while Kubrick's movie is important to my analysis here, it is not the only text under discussion. A comparative analysis of competing U.S. and Soviet efforts to claim Spartacus as cold war hero, this chapter reads Kubrick's 1960 film with and against Aram Khachaturian's and Yuri Grigorovich's 1968 ballet *Spartak* and concludes with the 1970 publication of the first *Spartacus International Gay Guide.* My analysis of the decade's fascination with Spartacus highlights the destabilizing effects of moving figures—those fraught constellations of antagonistic forces whose impact in large part derives from their ability to harness the power of irreconcilable tensions—on what seem, at least initially, to be straightforward narratives with unambiguous ideological aims. The transmission of the Spartacus story is best understood as a modal movement of progressively displaced emphases, a series of gestures in which a hero in a narrative is slowly transformed into a narrative of a hero. As Spartacus evolves from actor in the ancient chronicles to modern political symbol, cold war spectacle, and, finally, emblem of gay liberation, he does not emerge freshly conceived at each incarnation. Nor do the separate instantiations, or figurations, of his narrative add up to a single coherent meaning. Rather, each reappearance is coincident with a change in the terms of his signification and thus his significance. Forced to regain his footing on shifting terrain, Spartacus battles on.

Not surprisingly, even though their makers pledged fidelity to the most up-to-date scholarship on Rome in the first century before Christ, both the Soviet ballet *Spartak* and the American film *Spartacus* have proven to be as historically unruly and rebellious as the event they portray. Although those pledges did not prevent calculated allusions to fascism, McCarthyism, and civil rights, the issue is not simply the fact that, as Soviet and American productions, the productions don't tell the same story. Rather, each cold war Spartacus contains several different stories. Their lack of internal coherence, which has resulted in a wide variety of contradictory interpretations, illustrates the impossibility of accurately predicting an artwork's range of effects. As both a figure and a narrative at once political and aesthetic, Spartacus is an object lesson in the limitations of the dominant cold war view of the relationship between art and politics that informed American and Soviet programs of government arts patronage.

Although the problem of Spartacus's internal coherence reaches its highest pitch in the competing U.S. and Soviet cold war productions, it does not originate with them. Beginning with the ancient chronicles, there have been many efforts to tell Spartacus's story—to make the significance of his rebellion unambiguous and ideologically serviceable. These retellings are notable mostly for their disagreements, which range from obvious contradictions to subtle variations of tone and attitude, and discrepancies multiply as each contribution seeks to correct the perceived flaws of its predecessors.[1] Not until the Enlightenment was the Spartacus rebellion interpreted as a just blow for freedom; none of the classical sources contain a word of his direct speech or offer clear indication of the larger aims of the rebellion.[2] When Marx described Spartacus as a "real representative of the ancient proletariat," he was parsing this Enlightenment tradition in terms that forged a strong symbolic link between the gladiator and the European revolutionary left (Marx and Engels 126).[3] By the time of his verdict, however, Spartacus's significance as an avatar of freedom had been established under rather different terms in the United States, where Robert Montgomery Bird's enormously popular play *The Gladiator* struck poet Walt Whitman as a work "as full of 'Abolitionism' as an egg is of meat, . . . a play . . . calculated to make the hearts of the masses swell responsively to all those nobler manlier aspirations in behalf of mortal freedom!" (Lillard 15). The distance between proletariat and slave is not great, but Spartacus's imbrication in sentimental abolitionist discourse produces an American gladiator more steeped in nostalgia and family feeling than his European (later Soviet) counterpart, even as both the American and European Spartacus put implications of homoerotic "manlier aspirations" in play.[4]

As a figure, the nineteenth-century American Spartacus is an early indicator of an expansion in the terms of human freedom, one that accelerated through the twentieth century and finds forceful expression in Kubrick's film and Grigorovich's ballet via four interconnected topics or themes: (1) the central role of nostalgia in utopian thought; (2) the relationship of the progressive revolutionary project to utopian thought and nostalgia; (3) the appeal to art as mediator of nostalgia and revolution and the degree to which this appeal allows antagonistic forces to invade the category of the aesthetic; and (4) the role of sex in imagining and staging the fraught relations among art, nostalgia, and revolution. Cold war articulations of Spartacus forced a reckoning with art's riven, hybrid, contradictory, and pidgin status as mediator of nostalgia and revolution, past and future, political and personal. Those articulations in turn amplified art's powers of dissent, thus ushering once-abject subjects to the foreground of politics.

In January 1948, Soviet musicians assembled in Moscow at the behest of the Central Committee of the Communist party for a three-day conference, at the end of which Andrei Zhdanov condemned some of the nation's most celebrated composers for producing work marked by the "atonalism, dissonance, and disharmony" of the "formalist and anti-people school" (Werth 29).[5] A month after the conference, the Central Committee released its Decree on Music, which denounced the "anti-democratic tendencies" of twentieth-century Western art music as typified in the work of composers such as Stravinsky and the members of the second Viennese school. Among those Soviet musicians identified as most guilty of indulging in "formalist perversions" were Shostakovich, Prokofiev, and Khachaturian. Recalling a 1949 conversation with Khachaturian at a Moscow reception, British journalist Alexander Werth wrote, "The Decree had made a deplorable impression abroad, and had, of course, played into the hands of every kind of anti-Soviet propaganda."

> *Time* and *Life* and *Newsweek* had all become terrific Shostakovich fans, and defenders of the "persecuted musicians." Khachaturian, obviously sent to . . . do a little counter-propaganda among the foreign correspondents and diplomats, was perfectly willing to talk. His line was that "it shouldn't be taken too seriously": the Central Committee, in its Decree, had simply laid down certain principles and given certain indications, and it would now be for the composers themselves to sort out the good from the bad. And he added, a little wistfully: "There is going to be a reassessment of a lot of things; some of the works that I considered least important—such as some of my ballet music—will now be treated as important." (91–92)

Khachaturian began composing *Spartak* two years after his public chastisement had increased the importance of his ballet music. Politically, the context for *Spartak* could hardly have been more fraught: Khachaturian completed the score in 1954, a year after Stalin's death, and the ballet received its world premiere at the Kirov Theatre ten months after Khrushchev's famous secret speech to the party condemning the Stalinist cult of personality. Though Khachaturian did not begin composing the ballet until 1950, he had known for ten years that a politically significant job was before him. Nikolai Volkov had written the book for *Spartak* in 1938, when the Spartacus rebellion was enjoying a vogue as a subject among Soviet scholars charged with proving Stalin's version of the Marxist "stage theory" of human progress, which maintained that "the great slave uprisings of the declining Roman republic annihilated the slave-owner class and the slave-owner society" (Rubinsohn 6; Yuzefovich 207).[6] Between 1934 and 1937, Soviet historian A. V. Mišulin produced a series of books and essays casting the failed Spartacus rebellion as a forerunner of the ultimate Soviet victory. As Wolfgang Zeev Rubinsohn notes, these interpretations allegorized the Spartacus uprising (which Mišulin claimed was an actual revolution) to emphasize "the ideological foundation, the mass-organization, which means, in modern parallels, the Party."

> Just as in the Communist Party of the USSR the left-wing opposition (the Trotskyites) and the right-wing opponents (the Bukharin-Tomskij group) had hindered the Great Leader . . . in the execution of the plans conceived by his genius and sabotaged his actions, so too in Spartacus's uprising the "extremists of the left" (Crixus and Oenomaus; Castus and Gannicus) and the "petty bourgeois opposition" (the poor free-men) had hindered their Great Leader . . . Spartacus in carrying out his plans. Spartacus soon came to grief because of inadequate discipline and the splitting of his forces. Had he got rid of the opposition at the right moment, he would have had a chance of winning. From this it follows, according to empirical materialism, that the opposition must be relentlessly eliminated at the right moment, in order to save the revolution. So Mišulin, by the use of an example from ancient history, legitimized the elimination both of the Kulaks and of the opposition from within the Party. (8)

No doubt Volkov's choice of Spartacus as a subject for ballet reflected a genuine interest in the story itself. However, Rubinsohn's analysis suggests that it was also designed to please a regime that had begun to turn a wary eye on its artists, as the new Soviet history of Spartacus emerged concomitantly with the rise of socialist realist aesthetic theory and the growing power of Zhdanov.[7] Certainly, Khachaturian saw Spartacus as making special demands on the Soviet artist. In 1941, a year after accepting Volkov's invitation to take on the project, he described the ballet as "a monumental tale of the ancient uprising of slaves, a mighty avalanche in defense of the freedom of the individual, to which I as a Soviet artist wish to pay tribute and express my deep respect and admiration" (Yuzefovich 208). When he finally began composing the ballet in January 1950, two years after the Decree on Music, he did so under newly intensified pressure to prove himself as a Soviet artist.

The first production of *Spartak* opened at the Kirov on December 27, 1956, with choreography by Leonid Jacobson and scenery by Valentin Khodasevich. Askold Makarov danced the title role. In almost every register, the ballet was a classic exercise in socialist realism, a "historically concrete depiction of reality in its revolutionary development" targeted toward "the task of educating workers in the spirit of Communism" that took most of its narrative cues from the official Soviet history of the gladiators' rebellion (Bown, *Art under Stalin* 90). Spartacus suffers the humiliations of the slave market. Forced to kill in the arena, he is radicalized and leads his fellow gladiators in revolt. His defeat and death, though tragic, are depicted as regrettable but necessary sacrifices endured on the road to eventual (Soviet) liberation. Yet *Spartak* differs from

Mišulin's history in one key aspect. Spartacus is destroyed not by the combined antagonistic forces of the extreme left and the petty bourgeoisie but by sexual intrigue: Harmodius, the gladiator's "comrade-at-arms," is seduced by Aegina, the consort of Crassus, into betraying his fellow rebels to the Roman army (Shneerson 88).[8] This first articulation of a cold war Spartacus, then, illustrates how the individual figure, even in its subordination to the sweep of a spectacular collectivist narrative, retains its capacity to shape that narrative.

As the score neared completion, Khachaturian came to regard his responsibilities as a Soviet musician in terms that did not quite square with the requirements of the 1948 decree. In an essay published eight months after Stalin's death, the composer addressed the question of innovation in Soviet music—the very issue that had driven Zhdanov to denounce composers who "cater to the degenerate tastes of a handful of aestheticising individualists" (Werth 29). Khachaturian asked, "Can we Soviet composers say that our work meets the constantly growing cultural requirements of the Soviet people, that our accomplishments correspond to the greatness of the tasks set before us? No. We cannot say that." The problem, as he saw it, lay in the reluctance of Soviet composers to try anything new. The essay did not target Zhdanov specifically; in fact, Khachaturian dutifully paid his respects to "Comrade A. A. Zhdanov's words, 'The new must be better than the old, otherwise it makes no sense.'" However, he did not disguise his scorn for the music produced in the five years since the decree. Several times he asserted the importance of "creative individuality" and, denouncing the bureaucratic practice of vetting new works for ideological content, even praised the composers whom Zhdanov had censured:

> Pondering the paths of development of Soviet music, I cannot fail to turn my attention to the work of such splendid artists as Sergei Prokofieff and Dmitry Shostakovich. The best works of these composers move me, set my creative thoughts in motion, and stir my senses. . . . The time has come to revise our established system of institutional guardianship over composers. I will say more: We must resolutely reject the wrong practice of interference with the composer's creative processes by officials of music institutions. Creative problems cannot be solved by bureaucratic methods. (3–4)

The passion of Khachaturian's prose is remarkable, and his rebellious call for artistic freedom aligns suggestively with the subject of the ballet he was completing. Still, few would claim that the first production of *Spartak* constituted a clear break with *zhdanovshchina,* which continued to influence Soviet critics and artists well beyond the deaths of Zhdanov and Stalin. Almost certainly because of its subject, *Spartak* won the approbation of two state-sanctioned biographies of Khachaturian, both of which assert that the ballet's premiere received strong public and critical approval. However, biographers Victor Yuzefovich and Grigory Shneerson also admit that this first production had its flaws, which they attribute to its choreographic innovation. Indeed Jacobson, who had choreographed the first production of Shostakovich's *The Golden Age* in 1930, was not a favorite of Soviet authorities, who often found his work too experimental.[9] Jacobson's unusual choreography abjured the refined style and specialized vocabulary of classical ballet (*pointe* work in particular) in an effort to duplicate figures drawn from Roman vases and the Pergamon Altar—a move highly reminiscent of Vaslav Nijinksy's representation of antiquity in his 1912 ballet *L'après-midi d'un faune.* According to Yuzefovich, this was simply *too* innovative (218). For his part, Shneerson simply notes that after "the Soviet public acclaimed with enthusiasm the Kirov Theatre production," the ballet almost immediately received quite different choreographic treatments in new productions in Prague and Moscow (89).

Thus, *Spartak* was sent back to the studio for revision. Its second Soviet production, which premiered in 1958, was created for the Bolshoi Ballet. This version was choreographed by the celebrated Igor Moiseyev, director of the bravura folk dance troupe that was part of the first cultural exchange agreement between the Soviet Union and the United States.[10] Pointedly avoiding innovative gesture in favor of colorful scenes of massed movement, Moiseyev's approach nevertheless proved just as problematic as Jacobson's. Though supposedly "distinguished by grandeur, magnificence and splendour," Moiseyev's *Spartak* was "not entirely free from faults occasioned for the most part by an excess of superficial effects and certain naturalistic details (especially in the scene of the gladiators' fights), as well as by the preponderance of pantomime over dance" (Shneerson 90). This second major *Spartak* was scrapped after fewer than ten performances.[11]

Still, when the Bolshoi Ballet made its first U.S. tour in 1959 as part of the second U.S./U.S.S.R. bilateral cultural exchange agreement, the company brought with it excerpts from the Moiseyev production. Part of their "Highlights" program, these excerpts seem to have escaped the serious notice of U.S. reviewers, who were far more interested in Leonid Lavrovsky's *Romeo and Juliet*, the artistry of the legendary, if rapidly fading, ballerina Galina Ulanova, and the virility of the company's male dancers (whose "prudish" costumes prompted some derision).[12] Reviewers also noted the company's tremendous impact on the U.S. cultural scene. Nothing in American high or popular culture quite compared to the dazzling glamour of the Bolshoi Ballet, a glamour that seemed, to some U.S. dance critics, out of proportion to the quality of the choreography on display. Although coverage of the company's New York performances was intensive, with both the *New York Times* and the *New York Herald Tribune* giving front-page play to opening-night reviews, critical reaction to the choreography was mixed. Despite his enthusiasm for the Bolshoi's

Giselle, the *Times*'s *John Martin* had reservations about its *Swan Lake* and termed Yuri Grigorovich's *The Stone Flower* "dated" ("Dance: Classics," *New York Times,* May 3, 1959, p. 20X; "Ballet: 'Stone Flower,' *New York Times*, May 5, 1959, p. 41). Likewise, admiration for Ulanova did not keep the *Herald Tribune*'s Walter Terry from finding some of *Romeo and Juliet* "quite pedestrian" ("Dance: Bolshoi Ballet," April 18, 1959, p. 9).[13]

Though senior American dance critics gave scant attention to the excerpts from Moiseyev's *Spartak,* the ballet was important to the company, and its presence in the repertory caught the attention of Stan Margulies, then a production assistant with Kirk Douglas's Bryna Productions.[14] On May 16, 1959, Margulies wrote publicity agent Myer Beck with his latest idea for a promotional stunt for *Spartacus,* which was then being filmed in Hollywood: "When the Bolshoi Ballet arrives in Los Angeles, we are thinking about having the troupe visit the *Spartacus* set. This seems to be a natural and logical idea since they are dancing sections of their ballet about our hero on their 'Highlights' program. If they visit the set, we were then thinking that Kirk might present the man who dances the title role with a sword or a shield or some other gift from one Spartacus to another" (Douglas papers, box 33, folder 6). While there's no evidence that this plan was ever realized, Margulies's suggestion makes clear that Douglas and his staff were quite aware of the claim their film would make on competing views of the meaning and significance of Spartacus. Bryna officials knew not only about the salience of Khachaturian's *Spartak* in recent Soviet cultural history ("*their* ballet about *our* hero"): they also knew about Bird's play and Rosa Luxemburg's *Spartakusbund*, and they understood the interpretive issues at stake for their film.[15]

Four days after sending the memo to Beck, Margulies fired off a letter proposing a television special to publicize *Spartacus,* "which might have as its basic concept the age-old fight for freedom. . . . We thought we might possibl[y] try to tie this program in with a specific date familiar to the present audience—United Nations Day, which is celebrated in December, or possibly even connecting this early fight for freedom with our own Civil War, which will be marked by numerous centennial observances starting early next year."[16] Margulies offered some specific ideas about the programming for this television special: "Burl Ives and Harry Belafonte singing songs of freedom, . . . a Revolutionary War song, a Civil War song, etc. . . . ; Raymond Massey or Richard Boone doing a Lincoln speech . . . ; Stephen Vincent Benet's poem 'John Brown's Body,' [which] contains many stirring and effective passages. Some . . . set to music and arranged for a chorus by . . . Walter Schumann"; "dramatic incidents in our own history, ranging from Valley Forge to the flagraising at Iwo Jima"; "a special poem for the occasion" by Carl Sandburg ("he even might appear on the program to read it"); and a commissioned "freedom ballet" by Agnes de Mille. Margulies concluded, "It is possible to make such big concepts as freedom, America, and liberty exciting, dramatic fare, without pomposity or dullness" (Douglas papers, box 33, folder 7).[17]

It's an open question as to whether vaudeville is the best way to make "big concepts . . . exciting," but there's little doubt about the proposal's fundamental aim: to tie Spartacus to a uniquely American narrative of freedom, an aim articulated in the opening moments of the film itself, when the voiceover narration describing Spartacus as "dreaming the death of slavery 2,000 years before it would die" subtly casts the rebellion as a precursor to the Emancipation Proclamation. In a manner not so far removed from 1930s Soviet efforts to Stalinize the gladiator, the public relations staff of Bryna Productions worked hard to Americanize Spartacus. Notable among their efforts was a "library kit" for schools that included a commissioned pamphlet written by Brown University classics professor Charles Alexander Robinson, Jr. Titled "Spartacus: Rebel against Rome," it purports to explain the history behind the film. The first paragraph places the Spartacus rebellion in the context of "the eternal struggle for freedom and human dignity," noting that "the torch of liberty was kindled before the dawn of recorded history and has been carried forward through the ages by dedicated men, then passed on to new bearers when old hands faltered and dropped away, as in an everlasting relay race" (Douglas papers, box 66). Although Bryna paid Robinson 1,750 dollars for his article (about 14,000 dollars in current funds) staff members were not pleased with the job and the essay was rewritten (box 34, folder 12).[18] In fact, the passage about the "relay race" of the "torch of liberty" was inserted by Bryna copywriters at Margulies's request. Objecting to Robinson's original conclusion, he had proposed a revision that resembles nothing so much as an American version of Stalin's Spartacus: "His statement that Rome settle[d] down to a long period of peace and prosperity and that the slaves had better working conditions [after the rebellion] sounds like a dismissal of the Spartacus uprising. . . . Our conclusion, if it does not distort history too much and if Robinson will go along, is that Spartacus set in motion a chain of events that led to the fall of Rome and that is why he is remembered—an early important figure in the never-ending fight, etc." (box 33, folder 15).[19]

Kubrick's *Spartacus* has a long-acknowledged claim on cold war U.S. cultural history. Along with Otto Preminger's *Exodus,* it ended the thirteen-year-long Hollywood blacklist by publicly giving screenwriting credit to Dalton Trumbo, arguably the best-known and certainly the most prolific of the Hollywood Ten screenwriters who had refused to cooperate with the House Committee on Un-American Activities during its 1947 hearings on communist subversion in the U.S. film industry.[20] From the beginning, *Spartacus* was conceived as a star vehicle for Douglas, and he is frank in his memoir about wanting his movie to be known as the film that broke the blacklist.[21] Douglas himself had bought the film rights to Howard Fast's 1951 novel *Spartacus,* which Fast had conceived while serving a three-month sentence for contempt of Congress after refusing to give the House committee the names of contributors to the Spanish Refugee Appeal of the Joint Anti-Fascist Refugee Committee (Fast, *Being Red* 276). The film's leftist *bona fides* thus seem to be relatively uncomplicated, even overdetermined, and one might reasonably assume that its politics would have found fairly direct expression.

Once brought to life, however, Trumbo's *Spartacus,* not unlike Khachaturian's *Spartak,* made some unexpected moves. The film is less a testimonial to the left's eventual triumph over the forces of McCarthyism than a foreshadowing of the issues that would come to overwhelm and transform leftist politics in the turbulent 1960s. In crafting screenplay and score, Trumbo the blacklisted screenwriter and Khachaturian the chastised composer faced not only similar creative tasks (drawing on and working through past representations of Spartacus in order to bring him to modern life) but also similar professional and political obstacles. The work of both was scorned (in Trumbo's case, proscribed) for ideological reasons in the years leading up to their Spartacus assignments. Both men worked in nations that had come to believe in the strategic value of art. (In the United States in particular, that belief had the urgency of fresh discovery.) Neither Soviet cultural officials nor Bryna Productions had any wish to see *Spartak* or *Spartacus* in truly revolutionary terms, formally or otherwise. On the contrary, ballet and film were conceived as accessible exercises in cultural self-congratulation. The extraordinarily vexed production histories of both works, then, might be taken as their first metapolitical critiques of the regimes that had willed them into being.

Ideas about how to claim Spartacus for American liberty may have flowed smoothly from the public relations arm of Bryna Productions, but it was a different story for the film's principal creators, whose early disagreements about the nature and consequences of the gladiators' rebellion grew into furious acrimony. Memos circulating among Douglas, Trumbo, and Kubrick reveal how concerns over developing the strong individual characterizations and psychological interest so crucial to Hollywood cinema grew into heated disagreement over how those touches of pathos should read politically. In short order, Trumbo and Kubrick were at loggerheads. After a screening of the first cut, Trumbo fired off a scathing seventy-eight-page memo, "Report on *Spartacus,*" which castigated Kubrick for failing to make Spartacus sufficiently heroic (Trumbo papers, box 27, unnumbered folder).[22] Detecting in Kubrick's approach a whiff of Arthur Koestler's 1939 novel *The Gladiators,* a bitter, disillusioned treatment of the Spartacus rebellion written in the aftermath of the Moscow show trials, Trumbo argued vehemently against anything in the film he saw working against his and Fast's vision of what he called the "large Spartacus." In Duncan Cooper's view, Trumbo took offense at Kubrick's "fidelity to a bitter realism which spared the illusions of neither the left nor the right" but sought, by "graphically illustrat[ing] the violence and brutality of both the masters and the slaves," to "raise the question of whether even a noble goal like freedom can justify the human cost" (34). As is well known, Kubrick's vision did not prevail, and he quickly disowned the picture: the experience of making *Spartacus* led him to vow never to give up the right to determine the final cut.[23] Of course, his more critical view of Spartacus hardly stood a chance against the larger Bryna/Universal goal of portraying the gladiator as a forefather of American liberty. For Trumbo, however, Kubrick's approach to Spartacus felt like a personal insult, a mocking betrayal of the vision of human freedom for which he and Fast had sacrificed so much.

Yet as admirable as Trumbo's dedication may be to a film that has come to be read as not only a parable of and coda to the McCarthy era but also an allegorical endorsement of the civil rights movement, his "large Spartacus" bears a disconcerting resemblance to the Stalinist Spartacus.[24] In an effort to keep a scene that was ultimately cut, for example, Trumbo justifies Spartacus's killing of his erstwhile adjutant by asserting that the gladiator "execute[s] Crixus for the good of the whole"; the relationship between the two men, Trumbo notes, resembles the "war between brothers" of Stalin and Trotsky (Cooper, "Trumbo v. Kubrick" 35).[25] Trumbo worked strenuously to win Kubrick over to his own prudish, unabashedly homophobic notions of sexual decadence among the slaveholding Roman elite, notions that color Fast's novel as well. An undated thirteen-page memo schooled Kubrick on the social and political nature of the late Republic, tying the fall of Rome to the erosion of family values and a loss of religious piety: "The noble dignity of the Roman women had long since disappeared; countless divorces on slight or political grounds went hand in hand with loose intrigues and adultery. Family life in all classes was shaken to the foundation. . . . The old state religion, with its attendant priestly colleges, augurs, and auspices . . . had long since lost its moral force." Trumbo's memo consists mostly of stitched-together quotations from Henry Smith Williams's *Historian's History of the World* and an authority cited only as "Dill," presumably Samuel Dill, author of several histories of Rome published at the turn of the twentieth century. At one point, however, he does interject, in his own words, the claim that "most of the wealthy and noble Roman families showed their degeneration by their refusal to bear children. . . . This speaks a great deal for the sanctity of marriage as it existed at that time: it had, in practical effect, no existence at all" (Trumbo papers, box 24, folder 6).

Trumbo cared a great deal about the sanctity of marriage, at least as it affected *Spartacus*. He lobbied hard for the inclusion of a scene depicting a mass wedding within the rebel slave encampment on the eve of the disastrous final battle, an event prompted by Spartacus's decision to marry the pregnant Varinia (Jean Simmons) because "only with marriage and his father's name can our son be free!" (Trumbo papers, box 25, folders 1 and 2). The writer felt the scene was dramatically important and expressed considerable bitterness at Kubrick's strong resistance to it. In an undated memo, he wrote, "I admit . . . that there are many reasons why it is precisely this scene that may ruin our picture":

> It is, so far as I know, the first time that such a scene has been suggested for a motion picture. To do something that hasn't been done before is dangerous, contrary to the code, and probably subversive. We should therefore replace this affront to banality with a scene that has, by actual count, been tested before an audience 1,837 times—a man on the eve of battle cautioning his wife to see to it that his reputation is properly inflated in the mind of his surviving infant son.
>
> The scene implied that even slaves, sub-humans, despised and rejected and illiterate though they may be, can aspire toward the noblest concepts of their betters. These men and women are yearning toward the ideal of the family, of the dignity of a formal union between man and woman, of legitimacy for their children and the continuity of their seed. . . .
>
> My young confrere, Stanislav Kubrick, however, has an even better reason for eliminating the scene. It reminds him of the marriage of Adolph Hitler to Fraulein Braun. (box 24, folder 8)

Likening Trumbo's proposed eleventh-hour mass nuptials to the similarly melodramatic gesture of Hitler and Braun is certainly extreme, but Kubrick had a point. However sympathetic one may be to Trumbo's leftist politics and his difficult professional situation, the director's distaste for such kitsch is certainly understandable. Still, my point is not to praise Kubrick's proto–New Left suspicion of Trumbo's Stalinist nostalgia, even less to side with Trumbo's socialist-romantic narrative of heroic defeat against Kubrick's disconcerting, near-clinical fascination with cinematic spectacle.[26] It is more useful to consider the Trumbo/Kubrick conflict as registering an unusual moment when two classical Hollywood production values that usually operate comfortably in tandem—spectacle and nostalgia—separate and come into conflict. This conflict disfigured *Spartacus* while also intriguingly complicating it. In other words, the tension between spectacle and nostalgia became as productive as it was problematic, with many of those productive moments operating as immanent camp critiques of the film's conspicuous political righteousness.

The 1991 restoration and rerelease of *Spartacus* brought to the fore the film's second claim on cold war cultural history: the queerness of its storyline and characterizations. Previously acknowledged only indirectly, this aspect became much more apparent in the later version. In particular, the restoration of the snails and oysters scene between Marcus Licinius Crassus (Laurence Olivier) and the slave Antoninus (Tony Curtis), in which Crassus indicates his sexual interest in Antoninus ("My taste includes both snails and oysters"), snapped into focus an alternate register of meaning, not simply in this scene but in the film as a whole.[27] The scene was meant to present homosexuality in its usual guise as the morally repugnant ultimate limit of the master's power over the body of the slave while offering a certain voyeuristic titillation. In this it followed the lead of Fast's novel, where leering descriptions of homosexual liaisons among the Roman elite were ostentatious enough to draw critical notice, not all of it sympathetic to Fast's presumption. Reviewing the novel for *The Nation,* Harvey Swados singled out the book's sexual politics for particular scorn: "[Fast] has provided Spartacus with a lovely and loyal wife named Varinia, and as if to make sure that we will not miss the point, he has contrasted their splendid fidelity with the homosexual carryings on of the degenerate members of the master class" (331).[28]

However much Fast and Trumbo sought to harness homophobia to their cause, the effects of their efforts extended well beyond their moralizing intent, working not only to make homosexual passion visible (challenging enough in late 1950s Hollywood, with the double pressures of the Production Code Administration and the Roman Catholic Legion of Decency) but also to expand the terms in which human freedom might be signified. This expansion operated in part by articulating homoeroticism and the aesthetic together as realms beyond the control of Rome. Even without snails and oysters, *Spartacus* muses over the ways in which sexual and aesthetic experiences can be understood as political experiences—actions that catalyze and sustain dissent in the face of an implacably opposed power. And while the script and visual register provide plenty of food for thought in any consideration of the film's sexual politics, it is the music of *Spartacus* that literally underscores the connections linking aesthetic experience with sexual and political rebellion and brings those connections to the surface of audience awareness.

Often relegated to the status of "unheard melody," film music makes a powerful contribution to cinematic effects and meaning.[29] Even as they critique music's complicity with the administered aspects of commercial cinema, Theodor Adorno and Hanns Eisler acknowledge that it "bring[s] out [a] spontaneous, essentially human element" that cinema, in its reliance on mechanical reproduction, manifestly lacks. Motion picture music interposes "a human coating between the reeled-off pictures and the spectators, . . . breath[ing] into the pictures some of the life that photography has taken away from them" (59). For Adorno and Eisler, the greatest strength and deepest failing of film music lies in its ability to lend an appearance of life to the dead and deadening products of culture industry. To the extent that it lends the semblance of animation to the inanimate, however, film music also is profoundly utopic, mobilizing a range of effects that structure the viewer's understanding of utopia as either nostalgic (buried in an unrecoverable past) or progressive (promised in an impossible future).[30]

Alex North, composer of the score for *Spartacus,* came to Hollywood in 1951 after writing the incidental music for *Death of a Salesman.* A protégé of Elia Kazan, he immediately made his mark with the score to *A Streetcar Named Desire,* often described as the first jazz film score in Hollywood history. North scored more than fifty films before his death, including *Cleopatra, The Misfits, The Shoes of a Fisherman, Who's Afraid of Virginia Woolf?,* and *Viva Zapata!* As that last title indicates, his politics were, at least for a time, quite close Trumbo's.

The child of Russian-Jewish émigrés Jesse and Bessie Soifer, Alex North was the brother of leftist writer and editor Joseph North, whose journalistic affiliations included the *Daily Worker, New Masses,* and *Masses & Mainstream.* The lover of leftist dancer Anna Sokolow, Alex lived with her while he studied at the Moscow Conservatory of Music in 1934, and they toured Mexico together in 1939. He studied with leftist composer Aaron Copland and was a member of the leftist Composer's Collective, an affiliate of the Pierre Degeyter Club, the official musical organization of the American Communist party. North was a U.S. Army veteran and had been an employee of the Works Progress Administration's Federal Theatre project. Not surprisingly, he was also the subject of an eighty-six-page FBI file.[31] A memo within the file describes the bureau's reasons for interest in him, and it makes for sad but predictable reading, outlining a record comprised mostly of lists of leftist family members, friends, and acquaintances and reports of his attendance at meetings of various leftist organizations in the 1930s and early 1940s.

North was never called to testify before the House committee, which is something of a miracle. Nonetheless, the government made certain that North knew about its interest in him. An FBI agent interviewed him during his first year in Hollywood, asking pointed questions about his life during the 1930s. Responding to the agent's assumption that only strong political allegiance could account for his actions, North parried with an appeal to the realities of the performer's life, claiming that he participated in "various concerts and parties or rallies sponsored by such organizations as the Abraham Lincoln Brigade and the International Workers Order" on a solely "professional basis" as the paid musical entertainment (FBI, North file, September 3, 1954). He did manage to successfully deflect the agency's interest: a later memo indicates that his "activities have been reviewed in the light of the Security Index criteria and . . . he does not meet these criteria" (March 19, 1959). However, the tension of the 1954 interview is obvious: at one point North's wife blurted out that "she had never been a member of the Communist Party nor affiliated with it in any way whatsoever" (September 3, 1954).[32] North's career may have been launched by Kazan, but there is no evidence that he ever "named names" as his mentor had. Rather, the file indicates that the FBI had little luck in getting him to implicate past artistic associates (for instance, his former lover Sokolow) as Communist party members.[33] By the time he died, North had managed to almost completely erase any public trace of his leftist past. His September 11, 1991, *New York Times* obituary mentions his studies with Copland and at the Moscow Conservatory as well as his work with Sokolow's dance company, but there is nothing in the article to indicate that North so much as *had* a recognizable politics, let alone to reveal that, in 1951, such personal and professional affiliations were viewed as prima facie evidence of subversive political activity ("Alex North, a Film Composer, 80" B12).

Classical Hollywood film scoring practices are deeply indebted to the techniques of the Wagnerian *Gesamtkunstwerk,* and North made heavy use of them in the score for *Spartacus.* Chief among these techniques is the use of a *leitmotif* to identify specific characters, ideas, or circumstances in the drama, and North's score puts three motives into play: Spartacus's theme, the slaves' theme, and the love theme, actually identified in North's manuscript as "Varinia's theme."[34] This last theme was promoted as the *Spartacus* theme *tout court* after the film's release, and there is evidence that Universal International, if not Bryna Productions, hoped to squeeze a hit single out of it.[35] In a departure from usual Hollywood practice, however, North did *not* use Varinia's theme as the opening title music. Rather, the opening title runs over the Spartacus theme (first heard rumbling in the lowest registers of the orchestra as a kind of rhythmic motif in the kettledrums and basses), articulated in the context of something we might call the "Roman treatment": blaring, dissonant chords in the brass that don't quite add up to a melody. Strongly emphasizing Spartacus's theme (even giving it a brief contrapuntal treatment), the opening title music is martial, filled with tension, and rhythmically complex; a theme expressive of struggle, it is neither lovely nor aesthetic in the conventional sense, either melodically or harmonically. The mournful slaves' theme appears after the opening title, running beneath the film's voiceover introduction and through the brief scene establishing Spartacus's life in the Libyan mines before his selection for gladiator school by Lentulus Batiatus (Peter Ustinov).

Varinia's theme is not heard until sixteen minutes into the film, where it underscores her first encounter with Spartacus.[36] In its initial appearance the theme is carried not by the strings, in typical Hollywood fashion, but by the oboe, which imparts a pensive quality rather more somber than one would expect in a love theme. Its uncertain underlying tonality (the theme begins in a minor mode and ends in the parallel major) and halting rhythmic quality (only much later in the film does a triplet rhythm become clear) combine with the instrumentation to create a fragile, meditative effect. As the film continues, however—as Spartacus and Varinia become first rebels, then lovers, then parents—Varinia's theme undergoes a twofold transformation. First, it appears more and more frequently, beneath such a wide array of scenes that by the second half of the film it bears only a distant relationship to Varinia herself.

Second, its orchestration becomes more and more subject to Hollywood film score convention. As the film's exit title music, the theme has the last word in *Spartacus*, and by that point it has become Hollywood movie music of the most stereotypical kind. The oboe melody is given over to the violins, the somewhat modal harmonies are replaced by more familiar diatonic ones, and the waltz rhythm is unmistakable.[37]

This erasure of the theme's musically unconventional aspects (by Hollywood standards) accompanies its steady, progressive substitution for the Spartacus *leitmotif*, and the progress of the theme through the movie—its changes in orchestration and its appearance, especially in the last third of the film, in moments that have no clear connection to Varinia or "romance" conventionally (that is, heteronormatively) understood—charts a transformation in how utopia is imagined and articulated in *Spartacus*. This transformation is effected via the musical relationship North establishes between Varinia's theme and the slaves' theme, a melody that is similarly cast in a minor mode and that works as a musical bridge linking the Spartacus *leitmotif* and Varinia's theme. When Antoninus recites the nostalgic poem "Blue Shadows and Purple Hills," in which the dream of freedom is articulated as longing for a lost homeland, the relationship between these two themes is made clear. The slaves' theme leads directly into Varinia's music, now narratively recast as the love theme accompanying Spartacus and Varinia's tryst in the woods. Postulated first as a future goal entailing violent struggle and sacrifice, then, utopia in *Spartacus* grows to include moments recollected in the past and present amatory bliss.

To be sure, some of what I have just presented is simply evidence of the role a film's musical score can play in privileging the romantically tinged nostalgia that typifies Hollywood narrative. But there is more going on. For as its original orchestration and the circumstances of its earliest appearance hint, Varinia's theme signals a realm of experience not simply romantic but also sexual, poetic, and—this is music, after all—aesthetic. We initially hear the theme as accompaniment to Spartacus and Varinia's first conversation, a sexually charged exchange that is at once a deeply intimate expression and a public performance of their total lack of freedom. (Their encounter is watched by the leering Batiatus and the trainer Marcellus.) The rising importance of Varinia's theme over the course of the film thus signals not only the draw and drag of Hollywood-style romantic fantasy but also the impact of sexual and aesthetic experiences on political struggles. Additionally, and crucially, in the visual and narrative registers of the film, both Varinia and the poet Antoninus stand as figures for this imbrication of the sexual, the aesthetic, and the political. *Spartacus*'s first viewers were not introduced to Antoninus through his snails and oysters colloquy with Crassus, of course, but something like the erotic charge of that scene hovers over the first exchange between Antoninus and Spartacus, when the gladiator fingers Antoninus's fine white linen tunic and asks in amazement, "What kind of work did *you* do?" When Antoninus answers, "Singer of songs," Spartacus replies, "Singer of songs? But what *work* did you do?" Antoninus says, "Well, that's my work. I also juggle." Despite his seeming lack of real-world experience and gravitas (or because of it), Antoninus becomes Spartacus's chief assistant and advisor. He is the last surviving member of the slave army, the man Spartacus claims to love "like my son that I'll never see," whom he kills so as to spare him the agony of crucifixion. Arguably, although Varinia's theme serves as the musical sign of the film's blend of politics, sex, and aesthetics, Antoninus effects the transformation of the terms in which Spartacus (both the character and the film) imagines freedom. Deeply affected by Antoninus's poem, Spartacus begins to envision worlds of action and encounter beyond the exploitation of the arena and the terror of the battlefield: "He wants to fight. An animal can learn to fight. But to sing beautiful things, and make people believe them. . . ."[38]

Trumbo had a dim awareness of this queerly subversive linking of sex, politics, and the aesthetic, and it worried him—and not simply because Production Code Administration censors were likely to object. In his "Report on Spartacus," he launched a mighty effort to manage the sexual tenor of the scene in which Spartacus kills Antoninus. Kubrick's version, he felt, placed the relationship between the men in too tender a light. His comments, which begin with a quotation from the screenplay, are worth quoting at length:

> Spartacus (softly, hoarsely): And I love you—as I love the son I'll never see (face twitches). Go to sleep . . .
>
> We do not see his hands; but the movement of his body indicates that his right arm has made a short, swift, terrible motion. The light fades instantly from Antoninus's eyes. His head gently turns until his cheek touches the blood and sand of his last bed.
>
> Now what?
>
> I'm scared to death of the kissing, because of the homosexual desire Crassus has already shown for Antoninus, and Antoninus's own sombre, almost feminine beauty in these closing scenes. I almost feel that Spartacus has won as a kissing object that which was coveted by Crassus. More, I am compelled to wonder what Crassus, who is watching and who would have liked to kiss Antoninus in real life, thinks of this—and if his mere presence in the scene won't heighten the risk of homosexual implications. And finally, there may be some in the audience who will think we have shot these kisses almost as Spartacus's homosexual defiance of Crassus—his conscious assertion of victory over Crassus in the precise area of homosexuality. All of this may be far-fetched and wrong. But if there *is* to be kissing, I think you should dare only one—a very gentle, delicate brushing of the lips against the dead youth's forehead—a solemn, reverent farewell.
>
> And then what?

> Well, I can dream, can't I? I should like to see Spartacus stare down at Antoninus's dead face as if he were profoundly absorbed in a mystery (which he is)—the mystery of death. I should like to see him, frowning, thoughtful, his eyes drinking in the very face of death—as completely absorbed in the mystery of death as Olivier's close-ups in the scene show him to be absorbed in the mystery of Spartacus.
>
> Then, the trance broken, he looks about dazedly. He rises like a dream-walker, bends, picks up Antoninus's body, and starts out of the scene with it in a direction opposite, or at least different, from that where the watching Crassus stands.
>
> In the emotion of the moment, in the dazed wonder, in the almost hypnotic grip of what has happened and relief that it is over—he has departed from these tormentors. They no longer exist for him. He is wandering off with the body of Antoninus to hide it somewhere, to bury it perhaps.
>
> Then a guard, saying nothing, steps quietly in front of him. He looks at the guard questioningly. Then around—oh yes. He is here. And he is carrying the body of Antoninus in his arms. He looks across to Crassus. Now he knows exactly where he is and what he has done, and who has caused him to do it. He turns, walks slowly across to Crassus.
>
> His face is perfectly grave, perfectly impassive. He stands eye to eye with Crassus. Then, shockingly, he allows it to drop at the Roman's feet. And he says, quietly and without passion, as a simple statement of obvious fact: "He belongs to you now." (Trumbo papers, box 27, unnumbered folder)

Trumbo feared that Spartacus's kiss could be read as a sign of homosexual affection; yet the scene he proposed immediately after the kiss, which presents the relationship between Spartacus and Crassus as a kind of lover's quarrel over the body of Antoninus, is hardly free of homosexual inference. As it turned out, Trumbo didn't get his scene: Spartacus never dumps the body of Antoninus at Crassus' feet, nor did Kubrick choose to show Spartacus kissing Antoninus. Still, the final version does retains its queer pitch, for the music underscoring it is built around the intervals of Varinia's love theme—fragmented and displaced but audible and recognizable all the same.

Just as the blacklist legacy of the McCarthy years gives *Spartacus* audiences, both those of 1960 and those of today, an extra-cinematic context within which to interpret the film, so do the professional profiles—the inter-cinematic context, as it were—of three of the film's stars offer grounds for a queer reading of the film. In the case of the self-aware but miserably self-loathing Charles Laughton (Gracchus), the context was his own homosexuality.[39] For Tony Curtis (Antoninus) and Peter Ustinov (Batiatus), appearances in previous films had challenged heteronormative views of sexuality. Curtis had stepped into Crassus's bath and Spartacus's camp fresh from his turn as Joe/Josephine in Billy Wilder's *Some Like it Hot* (1959), while Ustinov's appearance as Nero in *Quo Vadis* (1951)—a wildly over-the-top performance, complete with lavender toga—had convinced some in Hollywood that the actor was gay.[40] Indeed, within the first ten minutes of *Spartacus,* Ustinov's Batiatus introduces what Richard Barrios has called the "pansy note," playing his opening scene as an interested inspector of men's musculature in the broadest manner possible. It is worth remembering that nothing at the start of the film indicates exactly *why* Batiatus is purchasing Spartacus, and Ustinov invites viewers to draw on their commonsense understanding—inflected as it would have been by their memories of his Nero—of the link between Roman slavery and homosexuality. Though viewers do quickly learn the purpose of Batiatus's purchase, Ustinov maintains his character's queer profile throughout the film, one strengthened by Kubrick's decision to cut scenes in which Trumbo established Varinia as a focus of Batiatus's sexual interest.[41] Given the character's profession and slave-owning status, Ustinov's and Kubrick's rendering of him as sexually irregular is hardly novel. What is novel is Batiatus's growth into a sympathetic character without the benefit of straightening out. Weaseling out of Crassus's demand that he identify Spartacus, Batiatus drives the cart bearing Varinia and her infant to freedom at the close of the film. His appeal depends upon a performance that emphasizes the roguish geniality typical of camp. Placed next to his performance in *Quo Vadis,* Ustinov's turn in *Spartacus* can be described as a kind of camp redemption.

Truly, the gay ethos of *Spartacus* runs deep, ranging from the stylized sketch of a naked, bare-bottomed gladiator that served as the film's logo to Crassus's obvious passion for the hero. As Varinia points out in the final reel, Crassus wants her only so that he may touch "something [Spartacus] had." Although she describes his feeling for Spartacus as "fear," Olivier's performance makes it clear that Crassus feels something other than fear for Spartacus. Even the celebrated first meeting between Spartacus and Varinia has its queer moment. "We recommend that you reconsider the line, 'I've never had a woman,' " Production Code Administration censor Geoffrey M. Shurlock wrote to Bryna officials after reviewing the script; clearly, he understood the line's double entendre.[42] Kubrick may have had this persistent queer undertone in mind when he claimed, in an astonishing statement that makes no literal sense, given the antiquity of the Spartacus narrative, that "we scrupulously avoided everything that's predictable in the story and the characterizations. For once, the audience doesn't know what's going to happen next" (Kubrick, *Spartacus,* disc 2).[43]

As his insistence on the mass-marriage scene and his anxiety about the death of Antoninus indicate, Trumbo was haunted by this unruly queerness, which perpetually threatened to wrest the film away from the heterosexual, pro-family, Old Left earnestness of his and Fast's conception and toward a quite different view of the relationship between Spartacus's figure and the narrative of freedom. The nostalgic spectacle of the Trumbo-Fast *Spartacus* sees public defiance and heroic loss as the wages of utopia. No less subversive, the spectacular nostalgia of the camp *Spartacus* looks toward a transformed future in smaller, more portable ways. The dissensual powers of art are not narrated but figured in a queer friction of resistance and accommodation. In such a context, proclaiming "I'm Spartacus" allegorizes not only a call for solidarity among dissidents in dangerous times: It points as well toward camp strategies of artfulness and artifice that never could be confused with the closet.

Although the excerpts from Moiseyev's *Spartak* failed to make an impact on U.S. dance critics during the Bolshoi's 1959 tour, the same could not be said for Jacobson's revamped production, which arrived in America in 1962 as part of the troupe's return engagement. This time U.S. critics were more attuned to the ballet, not only because of its appearance in the wake of Kubrick's blockbuster but also because the company eschewed the piecemeal highlights approach and mounted a full-bore Spartacus campaign. Like Lavrovsky's *Romeo and Juliet* three years earlier, Jacobson's revised *Spartak* was the showpiece of the tour, an evening-length production meant to impress U.S. audiences with the latest and best in Soviet ballet. To say that the ballet was failure would be an understatement. Terry was probably the kindest of the U.S. critics. His twenty-six column inches gleefully enumerated *Spartak*'s outsized production values: "more than two hundred performers, . . . a golden sedan sofa borne by husky servants, . . . a massed run of bearers of flaming torches, . . . opulent couches and thrones; weapons that range from short swords to javelins, tridents and shining shields and helmets; golden bowls to set our lovely blonde slaves a-staggering through halls dedicated to debauchery." Punctuating these descriptions was his verdict: "a really dreadful piece of choreography" ("DeMille Out-DeMilled" 1).

As a means of indicating the importance of *Spartak* to not only Soviet ballet but Soviet culture in general, the Bolshoi's advance publicity materials had made a point of mentioning the work's production history and its two earlier versions. This proved to be a serious mistake. Although the publicists meant to make this third production of *Spartak* look like a victory of Soviet dialectical aesthetics, one that had successfully synthesized the merits of its less-balanced predecessors, news of its vexed history led U.S. critics to conclude that enthusiasm for the work lay not with the artists but with the state. Both *Dance Magazine*'s Doris Hering and the *Times*'s John Martin likened *Spartak* to a doomed Broadway show. "*Spartacus* has a history not unlike that of a giant . . . musical that is subjected to constant tweaking on the road in heroic efforts to save the backers' investments and the reputations of authors, composers, and producers," Martin wrote ("About 'Spartacus'" 20X). Hering echoed, "the Bolshoi version of *Spartacus* was like a Broadway show that has been play-doctored to within an inch of its life during the out-of-town tryouts" ("And Still, the Chasm" 30).

However chastening this response may have been, the Soviets refused to give up on *Spartak,* and in 1968 the fourth revision assignment was handed to Yuri Grigorovich, who had become director of the Bolshoi in 1964 after a three-year term as ballet master at the Kirov. Grigorovich had come to the attention of Soviet cultural authorities in 1957 when he choreographed *The Stone Flower,* a ballet to a score by Prokofiev that struck the Soviets as thrillingly modern but failed to impress U.S. critics during the Bolshoi's 1959 tour. Compared to the work being done in the U.S. at the time by choreographers like Balanchine and Merce Cunningham, it is true that Grigorovich's choreography, with its reliance on traditional classroom passage work, is best described as "modernistic" rather than modern. Still, Grigorovich did have some understanding of the modern notion of dance as developed by Balanchine and Cunningham, one emphasizing clear lines (the dancer's figures) over mimed, linear storytelling, and though he could not abandon story, his work in crafting a new book for his *Spartak* did involve radical narrative reduction. He restructured the ballet as a performance for four soloists with corps, an approach that critic Luke Jennings calls "the four-sided construction favored by Grigorovich—good man, good woman; evil man, evil woman" (Jennings 76). Spartacus and his faithful Phrygia would be placed in opposition to Crassus and his scheming consort Aegina, a revision demanding a total transformation of the role of Crassus. In past productions the part had been "hardly danceable" or "played by an extra," a choreographic decision that sharpened the ballet's didactic point by placing the freely moving, freedom-loving Spartacus in opposition to an immovable, tyrannical Crassus (Yuzefovich 227). By contrast, Grigorovich saw the relationship between Spartacus and Crassus as not only an opportunity for political moralizing but also the emotional heart of the ballet. The cuts he proposed all aimed to focus attention on the relationship between these two men—a vision departing significantly not only from the previous choreographers' but also the composer's.

> The most difficult stage of the work . . . [was convincing] Aram Ilych that my ideas were correct and thereby win his support. The "battle for the notes," as we jokingly called it, was about to start. Every request to cut something caused bewilderment, a raising of eyebrows, and a hurt expression; then he would slowly start pulling at his suspenders—a sign of extreme annoyance. Funny misunderstandings occurred. When I showed Khachaturian the dance of the mutinous slaves and explained the place of the dance in the ballet, he asked, "But where are the women?" I explained that these were gladiators, slaves who had revolted. He thought a few seconds and again asked, "Yes, but where are the women?" (Yuzefovich 226)

More than a "funny misunderstanding," Khachaturian's question points to the source of the remarkable effectiveness of Grigorovich's production, which received tremendous international acclaim precisely because of its queer reversal of the usual figure-narrative relationship endemic to Soviet-style spectacle. Rather than being about the power and beauty of the Spartacus rebellion as precursor of the Bolshevik revolution, *Spartak* was about the power and beauty of the male figure. Offering "some of the most explosive choreography ever written for the male dancer," Grigorovich's ballet effects a radical revision of the convention of the single leading couple, redistributing the erotic tension that drives traditional nineteenth-century narrative ballet over two couples—or, to be more accurate, reinvesting it in two men, for, as Khachaturian correctly perceived, the women of Grigorovich's *Spartak* would never be taken for major figures in the ballet (Craine and Mackrell 216). His decision to make the male figure the center of *Spartak* is what most startled audiences both in the Soviet Union and in the West, what most accounts for the ballet's international acclaim, and what remains most modern about the work. With *Spartak,* Russian ballet finally abjured the Victorian sensibility that had sent its nascent dance modernism into exile (an exile that began with Nijinsky's dismissal from the Maryinsky for wearing an "indecent" costume in *Giselle).* It also registered the Soviet effort to create a ballet art that would, like the nation itself, make a unique claim on the modern that could not be confused with the Western, Balanchinian, "ballet is woman" aesthetic.

Moreover, Grigorovich's *Spartak* queered the Stalinist narrative of Spartacus, offering a new stage theory of human progress that seemed to both guarantee and subvert the authority and power of the Soviet state. Roman tyranny is matched by Roman vigor and glamour; in the climactic confrontation between Spartacus and Crassus, Spartacus chooses, inexplicably, to spare the Roman's life. Most striking are the bleak final moments of the work, which, by emphasizing the death of Spartacus and the grief of Phrygia (who has no children nor any prospect of them), refuse a consolatory gesture toward future freedom—a daring move, given the Soviet insistence on uplifting conclusions that, most famously, resulted in a happy ending for *Swan Lake.* By skirting still-influential Zhdanovian notions of proper communist art, Grigorovich produced a work that simultaneously acceded to and critiqued the artistic demands of the party. "Although impeccably Soviet on the surface, [the allegory in *Spartak*] worked both ways: was it the brave Thracians or the fascistic Roman legions who represented the Soviet state?" (Jennings 76).

Grigorovich's elevation of the male figure emerged within a Soviet Union of criminalized homosexuality and institutionalized sexual priggishness—conditions not all that different from those in the United States at the time, though by 1968 the Stonewall riots were only a year away. (Today, while much work remains to be done in the United States, homosexuals continue to be a persecuted minority in Russia.) In 1934 Maxim Gorky heralded article 121 of the new Soviet criminal code, which made sodomy an offense punishable by up to five years in prison, as "a triumph of proletarian humanism." Two years later Nikolai Krylenko, who held the position of people's commissar for justice, "announced that homosexuality was a product of the decadence of the exploiting classes; in a socialist society based on healthy principles, such people . . . would have no place" (Kon and Riordan 92).[44] Homosexuals were not liquidated as a consequence of this view, but they did become a particular interest of the state.

While Soviet homosexual repression should be understood as the deep narrative background to the moving figures of Grigorovich's *Spartak*, more general political and social events had roles to play, as well. Grigorovich's ballet appeared as the relative openness in Soviet cultural expression (the brief "thaw" ushered in by the death of Stalin) had almost completed its rapid contraction. Khrushchev's secret speech had near-immediate political and cultural consequences, most notably the October 1956 Hungarian uprising and the pressures that culminated in the building of the Berlin wall, and the reactionary narrowing of expressive freedom was well underway by 1963, when Khrushchev laid down his terms for proper Soviet cultural production. In tones reminiscent of Zhdanov's, he derided "the nauseating concoctions" of the sculptor Ernst Neizvestny, one of those "representatives of the world of art [who] . . . depict reality according to their own biased and distorted subjective impressions" ("Khrushchev on Culture" 9).[45] He attacked a film currently in production at Gorky Studios, Sergei Gerasimov's *Ilyich Zastava,* for its portrayal of confused youth that failed to properly condemn such "idlers and parasites" (11). Most importantly, he revisited and revised his earlier condemnation of Stalin, shifting much of the blame for the terror to Lavrenty Beria and issuing an explicit warning to artists who might wish to deal with this history in their work:

> The years of the personality cult indeed had grievous consequences. Our party told the people the whole truth about that. At the same time one must bear in mind and remember that those years were not a period of stagnation in the development of Soviet society, as our foes imagine. . . .
>
> That is why we say that writers who assess that particular stage in the life of our country from an extreme and one-sided angle, trying to make out that nearly everything was gloomy, and to paint everything in dark colours, are wrong. . . . After all is said and done, not everything in that particular period was bad; in that period of socialist construction too, the people showed heroism and for that reason we cannot blacken everything. (13)

Khrushchev's speech on culture appeared one year after he had allowed the publication of Aleksandr Solzhenitsyn's *One Day in the Life of Ivan*

Denisovich and one year before he was forced out of office and replaced by Leonid Brezhnev. While the unexpected and unwanted consequences of the thaw within the cultural life of the Soviet Union and its client states were not primary factors in his loss of power (the Cuban missile crisis, a failed agricultural policy, and difficulties with China were more important), his effort to reassert state power over artistic production signaled that Soviet authorities had come to see their loss of control over public discourse as unacceptable.

Awareness of this double history of sexual and cultural censorship fortifies a sense of Grigorovich's *Spartak* as a kind of queer critique, coded, like camp, to work both within and against the political and social background of the artwork. *Spartak* premiered on April 9, 1968; four months later Warsaw Pact tanks rolled into Prague, and the thaw was officially over. The ballet went on to win extravagant critical praise both at home and abroad, in part because its elevation of moving figure over narrative ground anticipated what might be called the politics of the figure that came to replace the grand, totalizing narratives of freedom that had collapsed in the movements of 1968.[46] What has been alternately praised and derided as identity politics—black power, feminism, gay liberation—can be understood as a move from a politics bent toward universal yet uniform freedom in some as-yet-unrealized utopian future to an idiosyncratic politics of Freedom Now. This was a sense of a freedom in and for the individual body, a freedom that, partly under pressure of an international arms race that seemed to preclude *any* future, let alone a better one, effects a transvaluation so that the ability of the figure to move both within and against the larger social narrative appears more attainable than any dreamed-for unity of individual and collective. Rather than symbolize the dedication to freedom in the long run by way of a teleological narrative of ultimate victory, Spartacus had come to figure something like a cultural expression of the Keynesian dictum that underwrote much of the cold war economic landscape: "In the long run, we're all dead."[47]

David Tuller has explained how minority sexual practices exercised in the face of ferocious Soviet opposition came to be seen as expressive of personal freedom precisely because they abjured the state's demanded contribution to the future utopia. "Soviet leaders valued the reproductive function as the source of new workers and soldiers, but they considered sexual passion a dangerous distraction from the only legitimate public or private goal: building a Communist future." The state's "unrelenting hostility toward same-sex love" derived from the belief that such passion "produced no offspring and so offered no revolutionary advantages" (3–4).[48] Yet far from crumbling away in the face of such implacable opposition, gay and lesbian life in Russia flourished by "slipping with cunning and wit from chamber to chamber, from mask to mask, from role to role" (275). Thus sex becomes linked to freedom (as the Russian heterosexual author Leonid Zhokhovitsky put it in an interview with

Tuller, sex *is* freedom), and thus the struggle for sexual freedom—freedom from the reproductive mandate, freedom from a heterosexual narrative of endless deferral toward the future—comes to stand, like Spartacus himself, as a symbol of the struggle for freedom as such.[49]

Given that my readings of *Spartacus* and *Spartak* have thus far explored a shared tension between linear, ideologically purposeful narratives and wily, artful, moving figures, one might be tempted to conclude that Kubrick's film and Grigorovich's ballet are in essence saying the same things about the political connections linking sex, art, and freedom. *Spartacus* and *Spartak* can both be seen as failed efforts to bind figure to narrative in the service of a particular ideological function (a view that, in the context of my larger argument about the relationship between art and politics during the cold war, makes them critically important failures), yet they do not employ the same *rhetorical* figure. Kubrick's film posits Spartacus as a metaphor of the struggle for freedom, while Grigorovich's ballet casts him as its metonym. Each figure in part arises in response to its cultural background. In the United States, a post-McCarthy embrace of resistant reconciliation (imaged in the last shot of the film) posits freedom as always pending outside the frame: Spartacus *is* the figure of longing for an ever-elusive freedom. In the Soviet Union, a post-Stalin, late-thaw reversal of the Luxembourgian transvaluation of defeat as victory casts the success of revolution for the state as the loss of freedom for the individual: here, Spartacus figures as one episode in a never-ending struggle. Insofar as it critically engages its background, however, each figure bears within itself the trace of its negation. Recognizing how Kubrick's film and Grigorovich's ballet reveal the same narrative as it splits into two distinct figures leads us to perceive that art's potent relationship to the political derives in no small degree from the protean nature of its figures.

As spectacle, the cold war Spartacus articulates a longing for freedom that uses the future perfect (it shall be so) to express grief for a vanished, no less imaginary past (it had been thus). There is no way to articulate such nostalgia for the future as a grammatically coherent narrative. It emerges only in figural flashes as history disintegrates into projections of longing. And so we arrive, in 1970, at the first edition of the *Spartacus International Gay Guide,* a vacation travel manual for gay men that, in pragmatic fashion, articulates the generative paradox of Spartacus as a revolutionary who urges flight from Italy as the most effective blow against the power of Rome. Published annually every year since, the guide casts a political aspect over gay recreation. The usual recommendations for hotels, restaurants, museums, beaches, and nightclubs are accompanied by careful analyses of the legal and social aspects of gay life in the proposed destination, analyses that frequently shade into pointed political commentary. Thus, for example, the guide's 2001–2002 discussion of vacation spots in the United States sarcastically observes that "it is true to say that the USA is known for its diversity" before launching into an analysis of the country's inconsistent hodge-podge of legislation pertaining to homosexuality. The guide includes a color-coded map identifying states in which "sodomy laws . . . apply to heterosexuals and homosexuals," those in which "sodomy laws . . . apply only to homosexuals," and "states where sodomy laws have been repealed through legislation or litigation." Here, *diversity* becomes another word for a legal incoherence that perpetuates injustice (Bedford 1131). In the *Spartacus International Guide,* the cold war's third (and arguably longest-lasting and most successful) Spartacus articulation, we see the ultimate consequences of this ancient narrative of failed rebellion for cold war art and politics. Catalyzed by the queer dissent of Kubrick's film and Grigorovich's ballet, Spartacus emerges as an avatar of gay liberation. Thus, the political merges into the personal; thus, dissent is rendered sensible; thus, the struggle continues.

7

From Art As Diplomacy to Diplomacy As Art

The Red Detachment of *Nixon in China*

At a preview performance a few months before the official unveiling of his first opera, John Adams joked that *Nixon in China* was "for Republicans and Communists" (Steinberg 115). He had a point: for a work with so much baldly political content, the precise nature of the opera's politics—in other words, its attitude toward that content—has proved elusive. The 1987 Houston Grand Opera world premiere left reviewers struggling to come to terms with what Alex Ross has called *Nixon in China*'s "studied ambiguity" (586). Some finessed the challenge by laying the entire enterprise at the feet of director Peter Sellars, a 1983 MacArthur Fellow with an established reputation for producing highly imaginative, seemingly parodic productions of classical operatic and theatrical works.[1] In 1987 Sellars was just coming off of a rocky two-year tenure as director of the Kennedy Center's American National Theater. The brilliant, astonishing stagings of the Mozart-Da Ponte operas that would win international acclaim were still a couple of years away, so his public profile at the time of *Nixon in China* was very much that of the *enfant terrible*, drawing the usual expressions of sober critical concern about lasting impact and seriousness of purpose. Reviewing the opera for the *New York Times*, senior classical music critic Donal Henahan leaped at the ready-made bait. Describing Sellars's work as "voguish and sometimes roguish" and flaunting his disdain for minimalist composition, Henahan slammed *Nixon in China* as a "visually striking but coy and insubstantial work . . . a Peter Sellars variety show, worth a few giggles but hardly a strong candidate for the standard repertory." A "serio-comic" bit of "campy fun," the opera certainly had nothing so substantial as a politics. Rather, *Nixon in China* was a "gentle put-on, a fantasy on the theme of Mr. Nixon's trip." Alice Goodman's libretto was little more than a "good-natured skit"; Adams's score amounted to "fluff" that "redefine[s] the concept of boredom" ("Opera: 'Nixon in China'").

Not all reviews were so dismissive. Just two months later, John Rockwell, also of the *Times,* took the occasion of the opera's restaging at the Brooklyn Academy of Music to proclaim it as "a stirring creation, full of . . . wit [and] . . . likely to last" ("Opera: 'Nixon in China'"). But even critics who admire *Nixon in China* are perplexed by what seems to be a deliberately casual approach to its enormously consequential subject. This approach is marked by intimate yet weirdly elliptical characterizations couched in a musical idiom whose promiscuous stylistic shifts make hash of the usual formal distinctions between art music and popular music. Daunted by the prospect of finding a stable political vantage point in such a shifting landscape, many reviewers who are favorably disposed toward the work have fallen in with Henahan's view of the opera as a genial sendup of the event even as they have striven to clarify that this in itself is no bad thing. Often invoked as Exhibit A in support of this judgment is the second act treatment of the command performance of the ballet *The Red Detachment of Women*, an apotheosis of Cultural Revolution earnestness that is both honored and skewered in the collaborators' fragmented, intertextually complex paraphrase, which has Richard and Pat Nixon inserting themselves into the dance and assigns the role of the evil landlord's "factotum" to the singer performing the part of Henry Kissinger (Adams and Goodman 206).[2]

The critical discourse surrounding the Metropolitan Opera's 2011 production of *Nixon in China* reveals how little key attitudes about the work have changed, even though the opera has gone on to enjoy an unexpectedly warm public reception. *Nixon* came to the Met by way of productions in Denver, Saint Louis, Chicago, London, Paris, Amsterdam, Bielefeld, and Edinburgh. The bravura coloratura aria "I Am the Wife of Mao Tse Tung" has become a staple of the audition circuit, and there are three recordings of "The Chairman Dances," an orchestral work that Adams describes as an outtake from the opera. *Nixon in China* itself has been recorded twice.[3] Clearly, Henahan's judgment fell wide of the mark: rarely has a contemporary composition passed into the repertory as rapidly or successfully. Yet even though the opera establishment's embrace of the work might seem to signal a consensus about not only its artistic merit but also its politics, *Nixon*'s take on political history continues to disturb, as indicated by the raft of contextualizing material in the Met's 2011 program notes and the reactions of the New York press.

Unquestionably, the best evidence of the opera's ongoing ability to stir up anxiety was Max Frankel's 2,000-word diatribe in the *Times.* A former executive editor of the paper, he had won a Pulitzer Prize for his coverage of Nixon's 1972 visit to China and felt compelled to correct what he saw as the opera's excessively blithe relationship to historical fact. Taking his cue from Met publicity materials that likened *Nixon* to other operas representing historical events, such as Verdi's *Don Carlo* and Mussorgsky's *Boris Godunov,* Frankel acknowledged that art and history can mix. But this can happen only, he insists, after a respectful number of years has passed, when a full appreciation of the historical event's meaning and significance has taken shape and properly ripened: "*Nixon in China* persuades me to take my stand with Shakespeare, who chose a century as the minimal safe distance between actual events and his iambic-speaking kings." Nevertheless, Frankel takes only the briefest pause before launching into a detailed discussion of how, given the chance, he would have chosen to handle an operatic treatment of Nixon's already highly-staged visit to China—a discussion that somewhat bizarrely concludes with the observation that this particular event lies beyond the capacities of art. "Yes, the Nixon trip was essentially just a piece of theater, but my out-of-sight interviews and ventures that week left me with a decidedly deeper drama than the Met's reproduction" ("A Witness Sees History Restaged and Rewritten").

Its journalistic hubris duly noted and set aside, Frankel's article remains instructive for the clarity with which it presents the fundamental interpretive error that has informed nearly every reading of *Nixon in China* since its premiere: the assumption that, in taking a key cold war event as its subject, the opera means to interpret that event as a historian would, showing how present conditions were shaped by past events and rendering a judgment on the political systems represented by the major players. In such a view, fidelity to the event is paramount. Because the historian aims to produce interpretations that are both influential and correct, accuracy in detail is a fundamental value. Even as they beetle over its narrative, however, issues such as the *realpolitik* of Chinese-American détente and Nixon's approach to diplomacy in the television age are not the central focus of *Nixon in China*'s historical vision. Rather, the opera's key interpretive investments are to be found in its subtle yet pointed interrogations of the era's ideologically-driven view of art as an instrument of political manipulation itself easily manipulable, a view informing both programs of cultural diplomacy and calls for cultural revolution. Adams was right: *Nixon in China* is indeed an opera for Republicans and communists, given that its central task is to highlight both parties' decades of effort to determine and delimit the range and political effects of art. Thus, I focus here not on the opera's fidelity to events or its characterizations of the Nixons, Henry Kissinger, Mao Zedong, Zhou Enlai, or Jiang Qing (Madame Mao) but on the setting, at the very heart of the work, of a signal moment in the history of cold war cultural diplomacy: that command performance before the Nixons and their entourage of *The Red Detachment of Women,* one of the most important works of state-sponsored art to appear during the cold war.

Itself a work claiming to represent history, *The Red Detachment of Women* first entered China's cultural landscape in 1961 as a film bent on honoring the Special Company of the Red Army's Second Independent Division, an all-women corps, which lost its 1931 engagement with nationalist forces on Hainan Island but whose early service to the revolution was later recalled and praised by Mao himself. The film presents that history through the experiences of the fictional Wu Qinghua, a peasant girl who joins the women's brigade after escaping her vicious landlord, Nan Batian. Over the course of the movie, the vengeful and impetuous Qinghua slowly becomes conscious of the crucial role that party discipline must play in bringing about the desired overthrow of Batian and the Guomindang. Under the patient tutelage of party secretary Hong Changqing, she advances so far in her thinking that she is able to step into Changqing's role as the ideological leader of the women's detachment after he is murdered by nationalist forces.

The Red Detachment of Women was an extremely popular film, so much so that, in 1964, work began on a ballet adaptation of the narrative. In May 1967, that ballet was named one of the eight *yangbanxi* (model performances) approved for presentation during the Cultural Revolution. An operatic adaptation of the same story was undertaken in 1972, evidence of not only the narrative's continuing appeal but also, as Paul Clark has observed, "the paucity of subject matter deemed reliable as politics and entertainment during those years" (68). By then the original 1961 film had been banned for failing to meet the party's formally established requirement that all cultural productions employ the "three prominences": "'Among all characters, give prominence to the positive characters; among the positive characters, give prominence to the main heroic characters; and among the heroes, give prominence to the central character'" (46). Because it had adopted the point of view and experiences of the imperfect Qinghua, the movie had failed to properly highlight the heroism of party secretary Changqing. The ballet sought to correct this error by emphasizing how the secretary's spectacular Joan of Arc–style execution (he is tied to a tree and burned alive, strains of the "Internationale" in the score emphasizing his political martyrdom) points the way toward eventual revolutionary victory (68).

There was more at stake in adapting *The Red Detachment of Women* from screen to stage than political correction of its narrative, however. Inspired by their subject and under tremendous pressure from Jiang Qing, the choreographers and dancers of Beijing's Central Ballet Company understood their task to be nothing less than the creation of an entirely new, uniquely Chinese approach to ballet. An art form with an extremely low cultural profile in

China, ballet had been deemed an ideal vehicle for Cultural Revolution, the perfect medium for demonstrating Red China's special capacity to appropriate and transform artifacts of Western modernity into avatars of collectivist utopia. Academies run by émigré dancers in Beijing and Shanghai had introduced ballet to China in the 1930s. (Among them was George Gonchorov's school, where Margot Fonteyn trained during the eight years her family lived in Shanghai.) But it was only when Soviet companies toured the country after 1949 as part of a larger program of Chinese-Soviet cultural diplomacy that ballet came to the attention of Chinese cultural authorities. Ten years later, the Central Ballet Company was founded in Beijing.

On the eve of the Cultural Revolution, ballet's reach remained limited, hardly extending beyond Beijing and Shanghai—a circumstance that actually worked in the art form's favor when Jiang Qing and her supporters sought to foster cultural productions with both nationalistic and ideological appeal. In their eyes ballet presented the perfect opportunity for a "modernizing and internationalizing ambition of cultural practice in the Cultural Revolution" (Clark 158). The chosen approach blended classical movement with martial arts gestures and ethnic dance patterns. Abjuring tutus and finely articulated *ports de bras* in favor of Chinese "pyjamas," military uniforms, and fists clenched in righteous determination, *The Red Detachment of Women* answered Mao's call for works of "revolutionary realism and revolutionary romanticism" that would direct popular cultural discourse into channels at once vernacular, internationalist, and politically correct (13). To this day, it remains a beloved work, as much for the fidelity with which it captures a particular historical articulation of Chinese cultural ambition as for its political message.[4]

A success with both audiences and government officials, the dance version of *Red Detachment* became the subject of a second cinematic treatment; the 1971 release and ensuing broad distribution of that film made the ballet one of the major cultural phenomena of the era.[5] It is no surprise that the work was chosen as the featured entertainment during Nixon's visit to China, for by 1972 *Red Detachment* was viewed as a masterpiece of the Cultural Revolution, perfectly blending Chinese and European theatrical traditions, nationalist fervor, and ideological rectitude into a subject of international fascination. Although Julia Kristeva's effort to read the import for Chinese feminism of the move from foot binding to *pointe* work was not entirely successful, there was no denying the appeal of the cover art of *About Chinese Women:* a photograph of the brave Wu Qinghua, *en pointe* in a bold arabesque, right fist clenched, left hand defiantly raising a red-flagged automatic pistol, gazing fearlessly forward into the future.[6]

According to Clark, Cultural Revolution efforts to create a uniquely Chinese and unquestionably communist art that would maintain the ferment of revolutionary politics, far from guaranteeing economic and political purity, actually laid the foundations for the decidedly capitalist forms and modes of cultural production and experience of today's China.[7] It is an unquestionably valid observation, one anticipated over twenty years ago by the treatment *The Red Detachment of Women* receives within *Nixon in China*. Something like a time-lapse presentation of key moments from the ballet (the whipping of Qinghua by Batian's minions; her rescue by Changqing and the refreshing of her spirit through a symbolic offering of a drink; Changqing's undercover reconnaissance of Batian's household; Qinghua's ideological errors on the road to class consciousness), the scene collapses two temporalities of *Red Detachment*'s production history: its creation at the command of Jiang Qing and its persistence through the state-directed turn to a market economy ushered in by Deng Xiaoping. As reconstituted by *Nixon*'s collaborators, the ballet is the scene of a double redemption: first of Wu Qinghua from a gruesome existence as the slave of Batian and then of the Chinese people from the equally horrifying excesses of the Cultural Revolution. This doubling is accomplished by the insertion of key political actors from the audience into the action of the ballet—not only the Nixons and Kissinger but Jiang Qing as well.

According to choreographer Mark Morris, *The Red Detachment of Women* "was always meant to be represented" in *Nixon in China*, and the four collaborators decided together "on the balance of the ballet within the context of the opera." Invited into the production "very early on," Morris brought to the task his memory of seeing *Red Detachment* in a television broadcast as a teenager. "In choreographing a paraphrase of that ballet," he recollected, "I purposely did not re-watch the ballet. I constructed the dance exclusively from my own recollection of my single viewing," which had left him "enraptured and inspired" (personal communication). That Morris's paraphrase manages to seem so faithful to the original without at any point directly quoting it testifies to the startling impact of *The Red Detachment of Women*'s adaptation of ballet's nineteenth-century form to mid-twentieth-century revolutionary content. The clenched fists, synchronously brandished rifles, and stage-devouring leaps serve less to point out new paths for ballet's development than to illuminate ballet's formal unconscious, its kinship with military discipline and militarized modes of expression usually kept well below the surface of the dance.

Morris may not have rewatched *Red Detachment,* but Goodman's libretto makes clear that at least one of the collaborators had carefully studied the work. Here we find the directions indicating when and how the Nixons, Henry Kissinger, and Jiang Qing should insert themselves into the ballet. Kissinger appears first in the guise of Lao Szu, "the landlord's factotum," a sexually aggressive sleaze who paws the imprisoned Qinghua and orders his "mercenaries" to "whip her to death" when she is recaptured after her escape (Adams and Goodman 206, 215). Pat Nixon enters next, leaping to the aid of the insensible

Qinghua ("They can't do that!"), followed by her confused husband ("It's just a play!") (215). In a gesture that repeats and revises a famous moment in the ballet, Pat hands party secretary Changqing the drink that revives Qinghua.[8] When Changqing, disguised as a merchant, enters Batian's mansion on his spying mission, he is accompanied by Nixon, who seems eager to become better acquainted with the intrepid party secretary (234). Minutes later, Jiang Qing rises from the audience to scold the dancer playing Qinghua, and the action of the ballet proper comes to an abrupt halt. The second act of *Nixon in China* concludes with the spectacular aria "I Am the Wife of Mao Tse Tung," sung by Jiang Qing over a Red Guard–incited riot. As the curtain falls on the mayhem, Zhou Enlai glares at Jiang Qing in anger and dismay.

Created at almost the exact midpoint of Deng's campaign to invent a market-friendly "socialism with Chinese characteristics," *Nixon in China*'s reimagining of *The Red Detachment of Women* tracks the ballet's political fortunes through the roles assigned to its interlopers. Kissinger and Jiang Qing signify the work's origins in the Cultural Revolution: Kissinger is called on to play the capitalist lackey that the revolutionary Red Guard undoubtedly said he was, while Jiang Qing performs her role as chief censor and executive director of the command cultural economy. Dick and Pat Nixon are the well-meaning, maybe-not-so-horrible-after-all American capitalists of the Deng era. Drawing these agents into the ballet's action highlights not only how the political valence of even an artwork built to serve a particular ideology may shift. It also illustrates art's power to make us forget where—and who—we are, a power related to art's capacity for sounding multiple frequencies at once. Thus the "studied ambiguity" of *Nixon in China* is not an effect of a reluctance to declare its political allegiance but rather of its dispassionate, metapolitical investigation into art's own ambiguous relationship to party politics. As both Richard Nixon and Jiang Qing were to learn, there is only so much that can be reliably stage managed.

In truth, the most profoundly troubling aspect of *Nixon in China* is less its "studied ambiguity" than its pointed questioning of the assumptions underlying the era's peculiar efforts to harness the political power of art. Appearing at the temporal margins of the cold war—two years before the fall of the Berlin Wall and the massacre at Tiananmen Square—*Nixon in China*, like Moore's "Combat Cultural," is a cold war work of art about the cold war use of art. As the opening salvoes of cultural combat were being fired, Moore's poem sounded the cautionary, skeptical note that *Nixon in China* picked up and amplified just before the curtain fell on an era that had begun in a thousand state-sponsored cultural blossomings. Those remarkable forced cultivations were fueled by a faith in the power of art to effect political change along predetermined ideological lines, only to be choked in the weedy entanglements of cultural revolution and culture war.

As Zhou Enlai observes in the opera's final aria, "Everything seems to move beyond our remedy." In an era when governments imagined art as a way of safeguarding their political futures even as they failed to deliver on their promises of healing a broken world, the metapolitics of the artworks themselves, more often than not, worked otherwise, quietly but persistently gesturing toward precisely that unrealized beyond. Furious exhortation or despairing judgment was not the point of those gestures. More often than not, their point was both more modest and more bold: to escape the cold, it's best to keep moving.

Notes

Preface

1. It was eventually published. See Kodat, "Dancing Through the Cold War."
2. I discuss this passage and Bourdieu's approach to the relationship between art and society in chapter 3.

Chapter 1 Combat Cultural

1. See Robinson, *The Last Impresario,* for a description of Hurok's persistence in arranging the Moiseyev tour (347–354). Soviet officials took strong exception to the stipulation in the 1952 Immigration and Naturalization Act (the McCarran-Walter Act) that Soviet visitors to the United States be fingerprinted. Hurok had secured Soviet approval for U.S. appearances of both the Moiseyev and the Bolshoi Ballet in 1956, but the tours were delayed until the fingerprinting requirement was abolished. The January 1958 bilateral exchange accord (the Lacy-Zarubin agreement) granted "unprecedented official status" to Hurok Attractions, Inc., by recognizing the impresario's right to work directly with the Soviet Union to arrange the Moiseyev appearances (Robinson 354). Prevots reports that ticket sales for the Moiseyev tour (which also included stops in Philadelphia, Chicago, Los Angeles, and San Francisco) topped 1.6 million dollars—almost 13 million dollars in 2013 terms (71).
2. The Moiseyev performance on *The Ed Sullivan Show* was broadcast on June 29, 1958, and repeated "by popular demand" on February 1, 1959 (tv.com; Prevots 73).
3. See Moore's May 4, 1958, letter describing the May 3 luncheon in Moran (766).
4. Moore rejected more than half of her published poetry in compiling her *Complete Poems* (Schulman xvii). For the earliest published version of "Combat Cultural," see *The New Yorker*, June 6, 1959. This was followed by the revision included in *O to Be a Dragon* (28–29) before the final version published in *Complete Poems* (199–200). Schulman republishes this version in her edited collection.
5. Gregory's "'Combat Cultural': Marianne Moore and the Mixed Brow" is the first analysis of the poem published since 1982 (208–221).
6. "Hometown Piece for Messrs. Alston and Reese" was written to celebrate the

Brooklyn Dodgers' 1956 World Series championship. Moore's first biographer calls it "close to doggerel" (Molesworth 392).

7. Nitchie misreads the poem's central image, describing it as "a wrestling dance involving either two identically garbed dancers or one dancer . . . wrestling with himself," even though "Two Boys in a Fight" concludes with its trick revealed (162). In seeing "Combat Cultural" as one of several poems treating opposition and integration, Hadas makes no mention of the event that occasioned it (70, 178–179). Phillips does anchor her reading in a discussion of the Moiseyev's 1958 Met season, though her description of the poem as "a *jeu d'esprit* on seeing and seeming" does not readily connect to her apologetic for its bluestocking "commentary on political issues" (216–219). Gregory's admirable essay grants the poem a certain seriousness of purpose. However, in describing it as one of a group of poems in which "high and low [-brow values] interpenetrate to create a thicker version of reality than either can provide alone," she, like Hadas, effaces its cold war aspect (212).
8. In one of the few negative reviews of the Moiseyev's 1958 visit, Sargeant calls the company's performance "the Russian equivalent of what goes on at the Radio City Music Hall . . . [with] something of the atmosphere of old-fashioned vaudeville" (82). Terry likewise comments on the troupe's tendency to play to the rafters ("The girls move with the precision of the Rockettes"), though he finds this admirable ("Dance: Russians Blaze").
9. Here I quote the final version of the poem as published in Schulman (317). Gregory's excellent discussion of Moore's interest in challenging "the view of the brows as a static binary of high vs. low (or static triad, when the middlebrow is included), and present[ing] them instead as a set of interactive cultural positions, which each individual may occupy serially or even simultaneously" is apposite here (214).
10. "Partisans," "City Quadrille," and "Two Boys in a Fight" were all included in *The Ed Sullivan Show* broadcast.
11. This particular post-Soviet program notes that the great success of "Two Boys in a Fight" during the company's 1958 season led to its being included in every subsequent U.S. tour. Moore's poem spells the name of the Samoyed people from whom the dance was allegedly drawn as "Nan-ai-ans." The current preferred English spelling of the name of this Siberian people is Nganasan.
12. "Two Boys in a Fight" can be seen in the Kultur International VHS recording of the Moiseyev's April 1994 appearance at Tokyo Bunka-Kaikan.
13. Hering praised the troupe's "exceptional rigor of technique" and "unremitting formality" (35). Shay's recent study makes clear how little Moiseyev's choreography has in common with actual folk dance. Since "Moiseyev used far fewer authentic elements than" has been claimed, "what the Moiseyev ensemble presents is not folk dance but ballet-based character dance in Moiseyev's unique stylization" (69–70).
14. Terry wrote, "Russian folk dance draws from many nationalities and many centuries of accomplishment. . . . The flashes of individual and group virtuosity . . . make Russian folk dances innately theatrical" ("Dance: Russians Blaze"). Martin observed, "The Russians are the dancingest people . . . in the world. . . . There are more than 180 different nationality groups in the Soviet Union, and from the evidence at least 179 of them must spend a liberal portion of their time dancing their heads off" ("The Dance: A la Moiseyev").

    Hirsch has described the dance section of the 1939 publication *Soviet Folk Art* as "a lucid metaphor" for a wider government-led effort to create an "ethnohistorical evolution" that would fuse the many ethnic, religious, and language groups of the Soviet Union into a single unified nation. While she does not describe this as an effort to privilege Russian folk dance above other traditions, her discussion of *Soviet Folk Art* notes passages in 1930s Soviet history textbooks that see "the transition from the Great Russian past to the Soviet Russian present" as indebted to "the Russian proletariat—the most 'progressive' part of the former 'oppressor' nation, the . . . heart of the new Soviet Russian nation, . . . first among equals" of the Soviet republics (268–270). As Shay notes, "neither Igor Moiseyev nor the government of the former Soviet Union was interested in [ethnic] verisimilitude. They wanted the spectacle of masses demonstrating support for an embodied representation of the Soviet system" (72). My thanks to Shoshana Keller for drawing my attention to Hirsch's study.

15. For the American reader, the history of the Nganasan after Russian contact invites comparison of the effects Soviet and U.S. policies of continental expansion and resource exploitation had on Arctic peoples. Parallels include disruption of seasonal migrations, ecological destruction, poverty, alcoholism, and increased infant mortality. See also Jones, *A Century of Servitude,* and Chance, *Arctic Circle.*
16. See her essay, "Anna Pavlova," published in the March 1944 issue of *Dance Index* and reprinted in *Complete Prose* (385–393).
17. In what appears to be the first draft of the poem that Moore showed to a reader, the comment "*I like this*; but if you think it better to leave out, OK" appears in the left margin of the first stanza. In the right margin, the entire stanza is bracketed and marked, "I don't have to keep this." On a later draft (one resembling the version of the poem published in *The New Yorker*), the first stanza is again bracketed and labeled "could be omitted" (Moore Collection).
18. For recent analyses of this program, see Osgood, *Total Cold War* (232–244) and Cull, *The Cold War and the United States Information Agency* (118–119, 172–173).
19. The "objective symbolic" of "Combat Cultural" is more than a little reminiscent of T. S. Eliot's "objective correlative": "a set of objects, a situation, a chain of events which shall be the formula" for producing emotion in a work of art (Kermode 48). It is reasonable to suppose that Moore expected her readers to make a connection between her term and Eliot's, but Eliot's concern is with inducing affect, Moore's with manifesting knowledge.
20. See Derrida, "Plato's Pharmacy," especially 75–94.
21. A rough draft dated February 19 and missing many of the final details of "Combat Cultural" concludes with this stanza:

    These battlers, dressed identically,
    (just one person) may by seeming twins,
    point a moral, I confess:
    you must cement the parts of any
    objective
    symbolic of *sagesse*.

    In the margin next to his stanza Moore wrote, "yes yes yes" (Moore Collection).
22. Typescript copy dated March 17, 1959 (Moore Collection). While not identified as such, this is almost certainly the typesetter's copy for *The New Yorker*.
23. However, see Miller ("Distrusting," 353–379), who makes a convincing case for Moore's 1943 "In Distrust of Merits" as a topical poem born of a "distrust both [of]

the public language of medal-giving and victories and . . . of righteous innocence" during World War II (372). Miller's reading makes it easy to detect in "Combat Cultural" a similarly distrustful view of the propagandistic powers ascribed to art in much cold war cultural diplomacy rhetoric.

24. See Fukuyama, *The End of History and the Last Man*. Broadcast in spring 1999, CNN's massive twenty-four-hour special *Cold War* is probably the most spectacular narrative of the period.
25. This review of Gaddis's *The Cold War* was first published in the *New York Review of Books* in March 2006 ("A Story Still to be Told"). The "one good woman" is Margaret Thatcher.
26. The writings of Koestler, Orwell, and Greene are exceptions that prove the rule. See, for example, Whitfield, *The Culture of the Cold War*. In *The Dancer Defects*, Caute ambitiously sets out to correct this cultural provincialism with a vast international catalogue of cold war productions in film, theater, dance, music, and the visual arts from the United States, the Soviet Union, France, Great Britain, West Germany, East Germany, Poland, and Czechoslovakia. Such a wide-bore approach, however, presents its own problems. See my review of Caute's study, "High Art in Low Times" (37–39).
27. See Guilbaut, *How New York Stole the Idea of Modern Art* and Rogin, "*Kiss Me Deadly*," republished as a chapter in *Ronald Reagan, the Movie* (236–271). Subsequent quotations are from this edition. I discuss the theoretical aspects of Guilbaut's study in chapter 3.

    The phrase "second cold war" describes the late 1970s–early 1980s return of "hard" cold war geopolitics (the Soviet invasion of Afghanistan and imposition of martial law in Poland, the American invasion of Grenada and covert funding of the Nicaraguan Contras) after the period of détente that had begun in the late 1960s. Westad's study significantly complicates the notion of détente underlying this phrase, showing that superpower political and military intervention in the affairs of nonaligned or developing nations (for example, Ethiopia, Chile, Angola, and Vietnam) was barely checked by nuclear nonproliferation agreements and pledges to promote peaceful international relations (SALT I, the Helsinki Accords) or improvements in U.S.-Soviet trade relations (increases in Soviet grain shipments to the United States, the Apollo-Soyuz test project).
28. See Jameson, *The Political Unconscious*.
29. See, for example, Schaub, *American Fiction in the Cold War*; Hixson, *Parting the Curtain;* Berghahn, *America and the Intellectual Cold Wars in Europe*; and several of the essays in Kuznick and Gilbert, eds., *Rethinking Cold War Culture*.
30. See Saunders, *The Cultural Cold War*; and Lasch, *The Agony of the American Left*. Some accounts of the history of the CIA's covert cultural and philanthropic funding credit the New Left magazine *Ramparts* with breaking the story. In April 1966 *Ramparts* published an article on CIA infiltration of the Vietnam Project at Michigan State University, an exposé that opened the door to more comprehensive New York *Times* coverage a month later. See Wilford, *The Mighty Wurlitzer* (237–240).
31. Perhaps not surprisingly, a fuller accounting of cold war culture begins to emerge when studies that are discipline- or medium-specific are read as discrete contributions to a larger narrative whole. Such studies include Prevots, *Dance for Export*; Craven, *Abstract Expressionism As Cultural Critique*; Nelson, *Pursuing Privacy in Cold War America*; and Von Eschen, *Satchmo Blows Up the World*.
32. Westad points out that the "new and rampant interventionism . . . after the Islamist attacks on America in September 2001" are less of "an aberration" than "a

continuation—in a slightly more extreme form—of U.S. policy during the Cold War. . . . The ideology of interventionism is the same, with the same overall aims: only by changing markets and changing minds on a global scale can the United States really be secure" (405).

33. Hofstadter's 1963 essay "The Paranoid Style in American Politics" is the classic historian's account of paranoid discourse in American politics, connecting its virulent mid–cold war manifestations (such as Goldwater's) to earlier varieties. For a strictly theoretical (almost resolutely anti-historicist) approach, see Sedgwick, "Paranoid Reading and Reparative Reading" (*Touching Feeling* 123–151). For a related, if differently inflected, theoretical approach, see Dean, "Art As Symptom." The phrase "hermeneutics of suspicion," now widely used to describe a certain prosecutorial style of cultural criticism, derives from Ricoeur's *Freud and Philosophy*, an analysis of a modern, secular "school of suspicion" rooted in the work of Marx, Nietzsche, and Freud. See also Gadamer, "The Hermeneutics of Suspicion." As both Ricoeur and Gadamer demonstrate, fundamental components of this mode of critique appeared well before the cold war, but the emergence of a definable school is a cold war phenomenon.
34. "Metapolitics is the discourse of the falseness of politics that splits every political manifestation of dispute, in order to prove its ignorance of its own truth by marking, every time, the gap between names and things, the gap between enunciation of some logos of the people, of man or of the citizenry and the account that is made of this, the gap that reveals a fundamental injustice, itself identical with a constitutive lie" (Rancière, *Disagreement* 82).

Chapter 2 History: From the WPA to the NEA (through the CIA)

1. For a comparative overview of government support of the arts, see the essays collected in Cummings and Katz, eds., *The Patron State.*
2. U.S. government arts patronage did not begin with Federal One, of course. Before the Depression, however, government support was limited to the commissioning of functional works with clearly patriotic or nationalist content (war memorials, monuments to dead statesmen, decorative paintings or murals in post offices and courthouses). Federal One set a precedent as the first government-funded program for the national creation and dissemination of autonomous artworks.
3. Saab sees Stieglitz in particular as "an important figure not only in introducing European modernism to New York audiences but also [in] applying these radical new styles in an American context" (6). Though she wrongly identifies the American Stieglitz as "German-born" (5), she is correct about the importance of European modernism to the formation of this desacralized American aesthetic.
4. Saab obliquely links the claims of Mumford and Dewey to Walter Benjamin's critical analysis of the "aura" of the artwork, first articulated in an essay drafted in Paris in the same year Federal One was established; see Benjamin, "The Work of Art in the Age of Mechanical Reproduction" (*Illuminations,* 217–251). However, the political point of her analysis depends on rooting this desacralizing impulse in uniquely American values. See Saab's brief discussion of the fetishization of the artworks' aura by nineteenth-century U.S. cultural elites and the accompanying footnote to Benjamin's essay (4, 187 n.17).
5. Szalay detects a similarly oppositional logic at work in New Deal efforts to reconcile art's double status as process and product: "Insofar as writers and artists did, invariably,

produce objects, the New Deal Arts Projects reasoned that the consumption of these objects should approach as closely as possible the conditions of their production. . . . Art would solve the problem of underconsumption by making consumption and production one and the same process, a temporally defined activity detached as much as possible from the determining equivocations of market demand" (6). For him this effort to align production and consumption so as to bypass commercial vagaries constitutes the politics of modern literature in the emergent welfare state.

6. For a discussion of the role theatrical art forms played in the settlement house movement, see Jackson, *Lines of Activity.*
7. See Wollaeger, *Modernism, Media, and Propaganda,* for a fascinating discussion of Orson Welles's unfinished feature-length Brazilian documentary, *It's All True,* commissioned by Rockefeller through RKO Pictures in 1941, shortly after he assumed leadership of the CIAA (221, 225, 245–251).
8. Henderson quotes from Creel, *How We Advertised America*. Scholars are unanimous on the importance of Creel and Bernays (who coined the phrase "the engineering of consent" to describe the work of public relations) in the rise of information services within modern U.S. diplomacy. See, for example, Osgood, *Total Cold War,* 19–25; Henderson, *The United States Information Agency,* 23–28; Cull, *The Cold War,* 6–9; Arndt, *The First Resort of Kings,* 27–36; and Wollaeger, *Modernism, Media, and Propaganda,* 7–8, 25, 263. A nephew of Freud, Bernays assiduously portrayed his techniques as applied psychoanalysis. He was a year old when his family moved to the United States from Vienna. In retrospect, his insistence on a close Freudian family connection has come to be seen as itself a clever bit of public relations work. See Tye, *The Father of Spin;* and Cutlip, *The Unseen Power.*
9. For an extended discussion of the American Ballet Caravan's South American tour, see West, "Todd Bolender with American Ballet Caravan."
10. The U.S. Information Agency (USIA) and the U.S. Information Service (USIS) sometimes appear to be interchangeable terms in public diplomacy scholarship. In brief, USIS refers to the overseas offices of information service housed within embassies, which sometimes included State Department staff. USIA designates the Washington agency officially charged with managing the international information service that, at its creation, was separate from State.
11. Faulkner also traveled to Paris in 1952 for the *Oeuvres du XXe Siècle* festival. While this was not a government-sponsored trip, his appearance had diplomatic overtones. Schwartz has claimed that Faulkner's rising reputation in the early years of the cold war was a function of an ideologically driven effort, jointly managed by government and cultural philanthropies such as the Ford and Rockefeller foundations, to promote "remote, complex, iconoclastic," and "inaccessible" modernist artwork that was seen as malleable to anti-communist political manipulation in ways that socially conscious 1930s realism resisted (5). In chapter 3, I discuss this claim in the context of Guilbaut's similar views of abstract expressionism.
12. For a comprehensive account of the Advancing American Art controversy, see Littleton and Sykes, *Advancing American Art.*
13. See Cull, 82–94, and Judt, *Postwar,* 224. Two excellent analyses of the political and aesthetic issues underlying the cold war revival of anti-communist anxiety about subversion in modernist visual art and literature are Mathews, "Art and Politics in Cold War America," and Filreis, *Counter-Revolution of the Word.*
14. Coined by Joseph S. Nye, assistant secretary of defense under Bill Clinton, *soft power* has become a catchall term for the range of initiatives previously described

as "public diplomacy," "cultural diplomacy," "citizen diplomacy," and "information service." The new term manages to be both more expansive (covering everything outside of direct military action) and more unilateral (exercises of power are not about dialogue or exchange). For recent discussions of this concept, see Nye, *Soft Power;* and Melissen, ed., *The New Public Diplomacy.*

15. Executive secretary to the MoMA board during the 1940s, Braden left the CIA in 1954 to become publisher of the Oceanside, California, *Blade-Tribune,* which he purchased with the help of a 100,000-dollar loan from Rockefeller. See McFadden, "Washington Columnist Got Rockefeller Loan to Buy Newspaper in California," 22.
16. See, for example, Saunders's description of the CIA's International Organization Division as "the nerve centre of America's secret cultural Cold War," a characterization that surely delighted Braden. Saunders's highly colored, stentorian style echoes Braden's, whom she interviewed extensively and whose voice is everywhere in her study, imparting a cloak-and-dagger dash to what, in less overwrought prose, would be tedious narratives of bureaucratic infighting. Though Caute takes issue with Saunders's work, he, too, seems rather enamored of Braden, going so far as to assert, inaccurately, that "in 1967 [he] was to blow the whistle on the CIA's cultural operations" (551). By contrast, Wilford entertains the possibility that Braden's 1967 *Saturday Evening Post* article was itself a CIA plant (following agency practice of ostentatiously dropping the cover of abandoned secret operations), though he does not completely discount the possibility that Braden's motives in publishing "I'm Glad the CIA is 'Immoral'" were sincere (244–248).
17. "Chronologically my work ends where Kozloff and Cockcroft begin, but conceptually I begin where they end" (Guilbaut 11). See Kozloff, "American Painting during the Cold War"; Cockcroft, "Abstract Expressionism, Weapon of the Cold War"; and Shapiro and Shapiro, "Abstract Expressionism."
18. Frascina describes the work of Kozloff, Cockcroft, the Shapiros, and Guilbaut as collectively articulating a single "revisionist thesis" (1–25).
19. See Kimmelman, "Revisiting the Revisionists"; Leja, *Reframing Abstract Expressionism;* Gibson, *Abstract Expressionism;* and especially Craven, *Abstract Expressionism As Cultural Critique.* For a recent reexamination of the politics of abstract expressionism, see Kuo, "Acting Out." See also Silliman, "AbEx and Disco Balls" for an inquiry into abstract expressionism's "gendered vicissitudes" and their connection to the sexual politics of the 1970s (321–325).
20. Ninkovich takes a middle path, adopting a similar view of the tactical value of secrecy—"open CIA financing would have automatically discredited such groups in the eyes of the rest of the world"—while granting Braden's claim that "Congress would probably have deemed many of the groups too liberal to merit public support" (18).
21. Braden's enthusiasm also ignores the international embarrassments that dogged CIA-sponsored programs no less than publicly funded government endeavors. These include Faulkner's drunken boorishness at the *Oeuvres du XXe Siècle* festival and Robert Lowell's psychotic break during a 1962 government-sponsored tour of South America. For a description of Faulkner's behavior, see Davenport-Hines, *Auden,* 280. For narratives of Lowell's collapse (which ended with his being removed from his Buenos Aires hotel in a straitjacket), see Hamilton, *Robert Lowell,* 299–303; and Mariani, *Lost Puritan,* 306–309.
22. "Incontestably, no one would devote himself to art without—as the bourgeois put it—getting something out of it; yet this is not true in the sense that a balance sheet

could be drawn up: 'heard the Ninth Symphony tonight, enjoyed myself so and so much,' even though such feeble-mindedness has by now established itself as common sense" (Adorno, *Aesthetic Theory,* 1997 13).

23. Pepsi was the official soft drink of the 1959 American National Exhibition in Sokolniki Park, Moscow, scene of the famous "kitchen debate" between Khrushchev and Nixon. See Hixson, *Parting the Curtain,* 194 and *passim.*
24. From a Department of State Airgram, December 17, 1964, signed by Cecil Sanford, American consulate general in Istanbul. It reported on the November 11–15, 1964, visit of Kirk Douglas under the State Department's American Specialists Program (which also sponsored Faulkner's tours in South America, the Far East, and Europe). The document is archived at U.S. Department of State/U.S. Information Agency, Bureau of Educational and Cultural Affairs, Special Collections Division, University of Arkansas, box 143, file 71. In future, I will cite materials from the archive as Cultural Affairs Collection, followed by box and file number.
25. Also noteworthy is Hafizullah Amin, fourth president of Afghanistan (and second president of its Communist Democratic Republic government), who became a Marxist while a graduate student at Columbia University (Westad 300).
26. Such events include the 1961 Middle and Far East tour of comedian Joey Adams, whose wife, Cindy Adams (in 2013, still a gossip columnist for the *New York Post*), published an irreverent diary of their travels that prompted dismayed members of Congress to question State officials about several of the department's internal protocols (Cultural Affairs Collection, box 47, file 6); Bill Evans's 1970 arrest at Kennedy Airport for heroin possession as he was about to depart for a State Department–sponsored appearance in Bucharest (box 57, file 20); and the 1976 publication of Thomas Gambino's *Nyet,* a memoir of his experiences as a staff musician with the Joffrey Ballet during its 1974 tour of the Soviet Union. The American Civil Liberties Union characterized State Department efforts to get Gambino to submit the manuscript to prepublication review as an attempt "to secure the right to censor . . . and sanitize the writings of American citizens" ("Musician Defying U.S. Rule on Official Tours Abroad" 2).
27. Internal embassy "progress reports" regularly described Graham's 1955 tour as a success, but, as Geduld writes, "reception was not clear-cut. . . . From Japan to Jakarta, local audiences misinterpreted fences, preachers, and frontiers in *Appalachian Spring* and found difficulties with the myth-based works" such as *Cave of the Heart* and *Night Journey.*

> In Japan, one reviewer interpreted the frontier narrative [of *Appalachian Spring*] as the Fall of Man. . . . A reporter from India wrote, "There must be something wrong with a gesture language that escapes one's grasp so totally. [*Appalachian Spring*] was like listening to an actor whose words cannot be heard in the stalls." Sexuality displayed by Graham in the classic Greek stories also presented problems. Writing that *Night Journey* "was [a] wrong conception to show the love-making between mother and son onstage," the Indian critic added that the work was a "jungle of movements that ought to be shunned"—a scathing blow. (64)

Another Indian reviewer wrote that the tour's arrangers should be "castigated" for booking Graham on the same evening as a performance of Indian dance. Despite this compelling evidence, Geduld concludes that the tour "served the State Department's foreign-policy objectives to repair international alliances and promote cultural convergences through high-art products" (71). This seemingly counterfactual interpretation illustrates the continuing force of the complicity thesis of modernist art in cold war cultural studies.

28. For analyses of jazz's cold war fortunes that are anchored in discussions of Conover's show, see Starr, *Red and Hot;* and Hixson, *Parting the Curtain,* 115–117.
29. For a fuller discussion of these concerns, see Kodat, "Conversing with Ourselves."
30. The Bolshoi arrived in New York two months after the February 1959 *Ed Sullivan Show* rebroadcast of the Moiseyev's appearance. *New York Times* music critic Harold C. Schonberg predicted that "the Bolshoi Ballet could well be the biggest box-office draw in the history of the entertainment business" (16). Indeed, every performance was sold out only days after tickets went on sale. To meet demand, the Bolshoi offered additional performances at Madison Square Garden after its Met season ended.
31. See Castle, *Billions Blunders and Baloney.*
32. Javits's article appeared a month before the publication of Moore's "Combat Cultural" in *The New Yorker* (see chapter 1).
33. Evidence of the importance of the cold war cultural front in the creation of the NEA/NEH is so substantial as to be virtually irrefutable, so I will not rehearse the details here. The two most comprehensive studies are Larson, *The Reluctant Patron;* and Binkiewicz, *Federalizing the Muse.* Together, they provide an excellent overview of the creation and early political fortunes of the NEA and the NEH, making clear that the emergence of a cultural front in the cold war was the key to conquering entrenched congressional hostility to government arts funding. Other important discussions include Taylor and Barresi, *The Arts at a New Frontier;* Biddle, *Our Government and the Arts;* Mark, *Reluctant Bureaucrats;* and Cummings, "To Change a Nation's Cultural Policy."
34. While he was on the staff of Senator Claiborne Pell, Biddle helped draft the legislation that led to the creation of the NEA. Deputy of the agency under its first chair, he became its chief during the Carter administration.
35. See Binkiewicz, *Federalizing the Muse,* for a description of the NEA's golden age during the Nixon years. Binkiewicz attributes the agency's steadily growing 1970s appropriations to Nixon's personal "desire to capture the issue of art funding from liberals . . . and to bolster his image as a leader and a benefactor" (223). However true this may be, those steadily increasing annual appropriations won congressional approval thanks to a growing bipartisan belief in the arts' contributions to détente. For "twigs for an eagle's nest," see Yeats, "To a Wealthy Man who promised a second Subscription to the Dublin Municipal Gallery if it were proved the People wanted Pictures," 107–108; and Straight, *Twigs for an Eagle's Nest.* Straight, who died in 2004, was deputy chair of the NEA from 1969 to 1978 but is probably best known for his work in journalism (he was publisher of *The New Republic* from 1945 to 1956) and espionage. After joining the Communist party while he was a student at Cambridge University in the 1930s, he became the sole American in the infamous Cambridge Spy Ring, whose members were recruited by art historian Anthony Blunt. See Straight, *After a Long Silence;* and Perry, *The Last of the Cold War Spies.*
36. In 1995, Congress cut the following year's NEA budget appropriation by 40 percent and eliminated most of the grant programs for individual artists. While budget allocations have since slowly risen and a few grants for individual writers, musicians, and folk artists do remain, most current funding is tied to programs in institutional stabilization, arts education, and community outreach.

37. In the aftermath of McCarthyism, the notion of the United States as a non- or post-ideological nation had considerable purchase during the cold war. For its classic articulation, see Bell, *The End of Ideology.*
38. Kennedy here alludes to the description, widely attributed to Stalin, of writers as "engineers of the human soul."
39. The exceptions are the Voice of America and the anti-Castro Radio/TV Martí, which continued under the specially created, semi-independent Broadcasting Board of Governors. In the wake of 9/11, Congress revived its interest in cultural diplomacy, and in October 2001, the Bush administration appointed advertising executive Charlotte Beers to the post of undersecretary of state for public diplomacy—testimony to the justice of Cull's and Arndt's diagnoses of a pervasive American inability to imagine cultural diplomacy as anything more than national advertising. See also Belmonte, *Selling the American Way,* especially 1–3, 178–185. In 2005, responding to widespread criticism that its efforts in cultural diplomacy were long on hype and short on substance, the State Department created the Rhythm Road, a deliberate effort to reproduce the jazz tours of the cold war. In early 2010, it followed up that initiative with DanceMotion USA, a program developed with the Brooklyn Academy of Music, for years a leader in U.S. dance programming. Three modern dance groups (presumably selected by the State Department in consultation with BAM) participated in the first year of the program. The San Francisco company ODC/Dance toured Thailand, Burma, and Indonesia; Evidence, a Brooklyn-based troupe, was sent to Senegal, South Africa, and Nigeria; and Urban Bush Women, also from Brooklyn, toured Venezuela, Colombia, and Brazil.
40. Contemporary evidence of the continuing importance of instrumentalist views of public arts patronage in the United States include efforts to create art zones to jumpstart urban commercial revitalization and appeals to the so-called "Mozart effect" as a rationale for arts education in the public schools.
41. O'Connor describes this text as "a revision and abridgment of the original report I submitted to the National Endowment in October 1968" (v). Slightly more than half of his recommendations urge the NEA to archive and preserve specific aspects of the WPA legacy. The first eight are much more comprehensive, outlining a plan for future action clearly rooted in the belief that art merits government support for its own sake: the NEA should (1) "give first priority . . . to the unknown and forgotten artist"; (2) adopt "as a basic criterion of support" an artist's "essential professional need irrespective of his present standing or acceptance in the art world or the style of his art"; (3) sponsor nonprofit galleries; (4) purchase works directly from artists and place them in public institutions; (5) avoid direct acquisition of work without providing for its proper disposition; (6) "establish extensive programs of grants, scholarships, and other awards to individual American artists"; (7) sponsor workshops giving artists "free access to the most advanced print shop, foundry, electronic, plastics and industrial equipment and technicians"; and (8) "sponsor a study of the cultural value of the visual arts with the purpose of promoting an increased understanding of those arts in our national life" (113–120).
42. Saunders adopts a similar view in her discussion of the CIA's covert cultural operations. This notion of abstract work as, by definition, non- or apolitical is indebted to Guilbaut's polemic against abstract expressionism (see chapter 3).
43. Something of this informs Steiner's *The Scandal of Pleasure.*
44. Income inequality began its rapid acceleration around 1981. See U.S. Census Bureau

data on income inequality, especially "A Brief Look at Postwar U.S. Income Inequality." According to that report, income inequality in the United States has been rising since 1968, when U.S. family income "was at its most equal" point since 1947. However, the pace picked up dramatically in the 1980s. Long noted by economists, the problem burst into public consciousness with the multiple Occupy movements of 2011–2012.

Chapter 3 Theory: Adorno and Rancière (Abstraction, Modernism, Gender, Sexuality)

1. "The core of the problem is that there is no criterion for establishing an appropriate correlation between the politics of aesthetics and the aesthetics of politics. This has nothing to do with the claim made by some people that art and politics should not be mixed. They intermix in any case; politics has its aesthetics, and aesthetics has its politics. But there is no formula for an appropriate correlation" (Rancière, *The Politics of Aesthetics,* 62).
2. See Morley and Chen, eds., *Stuart Hall,* for an excellent collection of essays assessing the various legacies of British cultural studies.
3. In their reviews of Jameson's *Late Marxism,* both Hullot-Kentor and Osborne take strong exception to Jameson's representation of Adorno's thought. For Hullot-Kentor, Jameson's engagements with Adorno are "uncomprehending" chiefly because "the idea of immanent criticism escapes Jameson" (*Things beyond Resemblance,* 223, 229). Osborne notes "an incompatibility between Jameson's method of reading and the philosophical position (namely, Adorno's) it is deployed to defend. . . . As a strategy for interpreting . . . it has something of the logic about it of burning the village to save it. If this is the price of Adorno's relevance to contemporary theory, irrelevance begins to seem the more critical option" (173, 177.)
4. As I mentioned in chapter 2, Von Eschen's study of the State Department's jazz tours represents an important departure from this view. Fosler-Lussier's "Cultural Diplomacy As Cultural Globalization" builds on Von Eschen's findings, though neither discusses the formal properties of the music itself. In visual art, Krenn's *Fall-Out Shelters for the Human Spirit* similarly tracks the lack of fit between government efforts to make art serve strategic cold war policy aims and the political goals of the artists who agreed to send their work abroad. Like Von Eschen and Fosler-Lussier, he offers little analysis of the art itself.
5. I specify *early* Bourdieu here, particularly *Distinction,* which has exerted tremendous influence among Anglo-American sociologists of culture. In my view, later work such as *The Rules of Art* offers a rethinking of some of the more categorical anti-aesthetic assumptions subtending his methodology. For an important critique of Bourdieu's approach to questions of aesthetic autonomy and value, see Loesberg, *A Return to Aesthetics.*
6. Working under the direction of Stanley N. Katz and Paul DiMaggio, researchers at the Princeton University Center for Arts and Cultural Policy Studies have been particularly productive in this field. For a definitive statement on the importance of Bourdieu's method to U.S. sociologists of culture, see DiMaggio, "Social Structure, Institutions, and Cultural Goods." Still, working papers published on the Princeton website (http://www.princeton.edu/~artspol/) testify to a range of interests and methodologies among the researchers extending beyond any strictly conceived Bourdieuvian approach.

7. For a recent example, see Grenfell and Hardy, *Art Rules.* Morris, *A Game for Dancers,* is a recent study of cold war dance that relies heavily on Bourdieu.
8. See especially Rancière, *The Philosopher and His Poor,* chap. 9, published in 1983, five years after Bourdieu's *Distinction.* Its belated appearance in translation means that Americans largely missed its timely critical engagement with Bourdieu's project and have mostly failed to appreciate the degree to which Bourdieu's later efforts to address art's politically emancipatory potential (most obviously in *The Rules of Art*) arose in response to Rancière's criticisms.
9. Rancière was one of the original contributors to the collectively produced *Lire le Capital* (1965). Brewster's redacted 1970 English translation of this text, *Reading Capital,* limits itself to the writings of Althusser and Balibar. Rancière's contribution to the original volume, "Le concept de critique et la critique de l'économie politique" was published separately in France after his 1969 break with Althusser (*Lire "le Capital" III*). It appears in English translation in Rattansi, ed., *Ideology, Method and Marx* and *Radical Philosophy* 7. For a description of Rancière's thought that explores how it is both indebted to and critical of his youthful Althusserian Maoism, see Reid's introduction in Rancière, *The Nights of Labor,* xv–xxxvii.
10. "The working-class café where the sociologist forces us to accompany him is, in spite of everything, of a slightly nostalgic kind. No Skai leatherette, pinball games, or juke-boxes; no consumers of strawberry milkshakes or young people with loud clothing; no calculations or dreams placed on horse races or lotteries. . . . [No] Portuguese, Yugoslav, North African, or black workers who form the core of our proletariat" (Rancière, *The Philosopher and his Poor,* 196–197). Rancière has little patience for what he sees as Bourdieu's "suppression of everything that could color or tattoo the simple face of [French] working-class identity" (197).
11. See especially Schwartz, *Creating Faulkner's Reputation,* chaps. 5 and 6.
12. For Eisenstein's theories of montage and its usefulness to political consciousness raising, see *Film Form,* especially 45–63, 72–83. The cultural criticism of the very literary-minded Lukács shows little trace of an active interest in cinema, although his earliest passion was theater. However, as a Communist party activist in Berlin from 1929 to 1933, he was well positioned to learn about Eisenstein's work: the director was in Western Europe from 1929 to 1930 and gave lectures on cinema in many cities, including Berlin. Soviet theories of how cinema might best meet its political responsibilities underwent many transformations between 1929 and 1938, when Lukács published his essay, and Eisenstein's vexed relationship with the party is well known. My point is to draw attention to what may be Lukács's indirect acknowledgment of Eisenstein's thought on this issue.
13. See Weinstein, *Unknowing,* for a reading of modernist fiction as rooted in a refusal of the realist confidence in progress toward a subjective coming into total knowledge, a refusal in part prompted by a recognition of the degree to which such confidence underwrites schemes of psychic, political, and economic domination.
14. Adorno did express impatience with much of what passed as psychoanalytic approaches to art: "For psychoanalysis, artworks are daydreams, . . . [reducing] artwork to crude thematic material, falling strangely short of Freud's own theory of the 'dreamwork'" (*Aesthetic Theory,* 1997, 8).
15. For a comprehensive discussion of Adorno's interactions with the members of the German radical student movement that also contextualizes the drafting of *Aesthetic Theory,* see Müller-Doohm, *Adorno,* 448–474. For a discussion of the difficulties of translating Adorno and the insufficiencies of the earliest English translations of

his work, see several of the essays in Hullot-Kentor, *Things beyond Resemblance,* as well as his translator's introduction to Adorno, *Aesthetic Theory,* 1997, xi–xxi. For a recent example of scholarship that takes the collectively authored *The Authoritarian Personality* as representative of Adorno's thought, see Genter, *Late Modernism.* Genter's profoundly mistaken description of Adorno as a critic whose "formalist modes of reading . . . treated the aesthetic object as an autonomous work disconnected from the distorting hand of mass society, . . . a form of experience distinct from the banalities of everyday life," illustrates how a certain fundamental incomprehension of Adorno's dialectical approach to cultural analysis persists (7).

16. See, for example, Hammer, *Adorno and the Political;* Jenemann, *Adorno in America;* Huhn, ed., *The Cambridge Companion to Adorno;* and Cook, ed., *Theodor Adorno.* Similarly important are Bernstein's exploration of Adorno's thought in the context of visual culture (*Against Voluptuous Bodies*) and Kaufman's Adornian examinations of Romantic, modernist, and contemporary poetry ("Lyric's Expression," "Poetry's Ethics?," and "Lyric Commodity Critique.")

17. Here, Sullivan and Lysaker quote Lenhardt's 1984 English translation of Theodor W. Adorno's *Aesthetic Theory* (328). More recently, Robert Hullot-Kentor has translated the sentence in the following way: "The categories of artistic objectivity are unitary with social emancipation when the object, on the basis of its own impulse, liberates itself from social convention and controls." (Adorno, *Aesthetic Theory*, 231).

18. As Hohendahl notes, "*Aesthetic Theory* as a whole maintains a critical stance toward the reality of advanced capitalism and tends to view the advanced work of art as a significant oppositional force. But this moment cannot, as Adorno's more dogmatic readers have suggested, be completely subsumed under the category of modernism (or, for that matter, of the avant-garde). It defies the logic of simple periodization"(215).

19. Rancière's thought here strikingly resembles Chakrabarty's observation that the alternative modernities of postcolonialism require us to "unlearn to think of history as a developmental process in which that which is possible becomes actual by tending to a future that is singular" and instead "learn to think the present—the 'now' that we inhabit as we speak—as irreducibly not-one" (249). In an essay in Rockhill and Watts's *Jacques Rancière,* Ross has described how this issue of the artwork's timeliness is, for Rancière, an aspect of the much larger question of the relation between history and emancipation:

> In the history of social formations, there is a multiplicity of times, some of which present themselves as repetitions, while others effect tesseracts, wrinkles that join the ancient with the contemporary—different times, as Rancière puts it, "telescoping" into one another. Thus the future appears in the present, the present repeats the past, and what some call anachronisms can inhabit an era. This is all very disturbing for those of us who learned to conceive of an "era" as one of those large, homogenous blocs or signifying totalities, as in the books we read as children, books with titles like *The Baroque Period,* where you are made to understand that the baroque period was baroque because back then scripture was baroque, legal systems were baroque, poetry and even the people who wrote it were baroque. (27)

The importance of this point for any rethinking of the politics of art during the cold war—which, like "the baroque," has been understood as a "homogenous bloc or signifying totality"—should be apparent.

20. See Rancière's discussion of the "heavy consequence" of Adorno's aesthetics of negation in *Aesthetics and Its Discontents,* 40–41, 99–103, 131. The critique has merit, even if at times it seems to traffic in the sort of *de rigueur* leftist dismissal of Adorno's pessimism described by Sullivan and Lysaker.
21. Hullot-Kentor quotes an unpublished review by Kracauer of Adorno's Kierkegaard study, which was published in 1933 and is considered his first substantive philosophical work.
22. "Geschichte zerfällt in Bilder, nicht in Geschichten" (*Gesammelte Schriften* 5, 596, my translation). In *Dreamworld and Catastrophe,* Buck-Morss translates the sentence as "History breaks down into images, not into stories" (68). In their English translation of the complete *Passagen-Werk,* Eiland and McLaughlin render the passage as "History decays into images, not into stories" (Benjamin, *The Arcades Project* 476). No English translation can capture the force of Benjamin's aphorism, which uses the single German noun, *die Geschichte,* in its double sense as both "history" and "story."
23. The English translation accurately captures the insinuations of Bourdieu's French (*La distinction* 444).
24. In the original French, "l'ensemble des différences socialement constituées entre les sexes" becomes "des infractions à la norme de la division du travail entre les sexes" (Bourdieu, *La distinction,* 445, 447).
25. The implicitly misogynistic aspects of Bourdieu's critique of aesthetic judgment have received little direct scholarly attention even as his investigations into cultural systems of social domination have attracted feminist interest. See the essays collected in Adkins and Skeggs, eds., *Feminism after Bourdieu* and also Moi, "Appropriating Bourdieu." For Bourdieu's own analysis of sexism, see *Masculine Domination.*
26. For a sample of scholarship conducted under the rubric of the new lyric studies, much of it combining historical and formal modes of analyses in ways that avoid historicist reduction, see various essays in *Publications of the Modern Language Association* 123, no. 1 (January 2008).
27. Hixson's *Parting the Curtain* makes the case for the importance of the cultural front in the collapse of the Soviet Union. Sherry's *Gay Artists in Modern American Culture* does explore the connection between the work of gay artists and the U.S. government's cold war cultural imperatives, but his study ends in a confused appeal to the "paradox" that "mid-century gay creativity occurred because of oppression, but also because oppression had limits, and for reasons having little to do with it" (238). So far, Jonathan D. Katz is the only other scholar to address the relationship between cold war art and homophobia; he has important things to say about the formal effects of the closet on work by gay artists such as Cage, Rauschenberg, and Johns, even if aspects of his readings tilt toward historicist symptomatology. See Katz's "Passive Resistance" and "John Cage's Queer Silence." I discuss this scholarship more thoroughly in chapter 5.

Chapter 4 Dancing: "Don't Act, Just Dance"

1. See Reed, *Art and Homosexuality,* for a superb reading of both questions. Though Reed understandably stops short of drawing a causal connection between the historically coincident births of modernism in the arts and the psycho-scientific postulate of a homosexual identity, his discussion of the large ground held in common by these two "ideas" makes compelling reading.

2. Examples of such scholarship include Homans's excellent *Apollo's Angels,* 448–539. Her observations build on Prevots's superb *Dance for Export.* See also Copel, "Modern Dance Humanism and the State Department's Agenda"; Windreich, "Cold War Exchange"; Geduld, "Dancing Diplomacy"; and Korppi-Tommola, "Politics Promote Dance." Kowal's *How to Do Things with Dance* should go far toward bringing dance studies to the attention of U.S. cultural studies scholars, though her decision to leave ballet out of her narrative gives the inaccurate impression that postwar modern dance constitutes the whole of cold war American dance modernism.
3. This extremely important essay also appears in Franko, *Migrations of Gesture,* ed. Noland and Ness, 241–258.
4. Macauley identifies Kistler as "the last dancer trained and promoted by George Balanchine." Kistler joined the New York City Ballet from its feeder academy, the School of American Ballet, in 1980. Balanchine died in 1983.
5. Similarly, Ruthanna Boris, who danced for Balanchine in the United States during the 1930s and early 1940s, recalls being told to "be a cold angel." See Tracy and DeLano, *Balanchine's Ballerinas,* 66.
6. Representative discussions of Balanchine's discouragement of role playing and emotional display in his ballets, described as both a liberation and a challenge, can be found in Ashley, *Dancing for Balanchine,* and in the conversations with Diana Adams and Violette Verdy in Tracy and DeLano, *Balanchine's Ballerinas.* In contrast, dancers antipathetic to Balanchine's aesthetic recall being told "don't think"—a phrase he certainly used and one as subject to interpretation as "don't act." The most notorious dancer's critique of the Balanchine aesthetic remains Kirkland's *Dancing on My Grave.*
7. For a representative sample of variations on "ballet is woman" that covers nearly every possible political permutation of the phrase, from sexist to separatist, see the pocket collection *Balanchine.* For a mining of Balanchine's aphorisms that shows the choreographer to be much more well read than commonly supposed, see Croce, "Balanchine Said."
8. In the words of Mary Ellen Moylan, "Never, never did [Balanchine] explain anything about any of his ballets, at least in my presence. He showed the steps. The steps explained. I think of it as, 'it is revealed, but never explained.' To me, that is Balanchine" (Belle, *Dancing for Mr. B.*).
9. Brown echoes dance critic John Martin's 1939 assertion that "the body is totally incapable of becoming an abstraction itself or of producing movement that is abstract, . . . the body cannot be separated from implied intent" (*Introduction to the Dance* 63, 125).
10. For important discussions of Dunham and Ailey, see Manning, *Modern Dance, Negro Dance;* Morris, *A Game for Dancers;* DeFrantz, *Dancing Revelations;* and Kowal, *How to Do Things with Dance.*

Chapter 5 Figures in the Carpet: Balanchine, Cunningham, "Persia"

1. See chapter 3 for discussions of the shift in Faulkner's literary reputation during the cold war.
2. Edel's *Henry James: The Untried Years, 1843–1870,* was published 1953. The acclaim that greeted his second and third volumes, *The Conquest of London, 1870–1881* and *The Middle Years, 1882–1893* (both published in 1962), confirms the canonization. Volume 2 received the Pulitzer Prize, while volumes 2 and 3 together won a National Book Award.

3. See *Hound & Horn*. Other contributors include photographer Alice Boughton and writers Lawrence Leighton, Francis Fergusson, Newton Arvin, H. R. Hays, and John Wheelwright.
4. High theory contributions to James scholarship include Felman, "Turning the Screw of Interpretation"; Todorov, *The Poetics of Prose;* Miller, "The Figure in the Carpet"; and Sedgwick, *Epistemology of the Closet.* Other important scholarship on Jamesian ambiguity published during the cold war and immediately afterward (when *closet* became the keyword replacing *ambiguity*) include Rimmon, *The Concept of Ambiguity;* Iser, *The Act of Reading;* and Savoy, "Embarrassments."
5. See, for example, Moon, *A Small Boy and Others;* Haralson, *Henry James and Queer Modernity;* Savoy, "Entre chien et loup"; and Ohi, *Henry James and the Queerness of Style.*
6. For a review of *The Worlds of Lincoln Kirstein* that emphasizes this aspect of the biography, see Kodat, "The Great Intermediate."
7. The estimated cost of *Figure* comes from Klass, "Finding The Figure in the Carpet" (48). Buckle and Taras report that Kirstein budgeted 50,000 dollars for the 1954 production of *The Nutcracker,* about 430,000 dollars in current funds (200).
8. Martin, whose early antipathy toward Balanchine is well known, described the ballet as "brilliant in detail but not terribly interesting as a whole" ("Ballet: A Novelty Bows"). Reports of the extra performance appear in Terry, "'Figure in Carpet' Featured by the City Ballet"; and Martin, "Ballet: 'Episodes, Part II.'"
9. This narrative of the loss of *Figure* draws from interviews with Barbara Horgan (July 1998) and Francia Russell (November 1998). Successfully reworked Balanchine ballets include *Mozartiana, Seven Deadly Sins, Divertimento No. 15* (originally *Caracole*), and the much-revised *Apollon musagète / Apollo.*
10. For a discussion of homophobic reactions to ballet during congressional debate of the legislation that created the National Endowments for the Arts and Humanities, see chapter 3.
11. Kirstein's four-part travel diary of the tour, originally published in the September–December 1941 issues of the monthly *American Dancer,* is reprinted in *Ballet: Bias and Belief,* 77–95. For a discussion of Rockefeller's Office of the Coordinator of Inter-American Affairs and its importance to the growth of cold war cultural diplomacy, see chapter 2.

    The New York City Ballet was Balanchine's and Kirstein's fifth attempt to establish an American ballet company. Efforts began in 1935 with the creation of the American Ballet and were followed by Ballet Caravan, American Ballet Caravan (merging the repertoire and personnel of the two failed predecessor troupes and created solely for the 1941 South American tour), and Ballet Society.
12. In retrospect, Kirstein's approach to this narrative of manly dancing seems seems almost entirely opportunistic and much less informed by a wish to forestall homosexual panic than Shawn's. For an important discussion of the rhetoric of the virile male dancer as it informed the writings and choreographic practices of Shawn and José Limón, both gay dancers who took pains to keep their sexual orientation secret, see Foulkes, *Modern Bodies,* especially chap. 4.
13. Sedgwick sees preterition as the operative rhetorical figure of Jamesian closeted narration (see *Epistemology of the Closet, chap. 4*). While I agree that preterition can forward an agenda of the closet, the practice of drawing attention to something by pretending to ignore it functions differently in literature than in ballet, where the body is always on display.

14. Morris, *A Game for Dancers,* and Kowal, *How to Do Things with Dance,* provide excellent analyses of the politically direct, activist dance works created by African American choreographers of the 1940s and 1950s such as Alvin Ailey, Katherine Dunham, Talley Beatty, Donald McKayle, and Pearl Primus. Though few of these choreographers were included in programs of cultural diplomacy (in fact Primus was placed under surveillance and had her passport revoked), their awareness of State Department eagerness to make dance serve an international political agenda led them to pursue their own politically charged choreographic projects, many of them directly addressing civil rights.
15. Kowal's view of Cunningham is an important recent exception to this trend. Sherry's superb *Gay Artists in Modern American Culture* does explore the connection between the work of gay artists and the U.S. government's cold war cultural imperatives but stops short of seeing the artwork itself as politically salient, preferring a more biographically centered narrative of gay artists' experiences as producers of cold war culture.
16. For a recent discussion of the 1962 tour, see Croft, "Ballet Nations."
17. See Von Eschen, *Satchmo Blows Up the World.* I discuss her thesis in chapter 2.
18. The main article jumps to A14–15; the two-page interior spread also includes three supplemental stories and a timeline.
19. *The New York Times* published Risen's analysis of Wilber's "Secret History" online in June 2000. To provide historical context, the site provides links to articles on Iranian politics that appeared in the *Times* between February 1949 and November 1954 (http://www.nytimes.com/library/world/mideast/041600iran-cia-index.html). For an illuminating discussion of the CIA's longstanding refusal to declassify documents relating to the coup and the *paper's* decision to publish Wilber's narrative electronically, see Byrne, "The Secret CIA History of the Iran Coup, 1953."
20. In 1935, the Anglo-Persian Oil Company was renamed the Anglo-Iranian Oil Company. In 1954 (a year after the coup), it became the British Petroleum Company (today's BP).
21. See Kinzer, *All the Shah's Men,* especially 6–7. He draws on Wilber's account and Roosevelt's *Countercoup* to craft a dramatic high-cold-war narrative of intrigue and espionage that stresses wily CIA persistence in the face of a string of setbacks over the coup's five days. Like Wilber and Roosevelt, he sees a "timid and indecisive" shah as a large part of the problem. In *The Life and Times of the Shah,* Afkhami takes strenuous exception to the histories of Wilber, Roosevelt, and Kinzer, offering a narrative of the coup emphasizing the volatile state of internal Iranian politics over CIA meddling and royal indecision. For other studies of the coup published since the appearance of "Secret History," see Byrne and Gasiorowski, *Mohammed Mosaddeq and the 1953 Coup in Iran,* and Bayandor, *Iran and the CIA.* Important analyses of U.S.-Iranian relations written before the appearance of "Secret History" include Saikal, *The Rise and Fall of the Shah,* and Bill, *The Eagle and the Lion.*
22. The obituary notes that "Don's celebrity as archeologist and scholar gave him a perfect cover" in his work for the CIA. See also Wilber, *Persian Gardens and Garden Pavilions.*
23. Though he does not directly accuse Pope of dealing in forgeries, Bloom writes that "it is difficult to believe that a man of Pope's knowledge and connections would not have known to question the origins of some of the objects he sold. . . . The most charitable interpretation is that he chose not to know what might do his business damage" (101). In 2010, Pope was the subject of an exhibition at the Art Institute

of Chicago, "Arthur Upham Pope and a New Survey of Persian Art," held to mark the reopening of the museum's Islamic art galleries, which Pope had helped develop (http://www.artic.edu/exhibition/Pope).

24. Pahlavi University was renamed Shiraz University after the 1979 revolution.
25. Werth's booklet, published in the wake of the Soviet Union's Central Committee Decree on Music, reproduces pertinent passages from the decree itself, and the phrases here are taken from it. I discuss the decree in more detail in chapter 6.
26. Letter on National Security League letterhead, to William J. Burns, July 11, 1922. The correspondent's name is blacked out. I obtained Pope's FBI file through a Freedom of Information Act request. It was not uncensored: it is agency practice to withhold names of still-living individuals identified in the documents, particularly informants and agents.
27. In a letter dated September 18, 1941, Hoover thanks Pope for the publication on German psychological warfare and expresses strong interest in the proposed volumes: "I would appreciate it very much indeed if arrangements could be made for us to secure a draft [of the planned] Russian Psychological Front. In the event the other material which you refer to is available, such as the instructions for spies which were smuggled out on microfilm, I would certainly like very much to receive it" (FBI, Pope file).
28. "Pope earned the undying enmity of several of his colleagues, notably Maurice Dimand, curator of the Metropolitan Museum of Art, and Mehmet Aga-Oglu, founder of the research seminary in Islamic art at the University of Michigan, for 'being in the trade'" (Bloom 101).
29. See Pope, *Maxim Litvinoff.*
30. The statement is undated and unattributed, but appears immediately after an August 8, 1950, office memorandum detailing a debriefing interview with Louis F. Budenz that identifies the ensuing statement as a "blind memorandum" dictated by him.
31. According to Klass, Pope had wanted to "rent the Metropolitan Opera House . . . and hire the New York Philharmonic. . . . He, Dr. Pope, would stand on the stage of the Met and lecture on the aesthetics of Persian art and its relationship to Western baroque art while gigantic slide projections of the Ardebil Carpet would be shown on a vast screen behind him and, simultaneously, the Philharmonic would play the overture to *Die Meistersinger* full blast—which would, he thought, illustrate the points he was making" (40).
32. Pope's articles are included in box 5, folder 93, titled "Figure in the Carpet," of the Kirstein Papers.
33. Kirstein's "The Diaghilev Period" first appeared in the *Hound & Horn* issue dated July–September 1930.
34. See Kopelson, *The Queer Afterlife of Vaslav Nijinsky,* especially 59–78; and Stoneley, *A Queer History of the Ballet.*
35. See Duberman, *The Worlds of Lincoln Kirstein,* 213–214, for a description of the Fokine study. The book also discusses Kirstein's long and tempestuous relationship with Romola Nijinsky.
36. "My work with George Balanchine since 1933 put me in touch with survivors of the Imperial School in Petersburg and members of the Ballets Russes in Western Europe. Pierre Vladimirov, who followed Nijinsky as first dancer at the Maryinsky Theater, and Anatole Oboukhov, who succeeded him there, both taught at our School of the American Ballet for many years. Madame Felia Doubrouvska (Vladimirova) and Madame Alexandra Danilova, veterans of renowned seasons in Russia

and throughout the world, still teach at the school, which bases its program and practice on theirs. From them I learned to ask questions and more questions about dancing and dancers. The replies I was given over the years furnish everything of value in this text" (Kirstein, *Nijinsky Dancing* 13).

37. I am grateful to Nicholas Jenkins for permission to quote the scenario.
38. Then, too, the notion that a "luminous and palpitating beauty" may find protective camouflage in its "dull reverse"—and that such beauty necessarily will assert its own overwhelming power—offers a view of the closet stressing its tactical and temporary nature over the immediate fact of its oppressive imposition.
39. For discussions of the politics of European *ballet de cour,* see Homans, *Apollo's Angels,* especially 11–34; Nevile, *Dance, Spectacle, and the Body Politic;* Franko, *Dance As Text;* and Hilton, *Dance of Court and Theater.*
40. "Camp is a form of historicism viewed histrionically" (Core 7).
41. Several of the reviews cited by Reynolds link the opening of *Figure* to *Serenade* (204), as did Russell and Verdy in separate interviews (November 1998 and August 1999). Created in 1934, a year after Balanchine's arrival in the United States, *Serenade* has been described as "the Rosetta Stone for a new kind of dancer, the American classical dancer" (Bentley, "The Ballet That Changed Everything"). The phrase has the virtue of encapsulating many years' worth of critical and scholarly writing about a ballet that is widely recognized as a masterpiece of twentieth-century choreography.
42. Reynolds describes a bravura passage in which "multiple pirouettes by the entire ensemble on different counts . . . framed continuous turns by Verdy" (204).
43. According to Russell, "my own part . . . wasn't really wonderful, but it sort of served the purpose. [Balanchine] played around with the fact that I could turn equally well right and left and that was really all there was to it. . . . I had these enormous plumes on my head, . . . so I had to turn right and left with this thing just about ripping my head off" (interview, November 1998). Neither her variation nor Hayden's *pas de deux* with d'Amboise were included in the *Omnibus* broadcast.
44. For an indispensable analysis of the terms and consequences of Cunningham's calculated grafting of ballet and modern dance techniques, see Copeland, *Merce Cunningham.*
45. See chapter 3 for a discussion of Lukács's brand of Marxist cultural critique.
46. *Theater Piece,* Cunningham's Artaud-influenced collaboration with Cage, Rauschenberg, M. C. Richards, Charles Olson, and David Tudor during the 1952 summer school at Black Mountain College, is an important early effort in this vein. However, *Museum Event #1* was the first official company Event; it took place on June 24, 1964, at Vienna's Museum des 20. Jahrhunderts.
47. Roth's essay first appeared in *Artforum* in November 1977, but my quotations are from the version reprinted in Roth and Katz, *Difference/Indifference.*
48. See Lukács, "Realism in the Balance." I discuss this essay in more detail in chapter 3.
49. Most recently, Roth's essay was included in the catalog accompanying the 2012–2013 Philadelphia Museum of Art exhibition *Dancing around the Bride,* a remarkable show centered on Duchamp's *The Bride Stripped Bare by Her Bachelors, Even* (1915–1923). Also known as *The Large Glass,* the work was adapted by Johns for Cunningham's *Walkaround Time* (1968). In the catalog's introductory essay, Reinaldo Laddago characterizes Roth's essay as "superb" (41). Katz's essay is not included or even mentioned.
50. Quoted in Foster, "Closets Full of Dances," 172–173.

51. *Orghast at Persepolis,* a collaborative theatrical work by Peter Brook and Ted Hughes, was featured in the 1971 Shiraz Festival. Founded in 1942 by Mostafa Mesbahzadeh, the daily newspaper *Kayhan* was generally supportive of the Pahlavi regime and critical of the Islamic clergy. Mesbahzadeh left Iran in 1978; after the 1979 fall of the shah, the Islamic revolutionary government took over the paper. Today it serves as a mouthpiece for the Office of the Supreme Leader. Mesbahzadeh died in Los Angeles in 2006 (http://articles.latimes.com/2006/dec/05/local/me-mostafa5).
52. The National Iranian Radio and Television (NIRT) rather than the Iranian Ministry of Culture was charged with running the festival chiefly because the state telecommunications agency was headed by Farah Pahlavi's cousin, Reza Qotbi. See Afkhami, *The Life and Times of the Shah,* 415–416.
53. Produced by the exiled Hungarian troupe Squat Theater, *Pig, Child, Fire!* was denounced by Islamic clerics for depicting "lewd acts." Afkhami defends the play as an allegorical representation of the relationship between the Soviet Union and Hungary that had "no nudity . . . and no exceptionally lewd movements" (419). In contrast, the *New York Times*' theater critic described a version presented in Manhattan two months after the Shiraz performance as a "reprehensible" "throw-back to Happenings" whose "vicious, violent, lewd, and tasteless" moments were "more revolting . . . than revolutionary" (Gussow, "West 23rd Street Banned in Budapest").
54. A French video of the festival available on the YouTube channel maintained by Farah Pahlavi captures the immoderacy of both the celebration and Pahlavi self-regard (http://www.youtube.com/watch?v=orWZHn1NivI). Afkhami writes that the costs of the festival were primarily borne by private industry and that the Anniversary Celebration included an ambitious and successful plan to build 2,500 new schools, one for each year of Persian monarchy (408–409). He counters reports in Western media that placed the cost of the four-day celebration at about 300 million dollars; his estimates place expenses at no more than 22 million dollars (413–414). Whether these sums are 1971 or 2008 dollars is not clear.
55. The quotation appears on the second page of the airgram. The file also includes a translation of the September 20, 1972, *Borba* review from which it is taken. *Borba* was the official paper of the Yugoslav Communist League.
56. For the comparison to Brecht, see the translation in the file of Olga Bozickovic's September 21, 1972, review in *Politika:* "Cunningham's action reminds, in a certain way, of Brecht's principle about 'actor's alienation,' that is, about [the actor's] permanent self-observation and relation toward what he does or intends to do on the stage." For the comparison to Grotowski, see the file's translation of Muharem Pervic's September 22, 1972 review, also published in *Politika.* Both reviews are in the Cultural Affairs files.
57. The sum comes to about 33,500 dollars in current funds. It is unclear what other financial support, if any, the company received for the rest of the tour. Cultural Affairs files make no mention of any subsidy. Brown's memoir indicates that the contract with Brazil's Teatro Nôvo had no payment guarantee, with the theater providing only a share of the box office. The troupe lost 9,000 dollars (more than 60,000 dollars in today's currency) on that engagement (516). She also indicates that planned appearances in Colombia and Chile were "dropped for lack of sponsor resources" (513).
58. For a personal account of the gesture—the planning that led up to it, its intended

meaning, and its consequences—see Smith and Steele, *Silent Gesture.* For a discussion of the 1968 Olympic Games that places Smith's and Carlos's protest in a broader historical context, see Bass, *Not the Triumph but the Struggle.*

59. For a definitive account of the Tlatelolco massacre, see Poniatowska, *Massacre in Mexico.* See also Doyle's two postings on the National Security Archive website at George Washington University.
60. "E' ótimo saber que as pessoas approvam, desaprovam, aplaudem e vaiam o espectáculo. Gosto da censura do público, só não aceito a de nenhum tipo de govêrno." "Independente e Interdependente" (newspaper clipping, July 28, 1968). My thanks to Nelson Cárdenas for his translations from the Portuguese, which appear here and elsewhere in the chapter.
61. "Merce Cunningham Só Acredita Na Censura Do Povo" ("Merce Cunningham Only Recognizes Censorship by the Audience"). The article "Protesto Tem Vez Na Arte De Cunningham" ("There Is Protest in Merce Cunningham's Art"), appeared on July 26, 1968, in *Diário de Notícias* and also quotes the press conference remarks about censorship. An article appearing on the same day in *Jornal do Brasil* includes Cunningham's censorship quotation in the second paragraph.
62. "Nada há em matéria de arte—e de vida, também—quesói tão belo como a liberdade. . . . O verbo *to kick,* além de dar pontapés e bater com os pés, significa, nos EUA, objetar, reclamar, protestar, criticar" (review, *Correio da Manhã,* August 4, 1968).
63. A single trifold pamphlet preserved in the Merce Cunningham Dance Company Archive (hereafter cited as Cunningham Archive) indicates that appearances on August 6 and 9, 1968, at the San Martín Coronado included performances of *Field Dances, Nightwandering, Walkaround Time, Scramble, Winterbranch,* and *How to Pass, Kick, Fall, and Run.*

Chapter 6 Spartacus

1. See Shaw, *Spartacus and the Slave Wars,* for an excellent compilation of the ancient Spartacus narratives of Plutarch, Appian, Sallust, Livy, Orosius, Velleius, Florus, Athenaeus, Varro, Diodorus, Frontinus, Cicero, and Suetonius.
2. Shaw describes a sudden eruption of historical writings about Spartacus in France during the 1760s that informed Voltaire's famous description of the rebellion as "a just war, indeed the only just war in history" (19).
3. Letter from Marx to Engels, February 27, 1861, in Marx and Engels, *Selected Correspondence.*
4. Of the ancient chroniclers, only Plutarch describes Spartacus as having a wife; none mention any children. In Bird's *The Gladiator,* Spartacus comes outfitted with wife, child, and brother and with a vision of liberty rooted in a desire to keep that family intact. By contrast, Kellogg's popular 1842 declamation "Spartacus to the Gladiators" features a bachelor Spartacus galvanized into rebellion by the memory of the "sweet smile" of the "noble and brave" "boyhood" friend he is forced to kill in the arena (337–338).
5. Werth's booklet, published in the immediate wake of the Soviet Union's Central Committee Decree on Music, reproduces sections of the published proceedings of the conference as well as pertinent passages from the decree itself.
6. The date of composition of Volkov's book appears in Yuzefovich, *Aram Khachaturyan, 207.*

7. For a discussion of this period, see Bown, *Art under Stalin,* particularly his analysis of socialist realism, 89–95.
8. I am grateful to Carl Serpa for sending me a copy of Shneerson, *Aram Khachaturyan*.
9. Describing the desultory nature of Jacobson's career, *The Oxford Dictionary of Dance* observes that at one point he was kept from working for six years (Craine and Mackrell 254). Among Westerners, Jacobson is probably best known for *Vestris,* the brilliant solo that Baryshnikov danced when he won the 1969 International Ballet Competition in Moscow.
10. See chapter 1 for a discussion of the Moiseyev Dance Company's 1958 U.S. debut.
11. *The Oxford Dictionary of Dance* reports nine performances (Craine and Mackrell 446), while *The International Dictionary of Ballet* reports six (Bremser 1332).
12. Sargeant found the Bolshoi men "agreeably masculine" (145). Terry observed that, after viewing the highlights program, one "gifted young American male dancer" had announced, "I think I'll toss in the towel" ("Bolshoi Exciting in Variety Show," sec. 4, p. 5). However, Genauer complained that "even the most lithe and agile of the male dancers look squat and square in the curiously long, prudish tunics worn for most of their roles" ("Bourgeois Decor at Bolshoi," sec. 4, p. 1).
13. For the front-page coverage, see the April 17, 1959, final editions of the *New York Times* and the *New York Herald Tribune.* Subsequent reporting in the *Times* included Martin's reviews (April 18, 19, 22, 23, 24, 26, 29; May 1, 2, 3, 5, 6, 11, 17, 24) and Schonberg's profile, "Presenting Sol Hurok, Impresario." The *Herald Tribune*'s coverage included Terry's reviews (April 18, 22, 24, 26, 29, 30; May 1, 2, 3, 5, 10, 13, 17) and Levine's feature article, "Khrushchev's Prettiest Propaganda." Though he had little to say about ballet, Levine had strong opinions about Soviet cultural diplomacy. *The New Yorker, Time,* and *Newsweek* all offered special Bolshoi reports in their late-April issues. *Dance Magazine*'s advance coverage of the Bolshoi tour took up most of its April issue.
14. Margulies would go on to a highly successful career as a television miniseries producer, with credits including *Roots* and *The Thorn Birds.*
15. See, for instance, a letter from Margulies to Beck, September 3, 1958, in which he says he's found an "interesting fact" that "an obscure American dramatist named Robert Montgomery Bird wrote a play entitled 'The Gladiator' about our hero" (Douglas papers, box 33, folder 3); a memo from David Lipton to Margulies, September 17, 1959, offering "information about the Spartacus party in pre-World War I [*sic*] Germany" (box 33, folder 8); and a remarkable night cable from producer Edward Lewis to Soviet minister of culture Nikolai Mikhailov, March 16, 1959, proposing that Khachaturian compose and conduct the score for the film: "this project has been approved by . . . our State Department and we have also received encouragement from Boris Krylov in your Washington embassy, who suggested we cable you" (box 33, folder 5). Douglas indicates that Koestler's *The Gladiators* was another important precursor text. In fact, it provided the narrative for a competing Spartacus movie, a United Artist venture that would have starred Yul Brynner and been directed by Martin Ritt (Douglas, *The Ragman's Son,* 277–286).
16. The May 20, 1959, letter was addressed to Helen Deutsch.
17. Margulies also considered sinking 72,000 dollars of *Spartacus*'s advertising budget (about 577,000 dollars in current funds) into a ten-minute animated short that would promote the film by "dramatizing the origins, the restraints upon, and the purposes of, freedom in the growth and organization of civilization" (letter from

Herbert Klynn of Format Films, Inc., to Margulies, November 13, 1959, Douglas papers, box 33, folder 10).

18. Certified public accountant Benjamin W. Solomon's November 26, 1960, report on advertising expenses for *Spartacus* lists the payment to Robinson under "miscellaneous advertising" (Douglas papers, box 34, folder 12).
19. See the memo to Margulies, May 20, 1960, for the "relay race" passage (Douglas papers, box 33, folder 17). A later memo, May 26, 1960, indicates that Robinson had approved the changes (box 33, folder 18).
20. For useful memoirs and analyses of the blacklist and the era that spawned it, see Bessie, *Inquisition in Eden;* Caute, *The Great Fear;* Navasky, *Naming Names;* Ceplair and Englund, *The Inquisition in Hollywood;* Schrecker, *Many Are the Crimes;* and Humphries, *Hollywood's Blacklists.*
21. Stung that Preminger's announcement of Trumbo's work on *Exodus* preceded his own, Douglas claims the "first" for *Spartacus* by arguing that his decision to leave a pass for Trumbo at the gates to the Universal lot while *Spartacus* was in production should mark the point at which the blacklist actually was broken (*The Ragman's Son* 295–296).
22. Selections from this document were published as part of a several-article report in *Cineaste* on the occasion of the 1991 release of the restored print of *Spartacus* (Trumbo, "Report on *Spartacus*"). The scene-by-scene analysis included in the Criterion Collection's *Spartacus* DVD is drawn from that report (Kubrick, *Spartacus, disc 1*).
23. "*[Spartacus]*was the only one of my films over which I did not have complete control; although I was the director, mine was only one of many voices to which Kirk listened. I am disappointed in the film. It had everything but a good story" (Nelson, *Kubrick* 250). Kubrick later sharpened this criticism of the film to emphasize his dissatisfaction with Trumbo's script: "When Kirk offered me the job of directing *Spartacus,* I thought that I might be able to make something of it if the script could be changed. But my experience proved that if it is not explicitly stipulated in the contract that your decisions will be respected, there's a very good chance that they won't be. The script could have been improved in the course of shooting, but it wasn't. Kirk was the producer. He and Dalton Trumbo . . . had everything their way" (Phillips, *Stanley Kubrick* 145–146).
24. For a reading of *Spartacus* that notes its engagements with the burgeoning civil rights movement, see Wyke, *Projecting the Past, chap. 3*.
25. The defection and subsequent execution of Crixus was apparently never filmed.
26. This is Douglas's view; see *The Ragman's Son,* 296–297, as well as 304–305, where he calls Kubrick "a talented shit." At the film's original release, and even more so after the 1991 restoration, critics singled out Kubrick's battle scenes for particular praise. Especially impressive was the final battle, shot on location in Spain using regulars from Franco's army—perhaps one of the film's more pointed political ironies, given that Fast conceived the novel while he was imprisoned for supporting the Republican cause in the Spanish Civil War. *Spartacus*'s place as a footnote in the history of cultural diplomacy emerges here: Universal required the help of the U.S. embassy to hire Franco's soldiers. See letters between Bryna Productions officials and John Davis Lodge, U.S. ambassador to Spain, in Trumbo papers, box 33, folder 10.
27. In fact, the 1960 Production Code Administration–approved release print did contain the snails and oysters scene; it was cut to placate the Roman Catholic Legion

of Decency, which said the scene had to go before *Spartacus* could be approved for Catholic viewers (Barrios 273).

28. Fast claims that, because he had become "a notorious symbol of the Communist party," the novel *Spartacus* was "ignored" by reviewers for mass-circulation dailies and "praised to the skies" by critics of the left (*Being Red* 293). As Swados's review indicates, the truth is a good deal more complicated. The book was panned in the *New York Times* but received glowing notices in *Saturday Review* and *Library Journal*. For his part, Swados gives a respectful accounting of Fast's politics, if not of his artistry.
29. See Gorbman, *Unheard Melodies*.
30. See Flinn, *Strains of Utopia*. My reading of North's *Spartacus* score is indebted to this study.
31. Information about North's past was drawn from his FBI file, released to me in January 2002 after my Freedom of Information Act request. Accounts in Pollack, *Aaron Copland*, and Warren, *Anna Sokolow*, were also helpful. Warren writes that North so impressed his composition teachers in Moscow that "they paid him the great compliment of recommending him for admission to the League of Soviet Composers, the only American ever to have been so honored" (60). Information about North's membership in the Composer's Collective and the organization's connection to the American Communist party comes from Zuck, *A History of Musical Americanism*, 116–117. When releasing North's file to me, the FBI indicated it was holding back three of its eighty-six pages (personal communication, January 28, 2002).
32. This memo notes that North had been portrayed as a likely communist in a short notice published in the February 26, 1954, edition of the rightwing journal *Counterattack*.
33. The FBI's investigation of North included an interview with Sokolow in November 1955. (The name is blacked out of the document, but internal evidence points to her.) Like North, she describes her participation in leftist activities during the 1930s in pragmatic terms: "With the exception of a few gratis benefits for the VALB [Veterans of the Abraham Lincoln Brigade] and Russian War Relief, she was a paid performer at all functions sponsored by the CP and other similar organizations. She said that during that time employment in the entertainment field was difficult to obtain and when she was offered an opportunity to perform at CP rallies and other functions sponsored by such organizations as the International Workers Order (IWO) [and] the Joint Anti-Fascist Refugee Committee (JAFRC) she readily accepted that employment. She said that this was her primary reason for performing for these organizations" (FBI, North file, February 27, 1959).
34. North's *Spartacus* scores, sketches, and notes are in the North collection, box 10, files 37-40.
35. Included in North's sketches for the score is a version of the melody with lyrics by Johnny Mercer (North collection, box 10, file 37).
36. If one includes the musical overture in the movie's total running time, Varinia's theme isn't heard until twenty minutes into the film.
37. North did not write the concluding arrangement of the theme. According to Bill Rosar, the exit music was scored by Edward B. Powell, an orchestrator for 20th Century Fox who had worked for twenty-five years as chief orchestrator for Alfred Newman and also assisted North in much of his studio work. "Powell told me that North had a kind of neurotic quirk, that when he got to writing the end title to his scores, his mind would go blank and he couldn't do it. . . . I assume that's why

[Powell] was called in on *Spartacus*" (personal communication, November 24, 1998).

38. Some version of an encounter between Spartacus and a poet appears in every draft of Trumbo's screenplay, though with wildly varying treatments. In one draft Spartacus denounces a poet named Galba as "a pampered, petted house slave, fawning over your master and wearing fine clothes, while field slaves died under the lash! . . . You must learn something useful. You'll be trained to fight. To kill with the sword. We want men here, not poets." In this version, Varinia intercedes: "*I* want poets." At her urging, Galba recites a poem, leading Spartacus to declare that, after all, the poet will "*not* learn to fight! You will stay in the *rear* where no harm can come to you!" Galba protests, "But I *came* to fight!" (Trumbo papers, box 25, folder 1). A later version of the scene presents a Spartacus somewhat less hostile to the poet (now named Antoninus) who still decides to keep him out of battle: "We're not going to make a gladiator out of you. We'll do the fighting. You sing." Again, the poet protests, "But I *came* here to fight!" (box 25, folder 4).
39. For a discussion of Laughton's homosexuality, see Callow, *Charles Laughton.* Throughout the book Callow claims that Laughton's self-disgust fueled both his obesity and choice of roles. His sexuality, an open secret in Hollywood during his lifetime, was first discussed frankly in *Elsa Lanchester, Herself,* his wife's autobiography.
40. Ustinov was preceded in Nero's precincts by Laughton, who played the emperor in Cecil B. DeMille's *The Sign of the Cross* (1932). Both actors portrayed Nero as a perverted decadent. In an interview packaged with the Criterion Collection's DVD of *Spartacus,* Ustinov recalled a day during shooting when Universal's "publicity lady" advised him to stay away from the commissary: "Hedda Hopper's there and she doesn't want to see you," he remembered her saying. He recalled: "I wheedled it out of her that Hedda Hopper had said to someone that I was so brilliant in *Quo Vadis* I've got to be queer. Well, of course, I needed no second bidding, I went straight to the commissary, went up to her, and . . . behaved in the way of a rather gross English sergeant. And we never had that trouble again" (Kubrick, *Spartacus,* disc 2).
41. A remnant of these cut scenes appears in the final version when Batiatus confides to Gracchus that "you feel [Varinia] would surrender to the right man, which is . . . irritating," though the effect of this line without its original context does not indicate Batiatus's desire for Varinia as much as hint that he is not a "right man" (Kubrick, *Spartacus,* disc 1).
42. Shurlock's letter is dated August 14, 1958.
43. The source for Kubrick's quotation is not given.
44. In the Soviet Union male homosexuality was criminalized, whereas lesbianism was treated as a medical and psychological problem. On the history of Soviet antihomosexual legislation, see Kon, *The Sexual Revolution in Russia.*
45. *Encounter*'s history as a Congress for Cultural Freedom/CIA-funded journal is well known. (See chapter 2 for my discussion of the Congress for Cultural Freedom.) Khrushchev's comments come packaged in this pamphlet with a good deal of pointed commentary, but there is no reason to doubt the accuracy of the translation.
46. Barnes called the work "one of the great ballets of the 20th century" (14), Percival wrote that the Bolshoi's presentation of *Spartak* during its Covent Garden season "had the house cheering" ("London Dateline," 95), and an unbylined feature article in *Dance Magazine* called the ballet a "triumph" that "establishes Grigorovich as

possibly the most important of all the younger Soviet choreographers" ("The Bolshoi's New Hit," 60).

47. The famous quotation is from Keynes, *A Tract on Monetary Reform*, 80. I do not mean to privilege Keynes's own identity as a gay (and married) man as a generating condition of his critique of neoclassical economics, nor do I imply that there is something particularly homosexual about Keynesian theory in general. I am simply connecting the era's underlying economic logic with its emergent sexual politics.
48. See also Essig, *Queer in Russia*.
49. "It was easier for them to control someone who had a family because if they told you to do something you would do it to protect your family. . . . But I felt myself a free person, free from their morality. . . . Because every time I made love to one of my beloveds, we broke the boundaries and did what was forbidden—which was, of course, exciting. So although I was not a political dissident, I was what could be called a 'sexual dissident.' Because sex . . . is freedom" (Tuller 5).

Chapter 7 From Art as Diplomacy to Diplomacy as Art: The Red Detachment of *Nixon in China*

1. Early Sellars productions that sparked critical consternation include a production of *Anthony and Cleopatra* set in a swimming pool and a puppet rendition of Wagner's *Ring* cycle.
2. For recent examples of the tendency to lapse into bemused plot summary in describing the ballet and its relationship to the opera, see Tommasini's review of the 2011 Met production, "President and Opera, on Unexpected Stage," and Swed's review of the 2012 San Francisco Opera production, "Opera Review: 'Nixon in China.'"
3. "The Chairman Dances" has been recorded by the San Francisco Symphony (Nonesuch 79144-2), the Baltimore Symphony (Argo 444 454-2), and the City of Birmingham Symphony (EMI 55051). The original cast recording of *Nixon in China* was released in 1988 by Nonesuch (79177); a recording of the 2008 Colorado Symphony and Opera Colorado production was released in October 2009 (Naxos 8.66902-24).
4. In "Popular Culture and the Culture of the Masses in Contemporary China," Liu Kang analyzes the rearticulation of Cultural Revolution productions in popular Chinese culture following the economic restructuring undertaken by Deng Xiaoping. The article includes a brief discussion of *Red Detachment*.
5. The film of the ballet is available for viewing at https://archive.org/details/The_Red_Detachment_of_Women.
6. See Kristeva, *About Chinese Women*.
7. Clark notes,

> Instead of being a side track on China's road to modern wealth and influence, the Cultural Revolution is best understood as firmly part of the process. The powerful themes of the Cultural Revolution, including mass mobilization and the renewed push to combine Western and Chinese elements in a new-style mass culture, fit well with the previous decades' obsessions. Suffering subjected on some Chinese between 1966 and 1976 should not obscure these long-term continuities with the preceding and following decades. Instead of being perceived simply as a period of destruction or as an arena of factional political conflict,

> the Cultural Revolution can be seen also as an era of modern innovation and efforts at real change in China's cultural inheritance. Failed or half-hearted attempts to update cultural forms stuck in convention for artists and audiences gave way to an all-out shift to modern subject matter, forms, and values. The ultimate failure of these efforts or rejection of their absurd politics does not detract from the astonishing innovation and commitment they represented. The participants in these upheavals went on to grasp the opportunities provided with the economic changes after the 1970s. The ambition of Cultural Revolution culture continued to reverberate even in the art and writing in the 1980s onwards that seemed to utterly reject Maoist culture. (8–9)

8. This important bit of stage business, present in both in the original Houston Grand Opera production and the Met's revival, is an elaboration of the stage directions in the libretto, which simply calls for Changqing to offer the drink (Adams and Goodman 226). In the Houston and New York productions, Pat puts the glass into the party secretary's hand, which interrupts the gesture of her husband, who thinks what's being requested is a pistol.

Bibliography

Acocella, Joan. *Mark Morris.* New York: Noonday, 1993.

Adams, John. *Hallelujah Junction: Composing an American Life.* New York: Picador, 2008.

Adams, John, and Alice Goodman. *Nixon in China.* Vocal score. London: Boosey and Hawkes, n.d.

Adkins, Lisa, and Beverly Skeggs, eds. *Feminism after Bourdieu.* New York: Wiley-Blackwell, 2005.

Adorno, Theodor. "The Actuality of Philosophy." In *The Adorno Reader*, edited by Brian O'Connor, 23–39. Oxford: Blackwell, 2000.

———. *Aesthetic Theory.* Edited and translated by Robert Hullot-Kentor. Minneapolis: University of Minnesota Press, 1997.

———. *Aesthetic Theory.* Translated by C. Lenhardt. London: Routledge and Kegan Paul, 1984.

———. *Critical Models: Interventions and Catchwords.* Translated by Henry W. Pickford. 1963. Reprint, New York: Columbia University Press, 1998.

———. "Cultural Criticism and Society." In *Prisms*, translated by Samuel and Shierry Weber. Cambridge, Mass: MIT Press, 1967.

———. *Kierkegaard: Construction of the Aesthetic.* Translated by Robert Hullot-Kentor. Minneapolis: University of Minnesota Press, 1989.

———. "Scientific Experiences of a European Scholar in America." In *Critical Models: Interventions and Catchwords*, translated by Henry W. Pickford, 215–244. New York: Columbia University Press, 1998.

Adorno, Theodor, and Hanns Eisler. *Composing for the Films.* London: Athlone, 1994.

Adorno, Theodor, Else Frenkel-Brunswick, Daniel J. Levinson, and R. Nevitt Sanford. *The Authoritarian Personality*, abridged edition. New York: Norton, 1982.

Afkhami, Gholam Reza. *The Life and Times of the Shah.* Berkeley: University of California Press, 2009.

"Alex North, a Film Composer, 80; Had 40-Year Hollywood Career." *New York Times,* September 11, 1991, p. B12.

Althusser, Louis, and Étienne Balibar. *Reading Capital.* Translated by Ben Brewster. Brooklyn, N.Y.: Verso, 1970.

Anderson, Jack. "Dances about Everything and Dances about Some Things." In *Merce Cunningham: Dancing in Space and Time,* edited by Richard Kostelanetz, 95–100. New York: Da Capo, 1998.

Armstrong, Isobel. *The Radical Aesthetic.* Oxford: Blackwell, 2000.

Arndt, Richard T. *The First Resort of Kings: American Cultural Diplomacy in the Twentieth Century.* Washington, D.C.: Potomac, 2005.

Ashbery, John, and David Sorouchian-Kermani. "Taking Care of the Luxuries." *Saturday Review of the Arts,* November 4, 1972, pp. 60–63.

Ashley, Merrill. *Dancing for Balanchine.* New York: Dutton, 1984.

Auden, W. H. "Ballet's Present Eden: Example of *The Nutcracker.*" In *The Complete Works of W. H. Auden,* edited by Edward Mendelson, 3:393–396. Princeton, N.J.: Princeton University Press, 2008.

Balanchine, George. *By George Balanchine.* New York: San Marco Press, 1984.

Barnes, Clive. "Dance: Bolshoi's Stunning *Spartacus.*" *New York Times,* July 19, 1969, p. 14.

Barrios, Richard. *Screened Out: Playing Gay in Hollywood from Edison to Stonewall.* New York: Routledge, 2003.

Bass, Amy. *Not the Triumph but the Struggle: The 1968 Olympics and the Making of the Black Athlete.* Minneapolis: University of Minnesota Press, 2002.

Bayandor, Darioush. *Iran and the CIA: The Fall of Mosaddeq Revisited.* New York: Palgrave, 2010.

Bedford, Briand, ed. *The Spartacus International Gay Guide, 2001–2002.* Berlin: Bruno Gmünder Verlag, 2001.

Bell, Daniel. *The End of Ideology: On the Exhaustion of Political Ideas in the Fifties.* New York: Free Press, 1962.

Belle, Anne, dir. *Dancing for Mr. B: Six Balanchine Ballerinas.* New York: Seahorse Films/ WNET New York, 1989. Kultur Films DVD.

Belmonte, Laura A. *Selling the American Way: U.S. Propaganda and the Cold War.* Philadelphia: University of Pennsylvania Press, 2008.

Benjamin, Walter. *The Arcades Project.* Translated by Howard Eiland and Kevin McLaughlin. Cambridge, Mass: Belknap/Harvard University Press, 1999.

———. *Gesammelte Schriften* 5. Edited by Rolf Tiedemann. Frankfurt am Main: Suhrkamp Verlag, 1982.

———. "Theses on the Philosophy of History." In *Illuminations,* edited by Hannah Arendt, translated by Harry Zohn, 253–264. New York: Schocken, 1968.

———. "The Work of Art in the Age of Mechanical Reproduction." In *Illuminations,* edited by Hannah Arendt, translated by Harry Zohn, 217–251. New York: Schocken, 1968.

Bentley, Toni. "The Ballet That Changed Everything." *Wall Street Journal,* September 3, 2010. http://online.wsj.com/article/SB10001424052748703467004575463543929815752 .html.

Berghahn, Volker R. *America and the Intellectual Cold Wars in Europe.* Princeton, N.J.: Princeton University Press, 2001.

Bernstein, David W., and Christopher Hatch, eds. *Writings Through: John Cage's Music, Poetry, and Art.* Chicago: University of Chicago Press, 2001.

Bernstein, J. M. *Against Voluptuous Bodies: Late Modernism and the Meaning of Painting.* Stanford, Calif.: Stanford University Press, 2006.

Bessie, Alvah. *Inquisition in Eden.* New York: Macmillan, 1965.

Biddle, Livingston. *Our Government and the Arts: A Perspective from the Inside.* New York: American Council for the Arts Books, 1988.

Bill, James A. *The Eagle and the Lion: The Tragedy of American-Iranian Relations.* New Haven, Conn.: Yale University Press, 1988.

Binkiewicz, Donna M. *Federalizing the Muse: United States Arts Policy and the National Endowment for the Arts, 1965–1980.* Chapel Hill: University of North Carolina Press, 2004.

Bird, Robert Montgomery. *The Gladiator.* In *American Plays: Selected and Edited with Critical Introductions and Bibliographies*, edited by Allan Gates Halline, 153–198. New York: American Book Company, 1935.

Blackmur, R. P. *Studies in Henry James.* New York: New Directions, 1983.

Blake, Casey Nelson, ed. *The Arts of Democracy.* Washington, D.C.: Woodrow Wilson Center Press, 2007.

Bloom, Jonathan M. Review of *Surveyors of Persian Art: A Documentary Biography of Arthur Upham Pope & Phyllis Ackerman. Iranian Studies* 31, no. 1 (1998): 100–102.

"The Bolshoi's New Hit." *Dance Magazine*, May 1969: 60–62.

Bourdieu, Pierre. *Distinction: A Social Critique of the Judgment of Taste.* Translated by Richard Nice. Cambridge, Mass.: Harvard University Press, 1984.

———. *La Distinction: critique sociale du jugement.* Paris: Les Éditions de Minuit, 1979.

———. "La Domination masculine." In *Actes de la recherche en sciences sociales* 84 (September 1990): 2–31.

———. *Masculine Domination.* Translated by Richard Nice. Stanford, Calif.: Stanford University Press, 2001.

———. *The Rules of Art: Genesis and Structure of the Literary Field.* Translated by Susan Emanual. Stanford, Calif.: Stanford University Press, 1996.

Bown, Matthew Cullerne. *Art under Stalin.* New York: Holmes and Meier, 1991.

Braden, Thomas W. "I'm Glad the CIA Is 'Immoral.'" *Saturday Evening Post*, May 20, 1967, pp. 10–14.

Bradford, Gigi, Michael Gary, and Glenn Wallach, eds. *The Politics of Culture.* New York: New Press, 2000.

Bremser, Martha, ed. *The International Dictionary of Ballet.* Vol. 2. Detroit: Saint James Press, 1993.

Brenson, Michael. *Visionaries and Outcasts: The NEA, Congress, and the Place of the Visual Artist in America.* New York: New Press, 2001.

Brown, Carolyn. *Chance and Circumstance: Twenty Years with Cage and Cunningham.* New York: Knopf, 2007.

Buck-Morss, Susan. *Dreamworld and Catastrophe: The Passing of Mass Utopia in East and West.* Cambridge, Mass.: MIT Press, 2000.

Buckle, Richard, and John Taras. *George Balanchine, Ballet Master.* New York: Random House, 1988.

Byrne, Malcolm, ed. "The Secret CIA History of the Iran Coup, 1953." Electronic Briefing Book, no. 28. National Security Archive, George Washington University, November 29, 2000. http://www.gwu.edu/~nsarchiv/NSAEBB/NSAEBB28/.

Byrne, Malcolm, and Mark J. Gasiorowski, eds. *Mohammed Mosaddeq and the 1953 Coup in Iran* Syracuse, N.Y.: Syracuse University Press, 2004.

Cage, John. "In This Day." In *Silence: Lectures and Writing by John Cage*, 94–96. Middletown, Conn.: Wesleyan University Press, 1973.

Callow, Simon. *Charles Laughton: A Difficult Actor.* New York: Grove, 1988.

Castle, Eugene W. *Billions Blunders and Baloney: The Fantastic Story of How Uncle Sam Is Squandering Your Money Overseas.* New York: Devin-Adair, 1955.

Caute, David. *The Dancer Defects: The Struggle for Cultural Supremacy during the Cold War.* Oxford: Oxford University Press, 2003.

———. *The Great Fear: The Anti-Communist Purge under Truman and Eisenhower.* New York: Simon and Schuster, 1978.

Ceplair, Larry, and Steven Englund. *The Inquisition in Hollywood: Politics in the Film Community, 1930–1960.* 1980. Reprint, Champaign: University of Illinois Press, 2003.

Chakrabarty, Dipesh. *Provincializing Europe: Postcolonial Thought and Historical Difference.* Princeton, N.J.: Princeton University Press, 2000.

Chance, Norman. *Arctic Circle.* Storrs: University of Connecticut, January 1, 2009. http://arcticcircle.uconn.edu.

Clark, Paul. *The Chinese Cultural Revolution: A History.* Cambridge, U.K.: Cambridge University Press, 2008.

Cockcroft, Eva. "Abstract Expressionism, Weapon of the Cold War." *Artforum* 12 (June 1974): 39–41.

Cook, Deborah, ed. *Theodor Adorno: Key Concepts.* Stocksfield, U.K.: Acumen, 2008.

Cooper, Duncan L. "Dalton Trumbo vs. Stanley Kubrick." *Cineaste* 18, no. 3 (1991): 34–37.

Copel, Melinda. "Modern Dance Humanism and the State Department's Agenda: Raising U.S. Status in the World Community during the Cold War." In *Congress on Research in Dance: Conference Papers,* edited by Ninotchka Bennahum and Tresa Randall, 31–41. Tallahassee: Florida State University, 2005.

Copeland, Roger. *Merce Cunningham: The Modernizing of Modern Dance.* New York: Routledge, 2004.

Core, Philip. *Camp: The Lie That Tells the Truth.* London: Plexus, 1984.

Craine, Debra, and Judith Mackrell, eds. *The Oxford Dictionary of Dance.* Oxford: Oxford University Press, 2000.

Craven, David. *Abstract Expressionism As Cultural Critique: Dissent during the McCarthy Period.* Cambridge, U.K.: Cambridge University Press, 1999.

Creel, George. *How We Advertised America.* New York: Harper and Brothers, 1950.

Croce, Arlene. "Balanchine Said." *The New Yorker,* January 26, 2009, pp. 36–38.

Croft, Clare. "Ballet Nations: The New York City Ballet's 1962 State Department–Sponsored Tour of the Soviet Union." *Theatre Journal* 61 (October 2009): 421–442.

Cull, Nicholas J. *The Cold War and the United States Information Agency.* Cambridge, U.K.: Cambridge University Press, 2008.

Cummings, Milton C., Jr. "To Change a Nation's Cultural Policy: The Kennedy Administration and the Arts in the United States, 1961–1963." In *America's Commitment to Culture: Government and the Arts,* edited by Kevin V. Mulcahy and Margaret J. Wyszomirski, 95–120. Boulder, Colo.: Westview, 1995.

Cummings, Milton C., Jr., and Richard S. Katz, eds. *The Patron State: Government and the Arts in Europe, North America, and Japan.* New York: Oxford University Press, 1987.

Cunningham, Merce. *Changes: Notes on Choreography.* Edited by Frances Starr. New York: Something Else Press, 1968.

———. "The Impermanent Art." In *Merce Cunningham: Fifty Years,* edited by Melissa Harris, 86–87. New York: Aperture Foundation, 1997.

Cutlip, Scott. *The Unseen Power: Public Relations, a History.* Hillsdale, N.J.: Erlbaum, 1994.

Davenport-Hines, Richard. *Auden.* New York: Pantheon, 1995.

Dean, Tim. "Art As Symptom: Žižek and the Ethics of Psychoanalytic Criticism." *diacritics* 32 (summer 2002): 21–41.

———. *Beyond Sexuality.* Chicago: University of Chicago Press, 2000.

Debord, Guy. *The Society of the Spectacle.* Translated by Donald Nicholson-Smith. 1967. Reprint, New York: Zone, 1995.

DeFrantz, Thomas. *Dancing Revelations: Alvin Ailey's Embodiment of African American Culture.* New York: Oxford University Press, 2006.
Derrida, Jacques. "Plato's Pharmacy." In *Disseminations,* translated by Barbara Johnson, 63–171. Chicago: University of Chicago Press, 1981.
DiMaggio, Paul. "Social Structure, Institutions, and Cultural Goods: The Case of the United States." In *The Politics of Culture,* edited by Gigi Bradford, Michael Gary, and Glenn Wallach, 38–62. New York: New Press, 2000.
"Donald Newton Wilber, '29." *Princeton Alumni Weekly,* March 19, 1997. http://paw.princeton.edu/memorials/51/70/index.xml.
Douglas, Kirk. Papers. Wisconsin Historical Society.
———. *The Ragman's Son.* New York: Simon and Schuster, 1989.
Doyle, Kate, ed. "The Dead of Tlatelolco." National Security Archive, George Washington University, October 1, 2006. http://www.gwu.edu/~nsarchiv/NSAEBB/NSAEBB201/index.htm.
———. "The Tlatelolco Massacre: U.S. Documents on Mexico and the Events of 1968." National Security Archive, George Washington University, October 10, 2003. http://www.gwu.edu/~nsarchiv/NSAEBB/NSAEBB99/.
Duberman, Martin. *The Worlds of Lincoln Kirstein.* New York: Knopf, 2007.
"Dupes and Fellow Travelers Dress Up Communist Fronts." *Life,* April 3, 1949, pp. 42–43.
Eagleton, Terry. *The Ideology of the Aesthetic.* Oxford: Blackwell, 1990.
The Ed Sullivan Show. Aired on June 29, 1959, CBS. http://www.tv.com/the-ed-sullivan-show/moscows-moiseyev-ballet/episode/116166/summary.html.
Edel, Leon. *Henry James.* 3 vols. Philadelphia: Lippincott, 1953–1962.
Eisenstein, Sergei. *Film Form.* Edited and translated by Jay Leyda. New York: Harcourt Brace, 1977.
Essig, Laurie. *Queer in Russia: A Story of Sex, Self, and the Other.* Durham, N.C.: Duke University Press, 1999.
Fast, Howard. *Being Red.* Armonk, N.Y.: Sharpe, 1990.
———. *Spartacus.* 1951. Reprint, Armonk, N.Y.: Sharpe, 1996.
Federal Bureau of Investigation. Alex North file. Washington, D.C.
———. Personal communication. January 2002.
———. Arthur Upham Pope file. Washington, D.C.
Felman, Shoshana. "Turning the Screw of Interpretation." *Yale French Studies* 55/56 (1977): 94–207.
Filreis, Alan. *Counter-revolution of the Word: The Conservative Attack on Modernist Poetry, 1945–1960.* Chapel Hill: University of North Carolina Press, 2008.
Flinn, Caryl. *Strains of Utopia: Gender, Nostalgia, and Hollywood Film Music.* Princeton, N.J.: Princeton University Press, 1992.
Fosler-Lussier, Danielle. "Cultural Diplomacy As Cultural Globalization: The University of Michigan Jazz Band in Latin America." *Journal of the Society for American Music* 4 (February 2010): 59–93.
Foster, Susan Leigh. "Closets Full of Dances: Modern Dance's Performance of Masculinity and Sexuality." In *Dancing Desires: Choreographing Sexualities On and Off the Stage,* edited by Jane C. Desmond, 147–208. Madison: University of Wisconsin Press, 2001.
Foulkes, Julia L. *Modern Bodies: Dance and American Modernism from Martha Graham to Alvin Ailey.* Chapel Hill: University of North Carolina Press, 2002.
Frankel, Max. "A Witness Sees History Restaged and Rewritten." *New York Times,* Sunday, February 13, 2011. http://www.nytimes.com/2011/02/13/arts/music/13nixon.html?pagewanted=all&_r=0. 14

Franko, Mark. "Dance and the Political: States of Exception." *Dance Research Journal* 38 (summer–winter 2006): 3–18.

———. *Dance As Text: Ideologies of the Baroque Body.* Cambridge, U.K.: Cambridge University Press, 1993.

———. "Mimique." In *Bodies of the Text: Dance As Theory, Literature As Dance,* edited by Ellen W. Goellner and Jacqueline Shea Murphy, 205–216. New Brunswick, N.J.: Rutgers University Press, 1995.

———."Mimique." In *Migrations of Gesture,* edited by Carrie Noland and Sally Ann Ness, 241–258. Minneapolis: University of Minnesota Press, 2008.

Frascina, Francis, ed. *Pollock and After: The Critical Debate.* 2nd ed. New York: Routledge, 2000.

Fukuyama, Francis. *The End of History and the Last Man.* New York: Free Press, 1992.

Gadamer, Hans-Georg. "The Hermeneutics of Suspicion." *Man and World* 17 (1984): 313–323.

Gaddis, John Lewis. *The Cold War: A New History.* New York: Penguin, 2005.

Gambino, Thomas. *Nyet: An American Rock Musician Encounters the Soviet Union.* Englewood Cliffs, N.J.: Prentice Hall, 1976.

Geduld, Victoria Phillips. "Dancing Diplomacy: Martha Graham and the Strange Commodity of Cold-War Cultural Exchange in Asia, 1955 and 1974." *Dance Chronicle 33, no. 1* (2010): 44–81.

Genauer, Emily. "Bourgeois Decor at Bolshoi with Men in Prudish Tunics." *New York Herald Tribune,* April 26, 1959, sec.4, p. 1.

———. "Still Life with Red Herring." *Harper's* 199 (September 1949): 88–91.

Genter, Robert. *Late Modernism.* Philadelphia: University of Pennsylvania Press, 2010.

Gibson, Ann Eden. *Abstract Expressionism: Other Politics.* New Haven, Conn.: Yale University Press, 1997.

Gluck, Robert. "The Shiraz Arts Festival: Western Avant-Garde Arts in 1970s Iran." *Leonardo* 40, no. 1 (2007): 20–28.

Gorbman, Claudia. *Unheard Melodies: Narrative Film Music.* Bloomington: Indiana University Press, 1987.

Graham, William A., dir. "A Midwinter Night's Dream." *Omnibus.* Aired January 1, 1961, WNBC-TV. New York Public Library Dance Collection of the Performing Arts. 16 mm film.

Gregory, Elizabeth. "'Combat Cultural': Marianne Moore and the Mixed Brow." In *Critics and Poets on Marianne Moore: A Right Good Salvo of Barks,* edited by Linda Leavell, Cristanne Miller, and Robin Schulze, 208–221. Lewisburg, Pa.: Bucknell University Press, 2005.

Grenfell, Michael, and Cheryl Hardy. *Art Rules: Pierre Bourdieu and the Visual Arts.* Oxford: Berg, 2007.

Guilbaut, Serge. *How New York Stole the Idea of Modern Art: Abstract Expressionism, Freedom, and the Cold War.* Translated by Arthur Goldhammer. Chicago: University of Chicago Press, 1983.

Gussow, Mel. "West 23rd Street Banned in Budapest." *New York Times,* November 17, 1977. http://query.nytimes.com/mem/archive/pdf?res=FB0615F6355B1A7B93C5A8178AD95F438785F9.

Hadas, Pamela White. *Marianne Moore: Poet of Affection.* Syracuse, N.Y.: Syracuse University Press, 1977.

Hamilton, Ian. *Robert Lowell: A Biography.* New York: Random House, 1982.

Hammer, Espen. *Adorno and the Political.* New York: Routledge, 2006.

Haralson, Eric. *Henry James and Queer Modernity.* Cambridge, U.K.: Cambridge University Press, 2003.

Harris, Melissa, ed. *Merce Cunningham: Fifty Years.* New York: Aperture Foundation, 1997.

Hayden, Melissa. Interview. May 2000.

Hayot, Eric. *Chinese Dreams: Pound, Brecht, Tel Quel.* Ann Arbor: University of Michigan Press, 2003.

Henahan, Donal. "Opera: 'Nixon in China.'" *New York Times,* October 24, 1987. http://www.nytimes.com/1987/10/24/arts/opera-nixon-in-china.html.

Henderson, John W. *The United States Information Agency.* New York: Praeger, 1969.

Hering, Doris. "And Still, the Chasm." *Dance Magazine,* November 1962, pp. 30–34, 70–71.

———. Review of the Moiseyev Dance Company. *Dance Magazine,* June 1958, p. 35.

Hilton, Wendy. *Dance of Court and Theater: The French Noble Style, 1690–1725.* Princeton, N.J.: Princeton Book Company, 1981.

Hinkson, Mary. Interview. March 2000.

Hirsch, Francine. *Empire of Nations: Ethnographic Knowledge and the Making of the Soviet Union.* Ithaca, N.Y.: Cornell University Press, 2005.

Hixson, Walter L. *Parting the Curtain: Propaganda, Culture, and the Cold War, 1945–1961.* New York: Saint Martin's Press, 1997.

Hofstadter, Richard. *The Paranoid Style in American Politics and Other Essays.* New York: Knopf, 1965.

Hohendahl, Peter Uwe. *Prismatic Thought: Theodor W. Adorno.* Lincoln: University of Nebraska Press, 1995.

Homans, Jennifer. *Apollo's Angels: A History of Ballet.* New York: Random House, 2010.

Horgan, Barbara. Interview. July 1998.

Hound & Horn 7 (April–June) 1934.

Hughes, Allen. "Ford Fund Allots 7.7 Million to Ballet." *New York Times,* December 16, 1963, pp. 1, 42.

Huhn, Tom, ed. *The Cambridge Companion to Adorno.* Cambridge, U.K.: Cambridge University Press, 2004.

Hullot-Kentor, Robert. *Current of Music: Elements of a Radio Theory,* by Theodor W. Adorno. Malden, Mass: Polity, 2009.

———. *Things beyond Resemblance: Collected Essays on Theodor W. Adorno.* New York: Columbia University Press, 2006.

Humphries, Reynold. *Hollywood's Blacklists.* Edinburgh: Edinburgh University Press, 2009.

Iser, Wolfgang. *The Act of Reading: A Theory of Aesthetic Response.* Baltimore: Johns Hopkins University Press, 1978.

Isherwood, Christopher. *The World in the Evening.* 1954. Reprint, Minneapolis: University of Minnesota Press, 1999.

Jackson, Shannon. *Lines of Activity: Performance, Domesticity, Hull-House Historiography.* Ann Arbor: University of Michigan Press, 2000.

James, Henry. "The Figure in the Carpet." In *Complete Stories, 1892–1898,* pp. 572–608. New York: Library of America, 1996.

Jameson, Fredric. *Late Marxism: Adorno, or, the Persistence of the Dialectic.* New York: Verso, 1990.

———. *The Political Unconscious: Narrative As a Socially Symbolic Act.* Ithaca, N.Y.: Cornell University Press, 1981.

Jappe, Anselm. *Guy Debord.* Translated by Donald Nicholson-Smith. Berkeley: University of California Press, 1999.

Javits, Jacob K. "Plan to Aid Our Lagging Culture." *New York Times Sunday Magazine,* May 3, 1959, pp. 21, 24, 26, 28.

Jenemann, David. *Adorno in America.* Minneapolis: University of Minnesota Press, 2007.

Jennings, Luke. "Night at the Ballet: The Czar's Last Dance." *The New Yorker,* March 27, 1995, pp. 71–86.

Jones, Dorothy Knee. *A Century of Servitude: Pribilof Aleuts under U.S. Rule.* Washington, D.C.: University Press of America, 1980.

Judt, Tony. *Postwar: A History of Europe Since 1945.* New York: Penguin, 2005.

———. *Reappraisals: Reflections on the Forgotten Twentieth Century.* New York: Penguin, 2008.

———. "A Story Still to Be Told." *New York Review of Books.* March 23, 2006. http://www.nybooks.com/articles/archives/2006/mar/23/a-story-still-to-be-told/.

Katz, Jonathan D. "John Cage's Queer Silence; or, How to Avoid Making Matters Worse." *GLQ* 5 (April 1999): 231–252.

———. "Passive Resistance: On the Success of Queer Artists in Cold War American Art." *Image* 3 (December 1996): 119–142.

Kaufman, Robert. "Lyric Commodity Critique, Benjamin Adorno Marx, Baudelaire Baudelaire Baudelaire." *PMLA* 123 (January 2008): 207–215.

———. "Lyric's Expression: Musicality, Conceptuality, Critical Agency." *Critical Inquiry* 60 (spring 2005): 197–216.

———. "Poetry's Ethics? Theodor W. Adorno and Robert Duncan on Aesthetic Illusion and Sociopolitical Delusion." *New German Critique* 97 (winter 2006): 73–118.

Kellogg, Elijah. "Spartacus to the Gladiators." In *The Sixth Reader*, edited by George Stillman Hillard, 337–338. Boston: Brener, 1864.

Kermode, Frank, ed. *Selected Prose of T. S. Eliot.* New York: Harcourt Brace Jovanovich, 1975.

Keynes, John Maynard. *A Tract on Monetary Reform.* Basingstoke: Palgrave Macmillan, 1971.

Khachaturian, Aram. "Concerning Creative Boldness and Inspiration." *Current Digest of the Soviet Press,* December 30, 1953, pp. 3–5.

"Khrushchev on Culture." *Encounter,* pamphlet no. 9., 6–47. Translated and annotated by Walter Z. Laqueur, Ronald Hingley, Hugh Lunghi, H. T. Willets, George Katkov, Norman Erwin, Victor S. Frank, and Melvin J. Lasky. London, 1963.

Kimmelman, Michael. "Revisiting the Revisionists: The Modern, Its Critics, and the Cold War." In *The Museum of Modern Art at Mid-Century: At Home and Abroad. Studies in Modern Art 4*, series edited by John Elderfeld, 38–55. New York: Museum of Modern Art, 1994.

Kinzer, Stephen. *All the Shah's Men: An American Coup and the Roots of Middle East Terror* Hoboken, N.J.: Wiley, 2003.

Kirkland, Gelsey. *Dancing on my Grave.* Garden City, N.Y.: Doubleday, 1986.

Kirstein, Lincoln. *Ballet: Bias and Belief.* New York: Dance Horizons, 1983.

———. "The Diaghilev Period." *Hound & Horn* 3 (July–September 1930): 468–501.

———, ed. *Nijinsky Dancing.* New York: Knopf, 1975.

———. Papers. New York Public Library for the Performing Arts, Jerome Robbins Dance Collection.

———. *Thirty Years: Lincoln Kirstein's The New York City Ballet.* New York: Knopf, 1978.

Klass, Rosanne. "Finding the Figure in the Carpet." *Ballet Review* 41 (spring 1986): 38–52.

Kodat, Catherine Gunther. "Conversing with Ourselves: Canon, Freedom, Jazz." *American Quarterly* 55 (March 2003): 1–28.

———. "Dancing through the Cold War: The Case of *The Nutcracker.*" *Mosaic* 33 (September 2000): 1–17.

———. "The Great Intermediate." *Salmagundi* 157 (winter 2008): 188–198.

———. "High Art in Low Times." *Boston Review* 29 (October–November 2004): 37–39.

———. "Reviewing Cold War Culture with Edwin Denby." In *American Literature and Culture in an Age of Cold War,* edited by Steven Belletto and Daniel Grausam, 37–58. Iowa City: University of Iowa Press, 2012.

Koestler, Arthur. *The Gladiators.* 1939. Reprint, New York: Macmillan, 1967.

Kolodin, Irving. "Music to my Ears: Balanchine in Persia—Walter's 'Lied.'" *Saturday Review,* April 30, 1960, p. 34.

Kon, Igor. *The Sexual Revolution in Russia: From the Age of the Czars to Today.* Translated by James Riordan. New York: Free Press, 1995.

Kon, Igor, and James Riordan, eds. *Sex and Russian Society.* Bloomington: Indiana University Press, 1993.

Kopelson, Kevin. *The Queer Afterlife of Vaslav Nijinsky.* Stanford, Calif.: Stanford University Press, 1997.

Korppi-Tommola, Riikka. "Politics Promote Dance: Martha Graham in Finland, 1962." *Dance Chronicle* 3 (January 2010): 82–112.

Kostelanetz, Richard, ed. *Merce Cunningham: Dancing in Space and Time.* New York: Da Capo Press, 1998.

Kowal, Rebekah J. *How to Do Things with Dance: Performing Change in Postwar America.* Middletown, Conn.: Wesleyan University Press, 2010.

Kozloff, Max. "American Painting during the Cold War." *Artforum* 11 (May 1973): 43–54.

Krenn, Michael L. *Fall-Out Shelters for the Human Spirit: American Art and the Cold War.* Chapel Hill: University of North Carolina Press, 2005.

Kristeva, Julia. *About Chinese Women.* Translated by Anita Barrows. New York: Urizen, 1977.

Kubrick, Stanley, dir. *Spartacus.* 1960. New York: Criterion Collection, 2001. DVD.

Kuo, Michelle. "Acting Out: The Ab-Ex Effect." *Artforum International* 49 (summer 2011): 314–315.

Kuznick, Peter J. ,and James Gilbert, eds. *Rethinking Cold War Culture.* Washington, D.C.: Smithsonian Institution Press, 2001.

Laddago, Reinaldo. Introduction. In *Dancing around the Bride: Cage, Cunningham, Johns, Rauschenberg, and Duchamp,* edited by Carlos Basualdo and Erica F. Battle, 39–42. Philadelphia: Philadelphia Museum of Art, 2012.

Lanchester, Elsa. *Elsa Lanchester, Herself.* New York: Saint Martin's Press, 1983.

Larson, Gary O. *The Reluctant Patron: The United States Government and the Arts, 1943–1965.* Philadelphia: University of Pennsylvania Press, 1983.

Lasch, Christopher. *The Agony of the American Left.* New York: Knopf, 1969.

Leja, Michael. *Reframing Abstract Expressionism: Subjectivity and Painting in the 1940s.* New Haven, Conn.: Yale University Press, 1993.

Levin, Thomas Y. "Dismantling the Spectacle: The Cinema of Guy Debord." In *On the Passage of a Few People through a Rather Brief Moment in Time: The Situationist International, 1957–1972,* edited by Elisabeth Sussman, 72–123. Cambridge, Mass: MIT Press, 1989.

Levine, Irving R. "Khrushchev's Prettiest Propaganda." *New York Herald Tribune Sunday Magazine,* May 19, 1959, pp. 12, 14–15.

Li Cunxin. *Mao's Last Dancer.* Camberwell, Australia: Viking Penguin, 2003.

Liu Kang. "Popular Culture and the Culture of the Masses in Contemporary China." *boundary 2* 24 (autumn 1997): 99–122.

Lillard, Richard G. "Through the Disciplines with Spartacus: The Uses of a Hero in History and the Media." *American Studies* 16 (fall 1975): 15–28.

Littleton, Taylor, and Maltby Sykes. *Advancing American Art: Painting, Politics, and Cultural Confrontation at Mid-Century.* 1989. Reprint, Tuscaloosa: University of Alabama Press, 2005.

Loesberg, Jonathan. *A Return to Aesthetics: Autonomy, Indifference, and Postmodernism.* Stanford, Calif.: Stanford University Press, 2005.

Love, Kennett. "Shah, Back in Iran, Wildly Acclaimed; Prestige at Peak." *New York Times,* August 23, 1953. http://www.nytimes.com/library/world/mideast/082353iran-shah-return.html.

Lukács, György. "Realism in the Balance." In *Aesthetics and Politics: Ernst Bloch, Georg Lukács, Bertolt Brecht, Walter Benjamin, Theodor Adorno,* translated by Ronald Taylor, 28–59. London: Verso, 1980.

Macauley, Alastair. "A Long Goodbye from the Last of Balanchine's Ballerinas." *New York Times,* June 28, 2010. http://www.nytimes.com/2010/06/29/arts/dance/29kistler.html?ref=darci_kistler.

MacFarquhar, Roderick, and Michael Schoenhals. *Mao's Last Revolution.* Cambridge, Mass.: Harvard University Press, 2006.

Manning, Susan. *Modern Dance, Negro Dance: Race in Motion.* Minneapolis: University of Minnesota Press, 2004.

Mariani, Paul. *Lost Puritan: A Life of Robert Lowell.* New York: Norton, 1994.

Mark, Charles Christopher. *Reluctant Bureaucrats: The Struggle to Establish the National Endowment for the Arts.* Dubuque, Iowa: Kendall/Hunt, 1991.

Martin, John. "About 'Spartacus': Can It Be Understood though Disliked?" *New York Times,* September 23, 1962, p. 20X.

———. "Ballet: 'Episodes, Part II.'" *New York Times,* April 18, 1960, p. 36.

———. "Ballet: A Novelty Bows." *New York Times,* April 14, 1960, p. 36.

———. "Ballet: 'Stone Flower.'" *New York Times,* May 5, 1959, p. 41.

———. "The Dance: Iranian City Ballet Spectacle Sponsored by Shah." *New York Times,* April 10, 1960, sec. 2, p. 14.

———. "The Dance: A la Moiseyev." *New York Times,* April 20, 1958, p. 19X.

———. *Introduction to the Dance.* 1939. Reprint, Princeton: Dance Horizons, 1965.

Marx, Karl, and Frederick Engels. *Selected Correspondence of Karl Marx and Frederick Engels, 1846–1895.* Translated by Dona Torr. New York: International, 1942.

Mathews, Jane de Hart. "Art and Politics in Cold War America." *American Historical Review* 81 (October 1976): 762–787.

McBride, Patricia. Interview. June 1999.

McCormick, Seth. "Neo-Dada, 1951–54: Between the Aesthetics of Persecution and the Politics of Identity." In *Communities of Sense: Rethinking Aesthetics and Politics,* edited by Beth Hinderliter, William Kaizen, Vered Maimon, Jaleh Mansoor, and Seth McCormick, 238–266. Durham, N.C.: Duke University Press, 2009.

McDonald, William F. *Federal Relief Administration and the Arts: The Origins and Administrative History of the Arts Projects of the Works Progress Administration.* Columbus: Ohio State University Press, 1969.

McFadden, Robert D. "Washington Columnist Got Rockefeller Loan to Buy Newspaper in California." *New York Times,* October 13, 1974, sec. GN, p. 22.

Melissen, Jan, ed. *The New Public Diplomacy: Soft Power in International Relations.* New York: Palgrave, 2005.

Merce Cunningham Dance Company Archive. New York Public Library, Jerome Robbins Dance Collection.

Miller, Cristanne. "Distrusting: Marianne Moore on Feeling and War in the 1940s." *American Literature* 80 (June 2008): 353–379.
Miller, J. Hillis. "The Figure in the Carpet." *Poetics Today* 1, no. 3 (1980): 107–118.
Moi, Toril. "Appropriating Bourdieu: Feminist Theory and Pierre Bourdieu's Sociology of Culture." *New Literary History* 22 (autumn 1991): 1017–1049.
Moiseyev Dance Company. Program notes. 1992.
———. "Two Boys in a Fight." West Long Branch, N.J.: Kultur International Films, 1994. VHS.
Molesworth, Charles. *Marianne Moore: A Literary Life*. Boston: Northeastern University Press, 1991.
Moon, Michael. *A Small Boy and Others: Imitation and Initiation in American Culture from Henry James to Andy Warhol*. Durham, N.C.: Duke University Press, 1998.
Moore, Marianne. "Combat Cultural." *The New Yorker*, June 6, 1959, p. 40.
———. *The Complete Poems of Marianne Moore*. 1967. Reprint, New York: Macmillan, 1982.
———. *The Complete Prose of Marianne Moore*, edited by Patricia C. Willis. New York: Viking, 1986.
———. *Dance Index* 3 (March 1944): 47–52.
———. "Hometown Piece for Messrs. Alston and Reese." *New York Herald Tribune*, October 3, 1956, p. 1.
———. *O to Be a Dragon*. New York: Viking, 1959.
———. Poetry manuscripts. Rosenbach Museum and Library, Marianne Moore Collection.
Moran, Eileen G. "Selected Letters of Marianne Moore to Hildegarde Watson, Edited, with a Critical Introduction." *Dissertation Abstracts International* 46 (February 1986): 2290A.
Morley, David, and Kuan-Hsing Chen, eds. *Stuart Hall: Critical Dialogues in Cultural Studies*. New York: Routledge, 1996.
Morris, Gay. *A Game for Dancers: Performing Modernism in the Postwar Years, 1945–1960*. Middletown, Conn.: Wesleyan University Press, 2006.
Morris, Mark. Personal communication. March 2013.
"Mostafa Mesbahzadeh, 97; Exiled Publisher of Iranian Newspapers." *Los Angeles Times*, December 5, 2006. http://articles.latimes.com/2006/dec/05/local/me-mostafa5.
Mulcahy, Kevin V., and Margaret J. Wyszomirski, eds. *America's Commitment to Culture: Government and the Arts*. Boulder, Colo.: Westview, 1995.
Müller-Doohm, Stefan. *Adorno: A Biography*. Translated by Rodney Livingston. Malden, Mass.: Polity, 2005.
"Musician Defying U.S. Rule on Official Tours Abroad." *New York Times*, January 28, 1976. http://query.nytimes.com/mem/archive/pdf?res=F40C14F73B58167493CAAB178AD85F428785F9.
Nabokov, Ivan, and Elizabeth Carmichael. "Balanchine." *Horizon* 3 (January 1961): 44–56.
Nadel, Alan. *Containment Culture*. Durham, N.C.: Duke University Press, 1995.
Navasky, Victor S. *Naming Names*. New York: Viking, 1980.
Nelson, Deborah. *Pursuing Privacy in Cold War America*. New York: Columbia University Press, 2002.
Nelson, Thomas Allen. *Kubrick: Inside a Film Artist's Maze*. Bloomington: Indiana University Press, 1982.
Nevile, Jennifer, ed. *Dance, Spectacle, and the Body Politic, 1250–1750*. Bloomington: Indiana University Press, 2008.
Ninkovich, Frank. *U.S. Information Policy and Cultural Diplomacy*. New York: Foreign Policy Association, 1996.

Nitchie, George W. *Marianne Moore: An Introduction to the Poetry.* New York: Columbia University Press, 1969.

North, Alex. North collection. UCLA Music Library, Special Collections.

Nye, Joseph S., Jr. *Soft Power: The Means to Success in World Politics.* New York: Public Affairs, 2004.

O'Connor, Francis V. *Federal Support for the Visual Arts: The New Deal and Now: A Report on the New Deal Art Projects in New York City and State with Recommendations for Present-Day Federal Support for the Visual Arts to the National Endowment for the Arts.* Greenwich, Conn.: New York Graphic Society, 1969.

Ohi, Kevin. *Henry James and the Queerness of Style.* Minneapolis: University of Minnesota Press, 2011.

Osborne, Peter. "A Marxism for the Postmodern? Jameson's Adorno." *New German Critique* 56 (spring–summer 1992): 171–192.

Osgood, Kenneth. *Total Cold War: Eisenhower's Secret Propaganda Battle at Home and Abroad.* Lawrence: University of Kansas, 2006.

Percival, John. "London Datelines." *Dance Magazine,* September 1969, p. 95.

Perry, Roland. *The Last of the Cold War Spies: The Life of Michael Straight.* New York: Perseus, 2005.

Phillips, Elizabeth. *Marianne Moore.* New York: Ungar, 1982.

Phillips, Gene D., ed. *Stanley Kubrick: Interviews.* Jackson: University Press of Mississippi, 2001.

Pollack, Howard. *Aaron Copland: The Life and Work of an Uncommon Man.* New York: Holt, 1999.

Poniatowska, Elena. *Massacre in Mexico.* Columbia: University of Missouri Press, 1991.

Pope, Arthur Upham. *An Introduction to Persian Art Since the Seventh Century A.D.* London: Peter Davies, 1930.

———. *Maxim Litvinoff.* New York: Fischer, 1943.

Posnock, Ross. "James, Henry." In *A Companion to American Thought,* edited by Richard Wrightman Fox and James T. Kloppenberg, 344–346. Oxford: Blackwell, 1995.

Prevots, Naima. *Dance for Export: Cultural Diplomacy and the Cold War.* Hanover, N.H.: University Press of New England, 1998.

Publications of the Modern Language Association 123 (January 2008).

Rancière, Jacques. *Aesthetics and Its Discontents.* Translated by Steven Corcoran. Cambridge, Mass.: Polity, 2009.

———. "The Concept of 'Critique' and the Critique of 'Political Economy.'" In *Ideology, Method and Marx,* edited by Ali Rattansi, 74–180. New York: Routledge, 1989.

———. "Contemporary Art and the Politics of Aesthetics." In *Communities of Sense: Rethinking Aesthetics and Politics*, edited by Beth Hinderliter, William Kaizen, Vered Maimon, Jaleh Mansoor, and Seth McCormick, 31–50. Durham: Duke University Press, 2009.

———. *Disagreement: Politics and Philosophy.* Translated by Julie Rose. Minneapolis: University of Minnesota Press, 1999.

———. *Dissensus: On Politics and Aesthetics.* Edited and translated by Steven Corcoran. New York: Continuum, 2010.

———. *The Emancipated Spectator.* Translated by Gregory Elliott. London: Verso, 2009.

———. *The Flesh of Words: The Politics of Writing.* Translated by Charlotte Mandell. Stanford, Calif.: Stanford University Press, 2004.

———. *Lire "le Capital" III.* Paris: Maspero, 1973.

———. "The Method of Equality: An Answer to Some Questions." In *Jacques Rancière:*

History, Politics, Aesthetics, edited by Gabriel Rockhill and Philip Watts, 273–288. Durham, N.C.: Duke University Press, 2009.

———. *The Nights of Labor: The Workers' Dream in Nineteenth-Century France.* Translated by John Drury. Philadelphia: Temple University Press, 1989.

———. "On the Theory of Ideology (The Politics of Althusser)." *Radical Philosophy* 7 (spring 1974): 2–15.

———. *The Philosopher and His Poor.* Translated by John Drury, Corinne Oster, and Andrew Parker. 1983. Reprint, Durham, N.C.: Duke University Press, 2004.

———. *The Politics of Aesthetics. Translated by* Gabriel Rockhill. New York: Continuum, 2004.

———. "The Politics of Literature." *SubStance* 33, no. 1 (2004): 10–24.

Reed, Christopher. *Art and Homosexuality: A History of Ideas.* New York: Oxford University Press, 2011.

Reynolds, Nancy. *Repertory in Review: Forty Years of the New York City Ballet.* New York: Dial, 1977.

Ricoeur, Paul. *Freud and Philosophy: An Essay on Interpretation.* Translated by Denis Savage. New Haven, Conn.: Yale University Press, 1970.

Rimmon, Shlomith. *The Concept of Ambiguity—The Example of James.* Chicago: University of Chicago Press, 1977.

Risen, James. "How a Plot Convulsed Iran in '53 (and in '79)." *New York Times,* April 16, 2000, pp. A1, A14–15.

Robinson, Harlow. *The Last Impresario: The Life, Times, and Legacy of Sol Hurok.* New York: Penguin, 1994.

Rockhill, Gabriel. "Translator's Introduction: Jacques Rancière's Politics of Perception." In Jacques Rancière, *The Politics of Aesthetics,* 1–6. New York: Continuum, 2004.

Rockhill, Gabriel, and Philip Watts, ed. *Jacques Rancière: History, Politics, Aesthetics.* Durham, N.C.: Duke University Press, 2009.

Rockwell, John. "Opera: 'Nixon in China.'" *New York Times,* December 6, 1987. http://www.nytimes.com/1987/12/06/arts/opera-nixon-in-china.html.

Rogin, Michael. "*Kiss Me Deadly:* Communism, Motherhood, and Cold War Movies," *Representations* 6 (spring 1984): 1–36.

———. *Ronald Reagan, the Movie: And Other Episodes in Political Demonology.* Berkeley: University of California Press, 1987.

Roosevelt, Kermit, Jr. *Countercoup: The Struggle for the Control of Iran.* New York: McGraw-Hill, 1979.

Ross, Alex. *The Rest Is Noise: Listening to the Twentieth Century.* New York: Picador, 2007.

Roth, Moira, and Jonathan D. Katz, eds. *Difference/Indifference: Musings on Postmodernism, Marcel Duchamp and John Cage.* Amsterdam: G+B Arts International, 1998.

Rubinsohn, Wolfgang Zeev. *Spartacus' Uprising and Soviet Historical Writing.* Translated by John G. Griffith. Oxford: Oxbow, 1987.

Russell, Francia. Interview. November 1998.

Saab, A. Joan. *For the Millions: American Art and Culture Between the Wars.* Philadelphia: University of Pennsylvania Press, 2004.

Saikal, Amin. *The Rise and Fall of the Shah.* Princeton, N.J.: Princeton University Press, 1980.

Sargeant, Winthrop. "Musical Events: Delightful *Shrew.*" *The New Yorker,* April 26, 1958, p. 82.

Saunders, Frances Stonor. *The Cultural Cold War: The CIA and the World of Arts and Letters.* New York: New Press, 2000.

Savoy, Eric. "Embarrassments: Figure in the Closet." *Henry James Review* 20, no. 3 (1999): 227–236.

———. "Entre chien et loup: Henry James, Queer Theory, and the Biographical Imperative." In *Palgrave Advances in Henry James Studies,* edited by Peter Rawlings, 100–125. Basingstoke, U.K.: Palgrave, 2007.

Schaub, Thomas Hill. *American Fiction in the Cold War.* Madison: University of Wisconsin Press, 1991.

Schiller, Friedrich. *On the Aesthetic Education of Man.* 1794. Reprint, Mineola, N.Y.: Dover, 2004.

Schonberg, Harold C. "Presenting Sol Hurok, Impresario." *New York Times Sunday Magazine,* April 26, 1959, pp. 16, 82.

Schorer, Suki. Interview. July 1999.

Schrecker, Ellen. *Many Are the Crimes: McCarthyism in America.* Boston: Little, Brown, 1998.

Schulman, Grace, ed. *The Poems of Marianne Moore.* New York: Viking Penguin, 2003.

Schwartz, Lawrence H. *Creating Faulkner's Reputation: The Politics of Modern Literary Criticism.* Knoxville: University of Tennessee Press, 1988.

Sedgwick, Eve Kosofsky. *Epistemology of the Closet.* Berkeley: University of California Press, 1990.

———. *Touching Feeling: Affect, Pedagogy, Performativity.* Durham, N.C.: Duke University Press, 2003.

Senie, Harriet F., and Sally Webster, eds. *Critical Issues in Public Art: Content, Context, and Controversy.* Washington, D.C.: Smithsonian Institution Press, 1992.

Shapiro, David, and Cecile Shapiro. "Abstract Expressionism: The Politics of Apolitical Painting." *Prospects* 3 (1976): 175–214.

Shaw, Brent D., ed. and trans. *Spartacus and the Slave Wars: A Brief History with Documents.* Boston: Bedford, 2001.

Shay, Anthony. *Choreographic Politics: State Folk Dance Companies, Representation and Power.* Middletown, Conn.: Wesleyan University Press, 2002.

Sherry, Michael. *Gay Artists in Modern American Culture.* Chapel Hill: University of North Carolina Press, 2007.

Shneerson, Grigory. *Aram Khachaturyan.* Moscow: Foreign Languages Publishing House, 1959.

Silliman, Amy. "AbEx and Disco Balls." *Artforum International* 49 (summer 2011): 321–325.

Smith, Tommie, and David Steele. *Silent Gesture: The Autobiography of Tommie Smith.* Philadelphia: Temple University Press, 2007.

Stapleton, Laurence. *Marianne Moore: The Poet's Advance.* Princeton, N.J.: Princeton University Press, 1978.

Starr, S. Frederick. *Red and Hot: The Fate of Jazz in the Soviet Union, 1917–1980.* New York: Oxford University Press, 1983.

Steinberg, Michael. "*Nixon in China* (1985–87)." In *The John Adams Reader: Essential Writings on an American Composer,* edited by Thomas May, 110–119. Pompton Plains, N.J.: Amadeus, 2006.

Steiner, Wendy. *The Scandal of Pleasure.* Chicago: University of Chicago Press, 1995.

Stewart, Susan. *On Longing: Narratives of the Miniature, the Gigantic, the Souvenir, the Collection.* Durham, N.C.: Duke University Press, 1993.

Stoneley, Peter. *A Queer History of the Ballet.* New York: Routledge, 2007.

Straight, Michael. *After a Long Silence.* New York: Norton, 1983.

———. *Twigs for an Eagle's Nest: Government and the Arts, 1965–1978.* New York: Devon, 1979.

Sullivan, Michael, and John T. Lysaker. "Between Impotence and Illusion: Adorno's Art of Theory and Practice." *New German Critique* 57 (autumn 1992): 87–122.

Swados, Harvey. "Epic in Technicolor." *The Nation,* April 5, 1952, p. 331.

Swed, Mark. "Opera Review: 'Nixon in China' by San Francisco Opera Hits Highs and Lows." *Los Angeles Times,* June 25, 2012. http://articles.latimes.com/2012/jun/25/entertainment/la-et-sf-opera-nixon-review-20120626.

Swenson, James. "*Style indirect libre.*" In *Jacques Rancière: History, Politics, Aesthetics,* edited by Gabriel Rockhill and Philip Watts, 258–272. Durham, N.C.: Duke University Press, 2009.

Szalay, Michael. *New Deal Modernism.* Durham, N.C.: Duke University Press, 2000.

Taylor, Fannie, and Anthony L. Barresi. *The Arts at a New Frontier: The National Endowment for the Arts.* New York: Plenum, 1984.

Taylor, Robert Lewis. "Profiles: Under the Rug—I." *The New Yorker,* July 14, 1945, pp. 28–32.

———. "Profiles: Under the Rug—II" *The New Yorker,* July 21, 1945, pp. 22–29.

Terry, Walter. "Bolshoi Exciting In Variety Show." *New York Herald Tribune,* May 3, 1959, sec. 4, p. 5

———. "Dance: Bolshoi Ballet." *New York Herald Tribune,* April 18, 1959, p. 9

———. "Dance: Russians Blaze; America on Fire Too." *New York Herald Tribune,* April 20, 1958, sec. 4, p. 6.

———. "DeMille Out-DeMilled." *New York Herald Tribune,* September 16, 1962, sec. 4, p. 1.

———. "'Figure in Carpet' Featured by the City Ballet." *New York Herald Tribune,* April 18, 1960, p. 8.

Todorov, Tzvetan. *The Poetics of Prose.* Translated by Richard Howard. Ithaca, N.Y.: Cornell University Press, 1977.

Tommasini, Anthony. "President and Opera, on Unexpected Stage." *New York Times,* February 3, 2011. http://www.nytimes.com/2011/02/04/arts/music/04nixon.html?pagewanted=all.

Tracy, Robert, and Sharon DeLano. *Balanchine's Ballerinas: Conversations with the Muses.* New York: Linden, 1983.

Trumbo, Dalton. Papers. Wisconsin Historical Society.

———. "Report on *Spartacus.*" *Cineaste* 18, no. 3 (1991): 30–33.

Tuller, David. *Cracks in the Iron Closet: Travels in Gay and Lesbian Russia.* Chicago: University of Chicago Press, 1996.

"2,500 Year Celebration of the Persian Empire." YouTube video, 12:44. Filmed in October 1971. Posted by EmpressFarahPahlavi, December 13, 2011. http://www.youtube.com/watch?v=orWZHn1NivI.

Tye, Larry. *The Father of Spin: Edward L. Bernays and the Birth of Public Relations.* New York: Crown, 1998.

United Press International. "Ruler of Iran Is Wounded Slightly by Two Bullets Fired by Assassin." *New York Times,* February 5, 1949. http://www.nytimes.com/library/world/mideast/020549iran-assassin.html.

U.S. Census Bureau. "A Brief Look at Postwar U.S. Income Inequality," June 1996. http://www.census.gov/hhes/www/img/p60–191.pdf.

U.S. Department of State. "The Rhythm Road." http://exchanges.state.gov/us/spotlight/rhythm-road-music-olympics.

U.S. Department of State/U.S. Information Agency, Bureau of Educational and Cultural Affairs. Cultural Affairs Collection. University of Arkansas, Special Collections Division.

Verdy, Violette. Interview. August 1999.

Von Eschen, Penny. *Satchmo Blows Up the World.* Cambridge, Mass.: Harvard University Press, 2004.

Warren, Larry. *Anna Sokolow: The Rebellious Spirit.* Princeton, N.J.: Princeton Book Company, 1991.

Weinstein, Philip. *Unknowing: The Work of Modernist Fiction.* Ithaca, N.Y.: Cornell University Press, 2005.

Werth, Alexander. *Musical Uproar in Moscow.* 1949. Reprint, Westport, Conn.: Greenwood, 1974.

West, Martha Ullman. "Todd Bolender with American Ballet Caravan." *Ballet Review* 38 (winter 2010–2011): 73–89.

Westad, Odd Arne. *The Global Cold War.* Cambridge, U.K.: Cambridge University Press, 2005.

Whitfield, Stephen J. *The Culture of the Cold War.* Baltimore: Johns Hopkins University Press, 1991.

Wilber, Donald N. *Persian Gardens and Garden Pavilions.* Rutland, Vt.: Tuttle, 1962.

Wilford, Hugh. *The Mighty Wurlitzer: How the CIA Played America.* Cambridge, Mass.: Harvard University Press, 2008.

Williams, Raymond. "The Future of Cultural Studies." In *The Politics of Modernism: Against the New Conformists,* 151–162. London: Verso, 1989.

Windreich, Leland. "Cold War Exchange: American Ballet Companies in the U.S.S.R." *Ballet Review* 37 (summer 2009): 57–68.

Wollaeger, Mark. *Modernism, Media, and Propaganda.* Princeton, N.J.: Princeton University Press, 2006.

Wyke, Maria. *Projecting the Past: Ancient Rome, Cinema, and History.* New York: Routledge, 1997.

Yeats, William Butler. "To a Wealthy Man who promised a second Subscription to the Dublin Municipal Gallery if it were proved the People wanted Pictures." In *The Collected Works of W. B. Yeats,* revised edition, edited by Ralph J. Finneran, 1:107–108. New York: Macmillan, 1989.

Yuzefovich, Victor. *Aram Khachaturyan.* Translated by Nicholas Kournokoff and Vladimir Bobrov. New York: Sphinx, 1985.

Zuck, Barbara. *A History of Musical Americanism.* Ann Arbor, Mich.: UMI Research Press, 1980.

Index

About the Author

CATHERINE GUNTHER KODAT is a professor of humanities and dean of the Division of Liberal Arts at the University of the Arts in Philadelphia. She has taught twentieth-century U.S. literature and American studies at Boston University, Boston College, and Tufts University. For more than fifteen years she taught at Hamilton College, where she served as chair of the English and creative writing department and director of the American studies program. A former Fulbright lecturer in American studies at Eötvös Loránd Tudományegytem in Budapest, Kodat also worked as a reporter at the *Baltimore Sun,* writing about urban affairs and serving as the paper's chief dance critic. Her essays on literature, dance, film, and music have appeared in *American Literary History, American Quarterly, Boston Review, Representations,* and *Salmagundi* as well as several edited collections.

CPSIA information can be obtained
at www.ICGtesting.com
Printed in the USA
LVHW092109060219
606655LV00002B/8/P